How Was It ...

Memorie

Rob Horlock

rob@intheforest.co.uk
www.20thcenturymemories.com

Contents:

Forword

Gladys Shaw sets the scene for this collection of 1940s memories with some random memories of the decade. Do these ring any bells with you?

Men working with picks and shovels were called 'navvies'
People walked miles to work
Guineas were used to price suits and costumes
Children played in the roads
Frozen ice in ice cream boxes on bicycles
Muffin man, tray on head, bell in hand
Milk delivered twice a day
Horse and cart to deliver milk and bread
Shire horses dressed overall to pull brewery carts
Bugs in houses and beds
Flea ridden dogs and cats, also children's hair
Outside toilets with several sets of holes, large to small
Lift up latch to toilet and kitchen doors
Skirts always below the knee
Copper boiled white washing and copper sticks
Green mesh safe for meat in the cellar
Chickens and pigs in back gardens, killed on the spot by a butcher
Home made lace collars and cuffs to match
Leather gaiters knee high, done up with a buttonhook.
'No spitting' signs in bus and trams
Spats and cravats and pomade for male dandies
Brylcreem for young lads
Women teachers were sacked when they married
'Disgraced' women gave up their babies to be adopted or sent to an orphanage
Buskers at pub doors, sawdust on pub floor with spittoons displayed
Voluntary run hospitals, babies born at home
Smog in cities
Cold water, the only tap in the house. Or use the water pump, or well
Maintained police boxes on street corners
Cobbled roads before tarmac
AA men saluting their badge as a car drives by
Men doffing their hats as a greeting
Chairs to sit on in the haberdashery and drapery shops
Home and Colonial shops

Introduction

'How Was It for You?' is a collection of hundreds of peoples' personal memories from the unforgettable decade of the 1940s. Whilst many of these memories are of experiences in World War Two, a host of other events in the decade are also recalled. Serious, sad, emotional and humorous stories and anecdotes are all recounted in a variety of styles.

If you lived through the 1940s, 'How Was It for You?' will certainly bring back many memories. If you can't recall the decade yourself, the book will give you an interesting snapshot of the life and times endured and enjoyed by your older friends and relatives.

The decade was, of course, dominated by World War Two, the world's bloodiest conflict. During the course of the war, 300,000 British servicemen and women were killed. Four million returned to 'civvy street' to pick up their lives. Many peoples' outlooks were changed forever and women, in particular, looked at the world through different eyes after the war.

Rationing was in force throughout the 1940s. In spite of (or perhaps, because of) this, the general health of the average person was better after the war than it had been at the start of the decade.

Princess Elizabeth married Philip Mountbatten in 1947; the wedding was a welcome break from post-war austerity and amongst the wedding presents was a gift from the Cabinet – all of their combined food coupons.

After the war, the electorate chose a socialist government and Churchill was defeated in the election of 1945. People looked forward to a better life. The National Health Service was launched and Social Security was introduced. Working class children with ability were given the chance to improve themselves with the introduction of the 11+ exam, the gateway to a Grammar School education.

The winter of 1947 was the worst of the century. The River Thames froze, industry was crippled and there were regular electricity cuts.

Further afield, Europe was divided in to the Capitalist West and the Communist East by an 'Iron Curtain.' The state of Israel was founded and China became a People's Republic led by Chairman Mao. India was granted Independence.

1940s Discoveries and Developments

Genes are made up of DNA	The Microwave Oven
The Transistor	The Computer
The Electronic Calculator	Rocket Propulsion
The Magnetic Tape Recorder	The Polaroid Camera
Streptomycin	The Hologram
Bar Codes	The Atomic Bomb
The Biro	

1940s Firsts

Non Stop Flight around the World	Organic Farming
Tupperware	Electric Guitar – The Les Paul
Prefab Houses	The Music Singles Chart (in the USA)
Oxfam Shop	The United Nations
Nuclear Reactor	Murray Mints
The 11+ Exam	The Morris Minor
The Launderette	The Bikini
Television	

1940s Anniversaries

50th of the first Automobiles to be manufactured in Britain (1895)

50th of the start of the Boer War (1899)

50th of the Bra (1893)

50th of the Dow Jones Share Index (1896)

100th of The Factory Act, limiting women and children to a 58 hour working week (1847)

100th of the Potato Famine in Ireland (1845)

100th of the launch of the first propeller driven ship, the Napoleon (1842)

100th of the publication of Karl Marx's Communist Manifesto (1848)

100th of the issue of the first Penny Black Stamp (1840)

100th of the Telegram (1844)

200th of the first public rendition of Rule Britannia (1740)

The Future:
In 1940, at the beginning of the decade, it would be:

21 years before Betting Shops became legal in Britain

26 years before England won Football's World Cup

31 years before Decimal Currency was introduced in Britain

32 years before Britain joined the EEC

33 years before VAT was introduced in Britain

34 years before the opening of Britain's first McDonald's restaurant

39 years before Margaret Thatcher became Britain's first woman Prime Minister

41 years before the appearance of the Personal Computer

62 years before the Euro replaced the national currencies of most EU member countries

The Bikini first appeared in 1946

The 1940s - Month by Month

1940

January
- The River Thames froze over for the first time since the 1880s
- Basic commodities including ham, sugar and butter were rationed

February
- German U boats were ordered to attack all shipping around the British Isles, including neutral vessels

March
- Meat rationing began

April
- Hitler's forces invaded Norway and Denmark

May
- Hitler's Nazi forces swept across France, Holland and Belgium, signalling the end of the 'Phoney War'
- Winston Churchill became Prime Minister
- The Local Defence Volunteer force was formed
- Nylon stockings went on sale in New York

June
- Over 300,000 Allied troops were evacuated from Dunkirk as Nazi troops overran Northern Europe
- Italy declared war on Britain
- Nazi troops occupied Paris

July
- The Local Defence Volunteers were renamed The Home Guard
- Germany invaded the Channel Islands
- Billboard magazine published the first music singles chart in the US, topped by Frank Sinatra

August
- Leon Trotsky was assassinated in Mexico by Stalin's secret police
- London was bombed for the first time
- At the beginning of the Battle of Britain, Churchill made his famous 'Never was so much owed, by so many, to so few' speech

September
- The George Cross and George Medal honours were introduced
- The London Blitz began

October
- Princess Elizabeth made her first public broadcast

November
- In The USA, Franklin D Roosevelt was re-elected for the third time
- The US Army Jeep was launched
- Coventry was flattened by the worst air raid of the war so far

December
- The heaviest air raid on London took place between Christmas and the New Year
- Anthony Eden was appointed Foreign Secretary

==================

A Slice of Life

Barry Chatfield recalls life in Hawkhurst

Sights, Sounds and Tastes

I lived 'in the front line' during the war, in the village of Hawkhurst, Kent, less than twenty miles from the south coast, where an invasion was considered possible. Because of this locality the war remained very real, from start to finish. In fact houses in our village were issued with an emergency food card which read as follows:

Food arrangements in case of Invasion:
1. Take a basket and tins and paper and your Ration Book.
2. Each person's ration consists of biscuits, corned beef, soup, sugar, condensed milk, margarine and tea
3. The cost per person is 10/- (50p). Pay if you can - if you can't, the money will be collected later, but be sure to fetch your rations.
4. These supplies are for eight days and they are your last reserves. Keep them as long as possible.
5. Carry on with your ordinary shopping as long as possible. The shops will have to be shut for a short time for stocktaking.
6. Keep a week's supply of flour for bread always in the house. The baker may not be able to get to you.
7. If you do have to use water other than main water, boil it for five minutes first.
8. Keep a large tin and adhesive plaster to put food in, in case of gas.

Here are some of my more vivid memories.

Sounds:
The air-raid sirens with their sinister wailing warning, heralding the approach of enemy aircraft. Since every village had a siren, in the stillness of the night, and with the wind in a certain direction, other distant warnings could be heard as well. The steady note of the All Clear was a very welcome sound. The sound of Big Ben striking. This signalled the start of the nine o'clock news on the radio, which everyone listened intently to.

Aircraft engine sounds. At first the sound of 'ours' seemed much the same as 'theirs', but people were soon able to recognise the harsher drone of a German Heinkel or Dornier, and hearing a lone one at night overhead was not a pleasant sound.

Sights:
There were plenty of those, but probably the most noticeable was the complete darkness at night. It was very dark. All houses had to make their windows light proof so that no light shone out. Doors had to be carefully opened if lights were on indoors. Buses, car and bicycle lights had to be masked, so that only a small amount of light was shown. No street lights, no cheerful displays in shop windows, and at Christmas time, definitely no twinkling lights from house windows, or outdoor positions. Obviously no firework displays on Nov 5th.

Without doubt however, the sights all children living in Kent will remember most vividly, will be watching the 'Battle of Britain' dog fights being fought out overhead during the long, hot September days in 1940. The blue skies were criss-crossed with white vapour trails, and streaks of black smoke, as the aircraft engaged each other. Spent machine gun cartridge cases pattered down, planes were crashing, and the pilots were baling out all over the sky. Once I remember counting five parachutes descending at the same time. They did not always open, or they were alight. There are three German airmen buried in our local cemetery. We children thought these battles most exciting, and did not seem to realize the dangers.

Tastes:

Many nice tastes gradually disappeared. Cakes and buns were rather tasteless, the ingredients were in short supply for families to make their own, but a great treat was to receive a food parcel sent from Canada or America. Relatives, or organisations like the Red Cross, or WI managed to send parcels containing exciting things like tinned fruit, tinned ham, dried fruit, chocolate and <u>tasty</u> fruitcakes. People always shared these goodies with friends and neighbours, often keeping them back for Christmas so that us children could benefit. There were however no bananas to be had for the entire time of the war!

Family Life and the Countryside:

Both rapidly changed. In the countryside, because an invasion was anticipated, in Kent and Sussex the direction arms on all signposts were removed. This was to confuse any spies, or parachutists, but it also made it difficult for any visitors not familiar with the area to find their way around. Concrete machine gun posts were constructed to guard important cross-roads, bridges or possible river crossings. Many still remain. Small units of soldiers set up search light positions, or anti-aircraft guns in the corners of fields, edges of woods or in farmyards. Most large country houses were taken over for soldiers to be accommodated, and off-duty soldiers (not always British) were a frequent sight in and around our village. Temporary airstrips were formed for fighter planes to operate from, or for returning bombers to make emergency landings if they needed to. Farmers erected sturdy posts in large flat fields to make it difficult for gliders to land with air-born troops. Stirrup pumps were issued for putting out any fires started by Incendiary bombs. They proved useful for watering the garden. In towns, huge piles of sandbags were placed around important buildings to protect against the blast from bombs. Yes, everywhere looked very different.

Memories of the 1940s

Mrs Laura Turner recalls an incident at London Zoo

Feeding the Bears

During the 1940s I joined the Land Army and was working on a large estate near Henley-on-Thames. I shared a room in a hostel with another Land Army girl.

One day we had a day off together so we went to London and visited Regents Park Zoo. We got talking to a keeper who invited us to watch him feed the polar bears. He took us into the feeding area where he placed the food on the ground. Before going to another gate where the bears were let out to feed, he requested that we stand outside the enclosure. As we left we walked out into the sight of crowds of people who had gathered to watch the polar bears being fed. You can imagine their surprise and amusement at seeing us instead, two Land Army girls!

Gordon Brown lived in Liverpool

Monkeys

The Second World War dominated my childhood. I invented my own seaside in the garden by cycling about a hundred yards on my three-wheel pedal bike to a site where workmen used to leave heaps of sand while building air raid shelters. I used to take my bucket and spade on my bike and fill my bucket and the take home the sand for sand pies. I wonder if the workmen wondered where their sand was going after they had gone home.

That was a way of making my own entertainment out of the sadness of war, which was brought home to me when my father came home on leave from his Royal Air Force station and took me to Liverpool. We went into Lewis's store, where there was a cage full of monkeys. I was laughing my head off at the monkeys and then my father and I left the store. Minutes later a bomb dropped on Lewis's. The store and the monkeys were destroyed.

Bill Luke recalls his early motoring days

Traffic Lights

Motorised vehicles were not much in evidence in 1941 as we came to a sign which said "Halt Major Road." After making sure the road was clear my friend and I carried on cycling towards home. Then we looked back to see a policeman trying to get our attention, so we waited until he caught up with us. He wanted to know why we had not halted, and even explained that if we had just touched the ground with one foot it would have been acceptable. After he had recorded our names, we thanked him for his advice. Then when I got home my Mother was in tears. A local policeman had called on her, checking up on my address. I got a summons for not conforming to traffic signs. Two weeks later on my 17th birthday, I was fined five shillings, by the chairman of the bench, a personal family friend, who indicated that he was aware that a car driver, had been stopped at the same road ends, but got off with a caution. Recognising the power of FreeMasonry gave me the grounds to be anti such secret societies for the whole of my life.

After the war a friend got a new motorbike, his pride and joy. He went to Middlesborough for the first time, and overtook what looked like a line of parked cars, until he got to the end, which was a set of traffic lights - on STOP! He was horrified, but his speed carried him through. As soon as possible he turned round and came back to his rightful place in the queue of parked vehicles. Unfortunately, a police car was in the queue and he was charged with failing to conform to traffic signs - for coming back, not for going through the lights!

Alan Birmingham lived on Canvey Island

GIs and Germans

I remember:

Travelling from Kings Cross to Newcastle on the Flying Scotsman in the days when every schoolboy's ambition was to be an engine driver. The train was packed with GIs, who plied me with unheard quantities of chocolate bars and sweets. I was very sick on Newcastle station.

Not being able to understand why the young German airman who was being given a cup of tea by my mum in our kitchen did not look frightening or wicked in any way; he looked just the same as us. Oh yes, he was in our kitchen because he had been captured and was waiting for an army escort. My dad was the village bobby.

Getting an extra six-week's holiday from school when the side of the corridor was blown out by the blast from a doodlebug.

We were a large family but never went short of meat, but it was always rabbit. They were everywhere on Canvey Island and very easy to catch.

Katie Smith recalls an incident in Malvern

A Stay in Malvern

Here is my story of a six-week stay in Malvern Cottage Hospital.

My parents luckily paid 6d a week into the hospital fund, this helped fund the running of the hospital, which had been given by Dyson Perrins for the people of Malvern. Dyson Perrins being of Worcester Sauce fame. The fact the 6d had been paid meant that I received FREE treatment and could stay for as long as necessary.

January 11th 1942, I was aged nine years old and rushed into hospital with appendicitis. Preparation for the operation included painting the face of my Teddy bear on my tummy with Iodine.

Our GP, who also performed the operation and the anaesthetist sprinkled the ether onto a mask, held over my nose.

Little did my parents at this stage know how seriously ill I was until the doctor had completed the operation. This was a burst appendix and Peritonitis (a condition that few recovered from prior to the use of antibiotics).

Luckily M&B was being used and thanks to these very painful injections plus the skill of our GP and caring, well trained nurses, after six weeks in bed and legs too weak to hold me up, I returned home.

Convalescence included food rationing, the Second World War, grandfather dying and Geoffrey Twitty my childhood hero taken to Canada to train in the RAF.

1942 was not a good year!

Margaret Chatters lived near Glasgow

Castle Wemyss

In 1941 we had the Blitz in Greenock where I lived and as the house was damaged, we moved down the Clyde coast to Wemyss Bay. In 1942 I joined the Wrens and in 1944 I got married. The date was the 8th June and we drank a toast to the boys who were involved in the D-Day Invasion. As my husband was chauffeur valet to Lord Inverclyde of Castle Wemyss, I spent the first three years of married life in the castle, as there were no empty houses on the estate. A most interesting time.

In 1946 King George VI and his Queen plus Princess Elizabeth and Prince Philip came to Wemyss Bay to join the Royal Yacht. It was a big Clyde festival. They slept in the Royal Train between Glasgow and Wemyss Bay as Lord Inverclyde was then divorced –

in those days the Royal Family did not stay with divorced people. Lord Inverclyde met them at Wemyss Bay station the following day.

In the years before I lived at the castle, many famous people stayed there. These included King Peter of Yugoslavia, in 1943 and the Emperor of Ethiopia, Haile Selassie who stayed there during his exile in 1936. I met his grandsons who were educated at Dollar Academy in the north of Scotland and who visited the castle on several occasions.

Muriel Stirling began work during the war

A Working Wage

My mother gave me 1/6d a week. From that, I saved 6d on a savings card, spent 6d and saved the other 6d for clothes. My first coat cost me one guinea and came from the Guinea shop. Shoes cost me 4/6d and were made of glove leather. My Robin Hood hat cost 1/6d and blew off the second time that I wore it. Not only that, it went straight under the wheels of a double-decker bus and was ruined; a whole week's wages gone in seconds!

I was married at a young age but the marriage was unhappy and didn't last long. My husband was in the forces and left me for one of his staff. Divorce was stigmatised, though and not readily accepted. When, some time later I met Bert, the man that became my second and dear husband I did not consider divorce for two years. In all that time Bert did not come inside my house. Even so, after my divorce I was reminded of the stigma by a certain gentlemen who I used to walk with to the bus stop, the manager of a department at the Co-op. "I would rather that you didn't walk with me" he declared, making me feel dreadful.

1940s Movie Stars

Jack Shepperd recalls an incident in London

Smog!

I came out from the cinema in Lewisham. The fog closed in around me, choking and penetrating every cavity in my exposed face, stinging my nose, streaming my eyes with tears. It was dense and a filthy dirty, greeny-yellowish colour that seemed to float on top of a cloud, mixing in with the fog and swirling around. It was peculiar to London and although I didn't know its name at the time, later we it called Smog.

The road led straight across the Heath to my house a short way away. Stumbling along with tarmac under my feet, I was pretty confident of getting home very soon. As I reached the top of the hill it became just the road and grass Heath with no houses or streetlights to break up the thick choking greeny-yellow 'Smog.'

I knew that all I had to do, to get back home was to keep my feet on the tarmac road. Within minutes however, still peering, coughing and spitting into the thick swirling, blinding, denseness and without even realising it, I was treading on the grass - now I was completely lost! My feet prodded around desperately searching for the tarmac road, but to no avail.

I stumbled on without any sense of direction, now feeling thoroughly miserable and wretched from the combined effects of Smog and the freezing cold wind.

I could barely see my feet through stinging streaming eyes and the thick green-yellowy mixture swirling all around me. So I just stumbled around blindly.

After an almost endless amount of time, I again felt gravel under my feet. The swirling fog lifted a little and I glimpsed water. Puzzled, I shuffled nearer to it, finding some granite stones edging the water. I followed the stones going round and realised in must be a pond.

Finally it hit me; this was the Prince of Wales pond on Blackheath, over three miles away from my house and in the opposite direction too! Luckily, the main road across the Heath was nearby. Following the traffic on it, I got back home only after a long, long time.

Stanley H Jones grew up in Trowbridge

Spitfire Week

The annual National Savings Week was a poor substitute for the usual pre-war carnival week in Trowbridge. Nonetheless, each year they provided that time of excitement so missing in our lives during the war. The week included special events, parades and military bands all intended to promote War Savings.

As Trowbridge was the home of a military barracks, I remember the parade being led by a top-class military band. Contingents from the armed services, the local Home Guard, Civil Defence and so on, all took part. Each year the week had a different name: 'Salute the Sailor', 'War Weapons Week' and 'Spitfire Week' come to mind. 'Spitfire Week' was especially important as Trowbridge contained several works where many of the parts were manufactured. These were moved to Trowbridge following the bombing of factories in Southampton.

Trowbridge was one of those towns completely taken over by the military during the war and the area where I lived was one huge 'tank park.' The preparation for the many campaigns and return from the battlefields saw many changes. I remember the soldiers training before they left for the continent prior to Dunkirk - and their return. Then there was the build up of British tanks and our forces defending us with the Germans threatening our shores. Later, the Americans arrived. Their large tanks lined Union Street and from our bedroom windows we could almost look down the turrets and watch as the soldiers prepared their equipment for battle. My dad was employed on Ushers transport (our local brewery) and after delivering beer to Bellefield House where many of their officers were stationed came back with tales of the luxurious food they were having! The GIs were however great and kept us supplied with gum!

Suddenly they had gone - the streets and lanes were strangely empty - and then we knew that D-Day had dawned - now the activity was in the air. Keevil Airfield which had always been so important during the war - Spitfires made in the Trowbridge area were assembled and tested there, but now lines of aeroplanes towing gliders were taking off all day. My most vivid memory is listening to the six o'clock evening news. There was a clear blue sky and as I listened to the voice of the newsreader coming through the open window to the back yard where I was playing so I watched the lines of gliders going over the town.

Alan Everson recalls his first job in Carshalton

The Milk Round

During the spring of 1943, at the age of twelve, I started working weekends on a milk round. In those days most milkmen employed a boy to assist him on Saturdays, which was the busiest day for collecting money. Although strictly against the Employment of Young Persons Act (or some similar piece of legislation), I also worked on Sundays in order to get the round finished as quickly as possible. The milkman I worked for, Bert Huggett, wanted me on both days for which he paid me five shillings (25p), but on top of this I made a few shillings in tips. Bert was a short, very thickset cheerful man in his fifties, who would frequently entertain me on the way back to the depot with his wide ranging repertoire of 'nonsense' rhymes, parodies of old music hall songs, and humorous recitations. He also had the intriguing habit of chewing tobacco.

Our round for the Express Dairy was, like most at that time, operated by horse and cart and we started some fifteen minutes drive from our depot at Carshalton. When the cart was fully loaded with crates of milk there was usually no room for me up front with Bert, so I made the journey standing on the rear step holding on tightly to the rail which ran round the roof. This was fine in the warm weather but on a cold winter's morning my hands would be frozen by the time we reached the start of the round. Only a complete sissy would have even considered wearing gloves, such items of clothing being only suitable for girls. Milk was 4½d a pint (roughly 2p) and very strictly rationed, the adult allocation being 2½ pints a week, so anyone living on their own would get only ½ pint for five days of the week and was forced to have two milkless days.

I very quickly learned how to handle the horse by helping to harness, lead, feed and drive, which I thoroughly enjoyed. Our regular horse was a light brown mare called Gypsy, very placid and a joy to work with, but on the days she was being rested we had a large grey called Desmond. Somehow he and I just didn't get on very well with each other, and after several attempts at tasting my flesh, did succeed on one occasion in ripping a large chunk out of the sleeve of my jersey. Another time when I was leading him by the head and trying to persuade him to turn a corner, he moved round suddenly and trod very heavily on my foot causing quite a painful bruise. This may not have been deliberate - although I wouldn't rule it out - but it certainly did nothing to improve our relationship.

Shortly after D-Day in June 1944 the Germans launched their much vaunted secret weapon, the doodlebug, as it became universally nicknamed. This sudden escalation of the war on our doorstep resulted in many families evacuating to safer parts of the country. With the resultant rapid decline in pupils, our school closed down, leaving me free to work six days a week on the milk round, to earn the princely sum of ten shillings. Each day as we worked our round we would find more and more houses unoccupied, with notes in the empty bottles to tell us they had gone away. We suddenly found ourselves with milk to spare, as our daily allocation remained the same. This was, of course, an unexpected bonus for our remaining customers who could suddenly enjoy the luxury of extra pints. Our last call on the round was an anti-aircraft battery army camp and the ATS girls would queue up to buy our surplus milk.

Eric Cornfield might have been famous in Welling

One Fine Day

Monday nights at The Embassy, Welling were becoming quite a feature for young people in this part of Kent. Amateur talent nights were bringing in ever larger crowds, and tonight was going to be my night. I felt it in my bones. The piano, bass and drums began the introduction to a slow rumba, and I began "When they begin the beguine ..." Two lovely chords from the brass section and we were off. The elation I felt with a first class band accompaniment was reflected in my performance.

"Till you whisper to me once more, Darling I love you." The tiniest hint of a sob in the "darling" and a certain hunger in the "love" and very soon it was over. The reception was everything I could have wished. As I stepped off the stage to enthusiastic applause the MC took the microphone and said "Well what do you think of that for Chick Henderson without the colouring?"

It was years before I found out that Chick Henderson was very fair. It was I who was the dark one.

I was on a 'high' that night, but within a very short time I was brought down to earth with a resounding bump. This is what happened. After the talent contest came the interval. It was quite usual for a number of patrons of The Embassy to nip across to The Nag's Head for some refreshment. I had even more reason to celebrate, so two or three friends and I made our way to the bar. As we entered three young ladies came squealing across the room towards me (this was before Frank Sinatra and 'bobby soxers' remember) patting me all over - well figuratively that is. I said, "Well thank you. You're very kind," or some such nonsense, and then ... Oh dear! "What did you think of the girl who sang 'One Fine Day'? Wasn't it awful?" As the word 'awful' left my lips, I realised I was looking straight into the eyes of the erstwhile Madame Butterfly.

"Er ... um ... Well, not awful, just unsuitable for that audience!"

It was no good. The damage was done, and I slunk off. I still go cold when I think about it sixty years later.

A few days after this event, I was in the shop's toilet, singing at the top of my voice, enjoying the resonance rebounding from the tiled walls, when in came the Branch Manager. "Gordon Bennet, have you got the croup?" he exclaimed!

"Flattery will get you nowhere," I rejoined pertly, while making my way to the door.

"Hang on" he said. "I want to talk to you." I waited outside, and when he came out he continued, "You think you can sing. Well I know someone who really can sing. He is understudy to Richard Tauber at the moment. I've told him about you and he wants to see you. Have you got the guts to go?"

"When?" I asked.

"Thursday night at eight."

At the appointed hour, I turned up at this gentleman's flat, (a handsome young Welshman I recall), and gave forth as he played the piano. The song was 'Rose Marie' and I gave it the full 'Nelson Eddy' treatment. As the music drew to a close the door opened and in came his pretty wife. "You really can sing can't you?" she commented.

"I like to think so" I replied self-effacingly.

"You go on thinking so. You have a fine voice, and don't let anyone tell you otherwise," was her reply.

He gave me a demonstration of his own ability, and very nice too! It was arranged that he would take me under his wing, commencing with a lesson on Monday 10th September 1940. Now why is that date so clear in my mind? On the 7th September the Luftwaffe threw everything they had into attacking London. The flames around Dockland leapt into the night, a beacon lighting the way for more waves of bombers. The noise and destruction was horrendous.

I turned up at the appointed time for my lesson and was met by a very disturbed young man. "I am sorry" he said, "But I have sent my wife and child to Wales and I shall follow as soon as I've finished packing. The best of luck to you."

"Oh well," I thought. "I've been here before and no doubt I'll be here again before I'm much older."

'Mary Lou' Potter lived in Totnes

A Privilege

I was a perfectly ordinary, only child born in 1926 with no idea what I should do when I left Totnes County School. I thought I might be a hairdresser.

Then one day several of us who were at Totnes were called to the 'Head's Room' and offered a scholarship to Dartington Hall. In those days, the founders, Dorothy and Leonard Elmhurst, were there with their social ideas of bringing the Arts back to the countryside. They had professional musicians before the war, Robert Masters and his string quartet and the Chekhov Theatre. But with the war, all had to leave. They had all the musical instruments, studios, pianos, etc and had the idea of training young people, straight from school to keep music going in conjunction with the rural music movement.

Imogen Holst, the only daughter of the composer of the 'Planets' etc, was in charge of music. Four of us went for interview and all were accepted. Gordon played trumpet and piano, Esther - flute and piano, Joan - piano and organ and I played piano and voice.

It was a wonderful experience. We sang, played in the orchestra and groups, and conducted local groups. We developed a small group of six to eight of us and sang from the clock tower in Dartington and in local churches - learning so much about the joy of music.

The scholarship was for one year but Joan, Esther and I were invited to stay a second year. By then, there were twenty of us. We had musical trips to Cambridge, the RMS headquarters, to an early production of Peter Grimes in London. I was sent for singing lessons with Julian Kimble in London every two weeks. It is difficult for me to say how privileged we were. We met great musicians - such as the Amadeus Quartet in their first years.

Imogen Holst was such a wonderful musician and friend and Dartington was full of impromptu music in those years. Full of joy!

Beryl Worthington recalls her Big Day

Lace and Tulle

I was married in Aug 1941 when clothes and materials were on coupons. For some strange reason lace and tulle could be bought without using any of these precious items. My mother made my wedding dress with a very full skirt in tulle and my two bridesmaids had turquoise lace dresses with big picture hats. We were lucky to get any presents and they were generally what the shops had left, completely useless at that time. I remember we had grapefruit spoons and a claret jug. The reception was held at home with whatever food we could get. We were lucky to have a honeymoon of one week at St Annes.

Norma Service remembers everyday life

Tinkers and Shire Horses

There are so many things that have vanished from everyday life. Remember when the tinkers used to sell wooden clothes pegs round the doors? We had an old man who used to come every year with a tray of knicker elastic, safety pins and bits and bobs. He always used to bring my gran an 'Old Moore's Almanac.'

All the delivery vans from the Co-op were pulled by Shire horses, the milk van, the bread van, even the coal and veg.

Sweets were very scarce and when our local shop got their quota, it caused great excitement. Several of us pooled our pennies and bought a stick of rock. This precious item was then broken up and shared out. Then, to make it last longer, we wrapped a piece in a clean hankie and sucked it through the cloth. This way it lasted twice as long and several pieces lasted several days. The downside was an awful lot of holed hankies!

Joyce Mellor found herself in Bromley

Sardines

I was at school during the 1940s and having in 1944 achieved the required Higher School Certificate Standard in English, French, Latin and Modern History, I decided that I would like to become a teacher. I applied to go to the Bishop Otter College at Chichester but the building had just been taken over by the RAF and was being used for planning purposes. We were therefore asked to report for teacher training to a college at Bromley, in Kent.

The previous students had been evacuated to a safe area and there was a shortage of domestic staff. We were told, "Domestic duty must come first." This meant that if one was in the kitchen peeling potatoes when the air-raid siren sounded one just carried on peeling. If one was having a history lecture then the students and staff would make for the air-raid shelters.

Because food was rationed we had to carry our personal portion of butter, jam, etc. a short distance outdoors from our sleeping rooms to the dining room. I was one of four people representing the students and at one meeting was asked by a member of staff if we could suggest any way of improving the meals or our domestic jobs. I remember suggesting that it would save washing up if we walked past the hatch with our mouths open instead of having to wash up dozens of willow pattern dinner plates each of which had held only a single sardine! One of the staff expressed her surprise and said a staff breakfast consisted of a kipper or bloater.

Our breakfasts did improve…

Roy Cox grew up in Hayes

The Concert Party

It all started on a January night in 1942. Two pals and myself decided to join 'Evelyn's Youth Centre' drama group. We enrolled and because I could do an Irish brogue, I was cast as an Irish doctor. On the way out we heard a piano playing. We popped in and saw a piano surrounded by ten to fifteen youngsters. The elderly gentleman in charge asked if we had come to join the Concert Party. We said no at first but were persuaded to join and from that day on we were hooked. We rehearsed three or four times a week and did our first show in June. We were a success and all of our shows were in aid of the Red Cross.

My brother-in-law was on the entertainment committee of a huge munitions factory in Hayes. He came to see us and asked if we would put on a show for the workers at lunchtime. We readily agreed and appeared about ten days before Christmas of 1942. The firm sent cars to pick us up. Before starting the show I peeped through the curtains and was stunned by what I saw – there were about 1,000 people in the audience! I was somewhat nervous. However, we did our show, which went off very well indeed. Molly Bodgi, a mezzo-soprano won a warm round of applause as did the dancers and pianist. I did my first number, then sang White Christmas and the audience all joined in. The applause was unbelievable, though I don't think it was for me, more for the song, by Irving Berlin.

The Concert Party

Doris Parr lived in Essex

Pyjamas and Harris Tweed

Classes at school grew larger, as evacuees joined our numbers. Male teachers disappeared into the Armed Forces. Air raid shelters were erected on the school playing field. Subjects such as French and German were removed from our school timetable, and soon even cookery classes had to be changed to House-wifery, as food became too precious for girls to experiment with, and we did boring things, like cleaning the gas cookers, instead.

When the evacuees arrived, mostly from Edmonton, and surrounding areas, my parents decided to take in a young mother with her tiny baby, John. Our father, who was by then in his fifties, rejoined the Army, but because of his age, was in charge of our local Home Guard. He was sometimes away, so I suppose the evacuee mother was company for our mum. I think her name was Sylvia, but we were not allowed to call her that. Our dad loved the Army. He had served in it for about twenty-eight years before the war, and when home, he kept a gun under the bed downstairs. It wasn't a revolver, I think it may have been a Sten gun. We were told not to tell anyone it was there. One early morning we were awakened by the sound of machine gun fire. It was a Jerry plane, swooping low and machine-gunning the workers of a local factory, as they left their cycles in the shed. Dad was in a fury over this, and, wearing his tin hat, but still in his pyjamas, he stood in the street firing with his gun at this plane. My mother implored him to come indoors and Yvonne and me stood at the front door, giggling at this amazing sight. Poor dad must have hit the plane, it was so low. Many cycles were damaged, but as far as I can remember, no one was hurt. Dad hated the Germans, and we thought we did too at that time. Only years later did we realise that the majority of them were no different in their ways from us.

One Saturday, when I was perhaps seventeen, an older girlfriend who had a brother living in Ilford, took me on the train to Ilford market, which she knew. We each bought a length of Harris Tweed, pre-war material of course, but we got it on the black market, as we did not give any coupons for it. We had our red clothing coupon books with us, and handed them to the stall owner, who pretended to cut coupons out then returned our books. We paid about £5 each for the tweed, which was a large sum in those days, and quickly departed to the home of my friend's brother, for a cup of tea. I expected the hand of the law on my shoulder for the rest of that day, and was glad when we got home that evening, having a guilty conscience about the whole procedure. My mother must have told my dad what we had done, for he told me severely that I was a traitor to my King and Country, making my guilt even worse. However I soon forgot my crime, and had the material made into what was then called a costume, which I wore for some years, but I never did anything like that again.

Leslie Oppitz was ahead of his time in Croydon

Pioneering Radio Days

I am sure I can claim to be one of the first pirate radio stations in the UK. It was almost at the end of the Second World War. I built a two-valve transmitter and strung an aerial along the garden. I sent out programmes twice a week for an hour during the evening. I played popular music (mostly big band stuff) using a throat mike to introduce them. I liked to think it encouraged people who were war-weary and I asked people to phone in requests. Being at the top of a hill I could cover a four to five mile radius. If my homemade transmitter gave trouble I switched to an army-type 'Walkie-Talkie'. The idea took off and people were phoning in with more requests - I played what I could but my record library of 78s was limited. Glenn Miller, Artie Shaw, Jimmy Dorsey, and so on.

All went well until I noticed this van with a rotating aerial on it going slowly up and down my street. When it hovered I disconnected and shoved the transmitter in a drawer. Next day when it hovered nearer I covered myself by hanging washing along the aerial.

'Radio Pandora', as I called myself, lasted long enough to give, I thought, a bit of fun to a lot of people.

I closed down later but when out locally I overheard two men in a shop who worked at the BBC monitoring station at Tatsfield, Surrey. They had clearly picked me up but in the euphoric days post WW2 they hadn't bothered to really chase it up.

Tatsfield did a tremendous job during the latter part of the war. It monitored German broadcasts seeking out very useful information. It also, I had understood, sent out a fake programme across Europe, called 'Soldaten Sender Calais,' with false news and German music to confuse the German military.

My own station 'Radio Pandora' of nearly sixty years ago may not be recalled by anyone today but may I claim to be the fore-runner of Radio Caroline and other off-shore pirate stations?

Mrs H Phillips recalls an amusing incident in Hertfordshire

What Colour is Your Vest?

I lived in one of the oldest cottages in Hertfordshire and we had to regularly have the chimney swept. There was a very good sweep in the village but he was so unreliable with his time. He had promised to come at 9am and so, oldest child off to school, toddler and I waited. The day wore on wearily until at 5pm he arrived. I was furious, my little girl watched as he prepared to start. She was giving him a very close inspection. At last he spoke to her and out she came with this wonderful gem back, "I bet your vest is black."

I think he was the dirtiest man she'd ever seen, but her comment made my fury disappear. The next time he was due, my neighbour and I decided to call him at the same time feeling there was safety in numbers. Alas we waited and waited, all day no sweep. He came a week late, this I'm afraid was the last straw. I sent away to a catalogue advertising sweep brushes and I became my own chimney sweep from then on. So my vest became as black as the sweep's!

Edna Turner lived in Devon

Memories of Devon

In 1945, when I was ten and in the top class at Junior School the headmaster decided to try an experiment, so everyone in 4a and 4b was allowed to go on a week's trip. This was to be a holiday and learning experience. We went to a small village in South Devon called Huccaby and stayed in the local village school. I think that water must have been short because our washing facility was across a small country lane, over a gate. It was a stream!

We had to be sure to be on the correct side of the cows who also used the stream. We only had two days of rain when we had to wear our boots to wash.

We all had a wonderful time with mattresses on the floor and spartan facilities but I am sure this helped us to become more worldly wise and tolerant.

Also when I was ten years old myself and four friends, one of whom was twelve, used to catch the train from Tavistock to Plymouth for 1/- return. We usually went on Saturday morning. We had to walk from the station into the city centre, past the badly damaged houses still left standing from the blitz. It was awful to see the belongings sometimes hanging over the edge of upstairs rooms and we often wondered where the occupants had gone. On our way we passed a fish and chip shop so we used to order our meal to eat, before we caught the train home.

In 1948, I was in the Girls Training Corps. We entered a team (nine girls and one officer) in a marching competition. However on the day, it rained really hard so the competition was held in a small hall. We started off very well but as we had to go around in small circles we were going faster and faster. We all realised this but the officer was afraid to lose marks and so we ended up almost running. However, as we were all in time with her instructions to "about turn," "left wheel" etc, we won the cup.

Judith Keel moved to Shropshire

Bishop's Castle

We moved from our home on the outskirts of Stratford-on-Avon just before the outbreak of the war. I was five and my sister Mary was not yet three. Our father had already joined up and was due to be stationed on the guns in Perry Park in Birmingham. I remember all the silver barrage balloons in the sky above the park and all the big guns in position, ready and waiting. Convinced that the war was going to happen and with concerns for our safety it was decided that we would have to move. As we had grandparents in Bishop's Castle, a small town in the south Shropshire hills, my father found a house there for us to live in. His fears must have been confirmed when a few days before our departure a plane came down in a nearby field narrowly missing our roof. It exploded in flames and the pilot was killed.

'The Old House' in Bull Street was our new home. It was right under the old castle walls. In fact, part of this wall formed the back of our small garden and towered above the house. At the front just across the narrow street was the stone built old town hall with a carved crest on the wall facing down the hill and wooden seats where the old men would sit. It was here that the air raid siren was installed and inside we were shown our air raid drill. The noise in the house when the siren went off was tremendous, as we were so close. Soon after our arrival we were issued with gas masks and I was very envious of my sister's mask which was brightly coloured and made her look like Donald Duck while mine was of the ordinary design and smelled strongly of rubber.

I displayed some odd behaviour at this time which I think shows that I was affected by what was going on. I remember going into a state where I wouldn't speak to anyone for hours, even days. I started to wet the bed and also to sleep walk or so I heard my mother tell my grandma. One night after we had been put to bed I woke up in the dark. I looked in mother's bedroom but she was not there. I went downstairs but there was still no sign of her. Very frightened, I opened the front door and went flying down the dark street barefooted and in my nightdress until I found my grandparent's house. I banged on the door and eventually it was opened by my mother who believing us to sleeping soundly had gone down there, no doubt to keep them company. I'm afraid that I must have given her a dreadful shock.

Unlike those in the large towns and cities there was never a real risk of food shortages, a rich and varied source of food came in from the countryside around. Farmwomen came door to door with large market baskets selling eggs, farm butter and cream, home cured bacon and ham, also watercress and duck eggs. Dubious characters arrived with rabbits, ducks and pheasants tied to the crossbars of their bicycles. I remember one man, obviously a poacher, who always kept a couple of ferrets up his trousers, which he was always pleased to show you! Such rabbit stews and pies we had with glorious redcurrant jelly. For me, that flavour has never been equalled.

Mother and our grandparents worked constantly to provide us with good nutritious meals. "Come on, eat up you are growing girls" they would say. Grandpa Cooke had for many years had a productive vegetable garden. A walled garden on the outskirts of the town, it had produced fruit and vegetables for his large family of children and now it did the same for us. A load of farmyard manure was delivered every spring and 'double dug' into the soil. Every kind of vegetable was harvested in season. He would always have the first new potatoes and young peas grown under cloches ready to go with the roast duck for lunch on Easter Day, followed by gooseberries made into a large tart. His runner beans were sliced as they were ready and laid in layers covered in salt in stone ware jars to use throughout the year. All the soft fruit was bottled or made into jam or chutney and stood in rows on cupboard shelves. Root vegetables were stored in sacking down in the cellar, apples on racks in the attic. Pears and tomatoes were picked early, wrapped in newspaper and stored in shoeboxes to eat on Christmas Day. His aim was always to grow and store enough to last until the crop came round again. On a heap of rotted manure he grew marrows and when they were still small he chose two, one for Mary and one for me. He wrote our names on them using a pin and as the marrows grew to full size our names, previously invisible, stood out large and clear and it seemed like magic.

As was only to be expected, we only saw our father very rarely during the war years. For several years he was stationed in the Orkney Islands, then later in Edinburgh. He sent us jumpers and Tammy hats from there in Shetland patterns, but they were very itchy! Mother sent him her home made Parkin and Mintoes and photographs of us. He also kept in touch by sending episides of 'The Chronicles of the Imp,' a story he wrote and illustrated himself about a mischievious imp who got into all sorts of scrapes and adventures and also his drawings of humorous nonsense animals. We eagerly looked forward to the arrival of the large brown envelope marked in blue by the censor.

THE PAVADROG

THE BLOWSPIKE

The BLUE FACE Snarfer

A selection of 'Animals'

There was a lot of poverty in the town and a very marked difference between the poor and the better off. Many children had no shoes, they had scabs from scabies and impetigo and played in the gutters. One woman gave birth every single year and had produced twenty-one children. People still lived in fear of the workhouse. By contrast, the owners of The Castle Hotel had a nanny for their two daughters who brushed their hair to shining perfection. One had flaxen and the other vivid auburn ringlets. I felt that my colouring was insipid by comparison, but was cheered when Nanny admired my mousey hair, describing it as 'ash blonde' and my eyebrows 'just like a film star's' and I clung on to this ray of hope for years. We had our hair wound up in strips of sheeting at night to make it curl. 'In rags' it was called and was supposed to make us look like the young Princesses, Elizabeth and Margaret. Like them we had matching outfits. Corduroy jodphurs were made in anticipation of pony riding but mine did not get any use for that purpose after I got thrown into a nettle patch on my first attempt. Instead they made very good cold weather wear during some of the very cold winters that we had at that time. We had a cleaner, an elderly woman who had always been in service, who always curtsied to father in his uniform, men doffed their caps and servicemen in uniform stood to attention and saluted. Even at that age I was very aware of the great differences between people's circumstances and I'm afraid to say that hardly a day went by when I didn't thank my lucky stars that some kind fate had allowed me to have the family that I did.

VE Day in 1945 came when we were at our boarding school in Church Stretton. It seemed to happen quite suddenly and will be remembered forever by us as the day when we ate our first banana. The father of a boy who had not seen his son since the day he left him at the school at the beginning of the war, flew in from the United States with a case full of bananas, some oranges and a lot of fireworks. He had brought enough for us to have a banana and half an orange each and we had a magnificent firework display that night which would have been seen for miles around. The first time that the night sky had been lit up in our part of the world for five years.

Alan R Irons holidayed at Tarbert

Tarbert, Loch Fyne

It was Tarbert; we must have been on holiday.

Tarbert - home to the silver darlings, so plentiful that the fishing boats were tied up in rows, side by side, eight or ten deep into the middle harbour, where the ruins of the old fort still stood. Not any more.

Tarbert - home to famous Loch Fyne kippers (the only kippers worth eating, really!) which uncle Archie used to send by bus to Edinburgh, a dozen pair at a time. I often wondered how they were still fresh when we collected them from the bus at St Andrew's Square.

Tarbert - where mackerel could be caught from the pier with a line and a piece of bread. Dad told me no one ate them – they were scavengers. And who eats scavengers? I still don't eat them. And the herring were plentiful.

Grandma lived two up in a tenement overlooking the pier, so we could watch the boats unloading their catch every morning, throwing the by-catch into the harbour where the gulls – and mackerel, of course - had a field day.

The milk cart came with a cargo of churns. We went down with a pan; the milkman dipped into a churn and measured out a quart. It was real milk, full of cream, straight from the farm just up the road.

One evening, we (my brother and I) were allowed to stay up late. We didn't really know why. But after dark, all the fishing boats, dozens of them, sailed into harbour, dressed overall, multi-coloured lights hung from stem to stern. They just kept coming. This was in June 1945, to celebrate VE day in May.

Norman Heath recalls his first payday

Paper Rounds and Pregnancy

When I reached the age of eleven I started an early morning paper round, at last I could earn some money. For doing the round I received the princely sum of five shillings. It was with great pride that I presented my first week's wages to my mum and dad. My dad then told me to give my mother 2/6d each week towards my keep.

I had a strange experience one morning whilst doing my paper round. The whole area was covered in strings of silver foil. I learned much later that it was dropped by German aircraft to foil our radar.

When I started work at fourteen my father said to me, "A third of your wages to your mother, a third to spend and a third to save." His other saying was, "If you can't afford it, don't go."

My partner that I have lived with for many years told me that when she married, in the 1940s, she and her husband lived with his parents. After a year of marriage she fell pregnant. She told her mother-in-law, whose reply was, "I didn't think my Bill was like that."

Olive Soutar lived in Pinner

Brownies and Guides

I became a Brownie during the War, at the age of eight. We lived then near Pinner, on one of the suburban estates that sprang up during the 1930s. A friend joined Brownies and took me along with her - 2nd Pinner Pack.

At that time the uniform was the brown dress with a brown linen hat, not unlike a sun hat. The older Brownies in the Pack had enrolment badges with a Brownie on a bar but the poor quality of metal during the War made it impossible to continue making these, so I had a square badge. These were only issued for about two years before being replaced by the oval badges, which then continued for a number of years. At the time I hated my enrolment badge but it now has some rarity interest.

I went to Guides at the age of eleven - 5th Eastcote Co. We wore blue linen dresses, pale blue ties, and the old big brimmed hats. Soon after I became a Guide we changed to navy blue berets and the old hats were collected up, to be sent to Guides overseas. The tie had to be very correctly folded to two and a half inches wide, and the length had to come three fingers width from the belt. The back of the tie had to be pinned down to the front of the uniform with a safety pin and, of course, it had to be tied with a reef knot behind the neck. We had inspection every week, which included checking that we had cleaned the back of our enrolment badges as well as the front, and had tied our shoelaces with reef bows. Sometimes we had pocket inspection to check we were carrying all the items considered necessary in case of emergencies.

We did some joint activities with another Company - 2nd Eastcote. Neither Company was attached to a Church but we sometimes attended Church Parade together. The Vicar was quite elderly and a bit doddery and invariably gave us back the wrong flags. We soon learnt to accept whichever flag he gave us and swap them as soon as we got outside the Church.

Living in suburbia we sometimes went to events in London. In (I think) 1947 we went to see a parade in The Mall of Guides from various countries who took part in an International Folk Dance Festival. Princess Elizabeth and Princess Margaret took the salute and drove down The Mall in an open carriage.

My mother was very worried about me going to camp as I liked to be neat and tidy, was a fussy eater and disliked insects. I was also a Londoner, with very little knowledge of the countryside. Mum never understood, and I can never explain, why I took to camping so thoroughly. My first camp was in 1947 at Charmouth. We camped on a farm where chickens scratched around in the yard and we fed waste food to the pigs. I clearly remember having kit inspection during the camp. We each had to lay all our personal kit out on a groundsheet and Captain checked that we had all the right things and that they were clearly marked with our names.

Another year I camped at Inkpen, near Hungerford. For a day out we visited Stonehenge, where there were no fences; the coach just pulled up at the side of the road and we all strolled across the grass to the Stones.

During most of my time as a Guide food was, of course, rationed and about two weeks before camp all our ration books were collected up to be able to claim the coupons for the time we would be away. We each took our own sweet ration in a tin, which were collected up, kept in the store tent and only handed out each day during Rest Hour.

In January 1949 a friend and I joined a group of Guides on a two-week winter sports holiday at the Guide Chalet at Adelboden, Switzerland (a big adventure in those days for fourteen-year-olds). We spent a night on a French train, sleeping on the seats, the floor and the luggage racks, arriving at dawn at Basle. We left the grimy French side of the station, walked past the border control and came to the clean Swiss side, where we had hot drinks, rolls and rich black cherry jam in the restaurant. (We came from a country where food was still rationed.) In Adelboden half the group stayed in a hotel in the village, the other half stayed at our chalet, and we swapped over halfway through.

Beryl Pearmain grew up in Belvedere

Baths and Beaches

From 1940 I lived with my parents in Belvedere, Kent. I remember going to a very cold building, where there were rows and rows of baths, with screens put around them. They were filled with something that smelled horrible. When I mentioned this to my mother as a teenager, I was told that the building was the public baths. Mum had received a letter to say she had to go there on a certain date. The local authorities were getting concerned at the number of lice and scabies they were having to deal with and it was thought that this was down to the way people were living in crowded air raid shelters and troops returning home on leave being infected. So anyone who had servicemen in the family had to report to the civic baths, where there were men and women to supervise them bathing, while all their clothes were disinfected. They also had to take a sulphur bath. Although we had a bathroom at home we still had to go, nobody was excused.

One day, both my mother and I were taken ill. My mother couldn't get out of bed and when she did manage it she couldn't walk. She used to suffer from Lumbago. It was my job to help to put these big plaster patches on her back, 'Thermagene' they were called. As mum couldn't get up and down stairs we slept in the front room under the piano. I don't know which of us was ill first, but my father came home on weekend leave from Lowestoft and found us lying on bedding all wrapped up from the cold. He lit the fire and made us comfortable and called a doctor. What he didn't know was that after he left his ship, all leave was cancelled, so he was posted as 'absent without leave.' He found out when the local police sergeant came knocking at the door. The military were called in and because of the situation he'd found us in, he was allowed a week's leave, but was told he was lucky, as the captain had put a good word in for him. As soon as we could be moved we were sent to live in Yarmouth so we could be near dad's base. Mum told me years later that I just escaped diphtheria. When I was better, mum borrowed a pushchair and used to wrap me up and take me along the seafront for some air. You couldn't go on a beach; it was all cordoned off with barbed wire and huge crosses. I got to know some of the soldiers that were patrolling and sometimes they pulled part of the wire back, so that mum and me could sit on the sand. We were the only ones there, not even the locals went near the beach.

As I got stronger my mother used to walk me to Lowestoft, where dad's ship was moored. We could only walk along one side of the river, the side where the ships were moored was guarded. One afternoon we went down there and a ship was preparing to leave. I can remember waving to the men on its deck. The next thing I knew my dad's head appeared and he was waving like mad. He wrote to my mother later to say how much it meant to the crew to have someone seeing them off.

Colin Bartlett recalls his early years on The Isle of Wight

Growing Up

I was born in East Cowes in1941 but my mother and I (my father was in the RAF) moved to Newport, five miles away, to avoid the bombing by the Germans. Their main target was J.S.Whites, the shipbuilders at the mouth of the River Medina but many of the bombs landed on the town, killing several people.

We moved into a small three-bedroomed terraced house in a row of four with an outside toilet and no bathroom. In the house next door lived my grandparents who I called nan and papa and their two daughters, my auntie Jean and my auntie Rona, I adored them all.

The houses had been built for a Royal Navy Captain during the First World War so the rents would provide an income for his wife and child if he was killed in action. Alas, he was and she used to come to the door each week to collect the rent.

I cannot remember our house very well as I spent most of my time in nan's. When you came out of our back door there was a gate in the fence that was the entrance to nan's back yard. In the yard was the huge cast iron clothes mangle and fixed to the fence was the meat safe with its perforated zinc covered door in which was kept the perishable foodstuff. The tin bath was also hung on the fence. The entrance to the outside toilet, complete with newspaper toilet paper, was also there. From the yard was the back door to the kitchen, which also served as the washroom. The kitchen contained a gas cooker, coal fuelled copper boiler to do the washing in which was also used to heat the water for the weekly bath. On the wall was nailed a wooden fruit box with a shelf in it, I remember it was painted brown. Papa kept his toiletries in here; his hairbrush (I don't know what the hairbrush was for as he was almost bald) and comb, cut throat razor, shaving soap and leather strop to hone the razor on. Hung on the box, on a nail was the same toilet paper that was in the outside toilet. This was used to wipe the soap off the razor when he was shaving. On the windowsill were papa's false teeth, in a cup of water with no handle. He only wore these when he went on holiday or to the cinema. The cinema was visited once a week with his neighbour. When papa came home from the cinema the teeth were always in his pocket wrapped in his handkerchief.

Mary Oldfield in Southampton recalls the war

In the Shelter

Soon after the war started we had a shelter delivered to our house. My dad, who by this time had joined the Home Guard, put it up in our back garden. When it rained, the shelter filled with water so when the raids got bad we went to the big shelter in Bitterne Road next to Minns, the butchers.

One night we went up to Harefield and settled down under a Monkey Puzzle tree. This seemed all right until a nearby ack-ack gun started going off and continued all night. The gunners said that we were safe where we were, though our house was only two streets away. A few days later we had a daylight raid and a bomb dropped on the wood yard, in our road. When we came out of our shelter all of the potatoes in dad's garden had been uprooted and all the apples had been blown off of the trees. All of the windows had been blown in but mum's bird was safe even though it was in its cage in the window. Unhappily, two days later our cat knocked the cage over and the bird died.

I didn't think anything could get any worse but one day soon afterwards I was in the garden when I saw a 'plane flying low overhead. I called mum and told her that it was a Spitfire. She came out to have a look just as the 'Spitfire' started shooting at us. Mum pushed me under the hedge and we stayed there until the shooting stopped. When we got up we saw that dad's bicycle was lying in the middle of the road and he was emerging from a neighbour's hedge. We all survived, thank goodness.

Patricia O'Driscoll lived in Manchester

Moss Side

I grew up in Moss Side, Manchester. I went to school at the Loretto Convent in Moss Lane. Moss Side was a place of fun, safety and happy days. I used to love going into Woolworth's Store on Alexandra Road, and would be drawn to the skipping ropes, jigsaws and books that were readily available for modest sums in those days.

I always will remember being taken to school every day, as Moss Lane was a very busy road, even then the traffic was busy. On my first day at school, this huge nun told me that there were too many Pats in the class and that I would have to be called Catherine at school. Oh God, how I hated the name for years.

My friend and I went to school one day, along Claremont Road, two girls about twelve years old and this 'person' approached us from inside the railings of Alexandra Park, and said to us "Would you like to come and play with me?" We reported this to our teacher who told the police, who came and interviewed us at the time. However, we heard nothing more about that episode.

Moss Side was a pure delight to me - a cornucopia of shops, merchandise, fun, games and enjoyment.

I now live in Ireland and I visited Manchester last year and the changes were remarkable to say the least - my beloved shops were gone, the whole landscape had been re-shaped and re-formatted into a new vista. The times they are a changing!'

John Dymock lived near Aylesbury

School Milk and Field Names

My uncle Walt delivered milk by courier-bike. Two large lidded cans complete with ladles - ½ pint and 1 pint. No milk bottles, the customer provided a jug. He always said, "It takes nine pints to make a gallon."

When free school milk first started he supplied the village school in the same way. The school mistress was most upset when the Education Authority decreed bottled, pasteurised milk be brought specially to the school. Uncle Walt's school milk deliveries came to an end.

Field names bring back memories. The first of these was called 'The Cream Ground.' This field was part of a friend's farm at Quainton. It couldn't have been better named. A lush meadow crossed by a stream, the grass was never brown and dry in hot weather. Many meadow flowers grew in this meadow and it was bordered by a wood to give shade to the cattle.

The second meadow has an interesting story attached to it. During the war the army son of a neighbour of my friends at Silford Ferris wrote to his mother and mentioned Joe's bottom field. Mother then knew where he was bound. The name of the field? Egypt.

Doreen Garner recalls an early memory in Coalville

New from Old

In 1943, I was about seven-years-old and clothing could only be got by having clothing coupons. I was growing that fast I was growing out of all my clothes. So my Gran went round the women in our family for their dresses they did not want. Then Gran put some newspaper for me to hold against myself and she cut round it for a pattern. In a few days I had some lovely new dresses made from those she had begged. Gran was a lovely sewer.

Connie Coates lived in the country

Candle in the Window

The winter of 1940 was long and dark, very dark because of the Government's restrictions. No light must be shown from streets or houses lest enemy aircraft be guided to their targets. A huge roll of blackout material was shown to the villagers. It was coupon-free, but not free of charge. Mother decided we would have to do without. After all, we had no gas or electric. We'd given up our oil lamps since the wartime paraffin made the wicks flicker and our clothes smell.

As we lived down a lane well away from civilisation, surely Hitler wasn't going to see our little light. I went to school in the dark and came back alone across the fields, groping my way completely unafraid. Home at last.

My dad put another log on the fire. A pan of soup simmered on the hob beside the big black kettle. Mother lit a candle in the kitchen so she could see to cut some bread. She brought in the tray and shut the door to keep us warm. We ate our supper, warming around the roaring fire. Dad sank into his chair with his mug of tea. He lit his pipe of homegrown tobacco and puffed away contentedly. We were at peace. Then we heard the latch clack open and the gate swing out as steps approached. A voice called out, "PUT OUT THAT LIGHT!"

Mother shifted first. She scooped up the mat she'd made to keep the draught out from the door and flung it on the roaring flames. There was a fizzly spit and steam sizzled from the up-turned kettle. We were plunged into smoke-filled darkness.

Then my dad leapt to the grate, stabbed his poker through the smoldering mat, and with equally foul curses at mother and at Hitler, charged out into the night, with flaming clumps of mat held aloft and sparking in his wake.

The ARP man, whoever he was, ran for his life. Dad fast after him swearing blood and threats and vengeance at people I never heard of, into the blackness of the winter night, shaking the sparks of our sooty doormat afore him away up the lane.

Meanwhile, our eyes streaming and quivering with fright, mother and I cleaned the hearth and soon had a bright fire burning. After a while, dad stomped back home and as he calmed, it seemed that the cursed warden never even had the cursed hell and damnation manners to shut our gate.

It was time we had a cup of tea. As dad settled back in his chair, muttering oaths at all and sundry, Mother crept into the kitchen to fill the kettle. The candle at the window was almost out, but still beamed defiantly across the fields. With trembling fingers, she snuffed it out and closed the door.

Geoff Bartlett grew up in Wednesbury

Bartlett's Bank

I was about six when the Second World War started. I must have been old enough to recognise what was going on and it seemed only days before we heard the sound of unsynchronised German bomber engines overhead.

My father was a carpenter/cabinet maker/property repairer and also the caretaker of the Midland Bank branch, which was quite a large branch for those days. The building was an old Coaching Inn converted to a bank and still had the stables and coach houses of its original purpose in reasonable condition plus three houses which were servants quarters I believe. We lived in one of these and my grandma in another.

All three houses were built onto the bank building in a large yard which was, I suppose, the coach turning area. Only ours had direct access to the bank main building, via a corridor and a locked door. We had the benefit of an inside toilet and would you believe a telephone, which I was scared of. My father had free use of the coach houses and stables for most of the time, which he used for workshops for his business.

Our address was Bank Buildings, 31 Market Place, Wednesbury and when asked by other kids where I lived had to say the bank. This brought the obvious reply 'Bartletts Bank' meaning Barclays Bank, of course.

I had to work hard from start of school days as we were responsible for cleaning and maintenance of the bank buildings and although we could and did, employ cleaners at times, my father was always broke and we had to do most of the work ourselves. This included scrubbing and polishing floors, polishing brass scales and large inkwells, etc.

It was not at all unusual for kids to have to work in those days as some of my schoolmates worked for their fathers driving horse drawn carts delivering bread, vegetables, milk and salt in large blocks and I used to envy them. I would have loved to drive a horse-drawn cart. It was also quite common to see steam-powered lorries still in use and later on of course, cars and lorries with large gasbags on the roof.

We didn't have to have an Andersen shelter as my friends did; the bank vaults were considered strong enough to take a direct hit so we used them. My father had to build a blast door to close off the vault we used and we spent many nights in there as did some close friends. The vaults consisted of two largish rooms/cellars with very large safes or strong rooms and one containing the boiler. Access to the vaults was via a stairway and a hand wound lift for carrying the cash trolley up and down.

Banks have changed enormously of course, but things that stick in my mind are the huge back to back desks and the enormous books in which accounting was done. These were about three inches thick and seemed about three foot by two, weighing a ton. They were kept in the book room, off our hallway. The first morning job for the clerks was to trolley these out for use and then do their work with occasional visits to the boiler for stoking. Typewriters were in abundance as were adding machines and comptometers.

Mike Minson spent the war years in East London, then Kent

Bombings and Brick Dust

When war broke out my mother and I were immediately evacuated to Cheltenham Spa, leaving my father behind in London. He had a reserved occupation – a bus driver – and so had not been called up. The 'Phoney War' then ensued and before long my mother decided to chance it and return to London, an action which nearly cost us all our lives. In late 1940 when the blitz began we were living in a terraced house in Forest Gate, East London. My father had taken the precaution of installing a Morrison Shelter in our living room and we were in it one night when the house next door took a direct hit from a land mine. The intervening wall collapsed, effectively burying us in our shelter. I can still taste the brick dust that filled the air and feel the terror of imminent death that gripped all three of us as we huddled there in the pitch darkness. However, the one-inch steel plate roof of our shelter held up and in the morning we were dug out, all unhurt.

As a result, we were forced to move to Barnehurst, in Kent and whilst there, my father lost his life as a direct result of German action. Whilst moving very heavy furniture out of my grandparents' bombed out house, he physically damaged one of the valves in his heart and three months later he was dead. He was only thirty-one and not only was my poor mother devastated, she found herself a widow with a five year old and a widow's pension of ten shillings per week! She was forced to take in lodgers so we could survive and times were indeed very hard.

Shortly after my father's death my mother took me to visit her sister in Hackney, my aunt Flo. This meant a bus trip through the Blackwall Tunnel and on emerging at the other side, in the tunnel approach road, we were machine-gunned by a German fighter plane. He missed our bus but I can still see the chips flying out of the white brick tiles in the tunnel wall and those bullet holes stayed there for many years afterwards.

Some months later, now in 1944, we were visiting the same aunt and whilst in her living room we heard the growling motor of a V1 overhead – and then it stopped! The doodlebug crashed less then two hundred yards away and the blast left us deafened, shaken and again covered in brick dust. My aunt's open coal fire leapt out of the grate and deposited itself in the centre of the room and we rushed around like headless chickens putting it out. What had saved us was my uncle's foresight. He had put up a twelve-foot wall of sandbags inside the Victorian railings in their short front garden and these took the main force of the blast, otherwise I wouldn't be here now.

Joy Riley grew up in London

Entertainment

Aunt Janie and uncle Fred were the first in the family to acquire a wireless. This was a large box that needed an accumulator to store the electricity to operate it. Our first wireless that I recall was powered by electricity - very posh! It was an HMV 340 Wireless

Set and cost £13 4s 6d. Before that we had an HMV wind up gramophone. This became a firm favourite of mine and I would play the records over and over. The gramophone had to be wound up before a record could be played. If you forgot, the record revolved slower and slower and the tone became deeper and deeper. We had Charles Penrose singing 'The Laughing Policeman,' many by Gracie Fields and Shirley Temple and comic records by Will Hay and others.

At Christmas family gatherings, there was a certain amount of drinking but I cannot remember anyone actually being drunk. As I got older, I was allowed a glass of port and lemonade but I was only allowed to sip it. Dad did not drink at all. If he had a shandy he really thought that was living dangerously. I think mother and the aunts generally had gin and lime. Everyone was very merry but that was as far as it went. Perhaps there was not the money to buy enough to get drunk or perhaps they were just sensible drinkers. Smoking was the vogue then. The men, but not my father, smoked cigars and most of the ladies cigarettes. The air was thick and I can almost smell the room 'the morning after' if I try hard.

One Christmas I had a beautiful baby doll made of rubber. Quads had been born in St Neots, Cambridgeshire and had made quite a stir. Edmunds, the local department store, had commissioned four of these life-size dolls and dressed them up for display. When the display was over they sold them off. They were very dirty but being rubber they were easily washed and mum bought one for me. She made lots of baby clothes for it. Apparently on that Christmas morning I also had a little wooden monkey that climbed up a stick and I would not play with anything else much to mother's chagrin but I soon came to love that doll more than any other. It was so lifelike that I used to give old ladies heart attacks as I dragged it around by one leg with its head banging on the ground. I kept that doll for many years and my own children played with it too. But time eventually took its toll and first the arms and legs and then the rest of it just crumbled away. Alas it is no more.

Everyday entertainment was mainly through the wireless. Every evening we would all sit round and listen to our favourite programmes. Dick Barton, special agent, was a serial broadcast every evening at 6.45 - 7.00. Mrs Dale's Diary was on every afternoon and was, I suppose, the forerunner of the soap operas of today. Weekly programmes such as Henry Hall's Guest Night, Monday Night at Eight and ITMA (It's That Man Again) featuring Tommy Handley, were compulsive listening. There were only two radio stations, the Home Service and the Light Programme, now Radios Four and Two respectively.

By far the most popular 'outing' was to the pictures, as the cinema was called. Once the cinema opened, usually about 12.30, the programme ran continuously until about 10pm. You could go in at any time you liked and you just stayed until the film came to the part where you had come in and then you got up and left. This meant that you had often seen the end of the film first! The programme usually consisted of the main film, a B movie, the news and trailers of next week's programme. There may be one or two adverts but that was uncommon. If you were really lucky you might have a cartoon thrown in for good measure. This arrangement meant that people were coming and going quite often during the film but nobody seemed to mind.

My favourites were the films made by the Gainsborough studio. They had a group of stars, Stewart Grainger, Margaret Lockwood, Pat Roc, James Mason, Phyllis Calvert and Jean Simmons who appeared in many of their films. I think I probably saw every one of them. James Mason was usually the dark mysterious 'baddie' while Stewart Grainger was the dashing hero. A crowd of us would rush to the Gaumont cinema near Wood Green Tube station as soon as we left school to see the latest offering. Seats were priced at one shilling, front stalls; one and ninepence, back stalls and two and threepence in the circle. If we went as a family in the early evening, our special treat was to buy a bag of chips to eat on the way home.

I think everyone's first date was a visit to the pictures and the back row of the stalls was always full of couple kissing and cuddling and not taking much notice of the screen! The usherettes would shine their torches along the row from time to time to keep an eye on what was going on!

Live theatre was quite badly affected during the war and I didn't go very often. The Windmill theatre in London which 'specialised' in nude shows as long as the girls DID NOT MOVE was famous for its saying 'We never closed!'

The few live shows that I did go to were when I was taken by one of father's sisters to the Wood Green Empire. There is only one that I can remember and that was being taken to see 'Jane' of the Daily Mirror. Goodness knows why that should have been deemed suitable. 'Jane' was a strip cartoon character in the Daily Mirror and spent most of her time either very scantily clad or very modestly naked! I would read the cartoon every day when we had the Mirror passed on from Mrs Goodall next door. When she died I would cut out the cartoons from my grandmother's paper when we went there every Sunday morning. Anyway, off we went to see the famous 'Jane.' As was usual for the star of the show her act was last on the bill and after singing a couple of songs in evening dress, she went behind a screen and took off her clothes in silhouette. That was really racy in those days!

Brian Moran lived in East London

Land Mines and Telegrams

In the May we had a German plane come over with smoke coming from one of its engines. As it came towards us in the distance two parachutes opened up in the clear blue sky. The Home Guard, thinking they were the German crew bailing out, started to wave their guns about hoping to capture them when they landed. Someone with binoculars said they are not Germans but land mines coming down. I have never seen people run so fast for cover in my life and that included me. One of the bombs fell in the graveyard at the back of us and the other, thank God, got hooked on a tree outside the main gate swinging to and fro only inches off the ground. We were all evacuated from the building while the bomb disposal unit came and took it away.

To add interest to our lives the enemy started to use new weapons called V2 long-range rockets. These gave no warning of their approach at all, these rockets went up into the atmosphere well over 40 miles and fell out of the sky towards earth at speeds in excess of 1,000 miles per hour. This is faster than the speed of sound so the bomb with its one ton warhead landed, exploded and caused the damage before you heard it coming.

The first of these V2 rockets fell in Leyton, near the entrance to the town hall grounds. The crater was oval in shape and measured fifty-three feet long and eighteen feet deep. Twenty-four houses were demolished, seven people killed and seventy-three were injured.

The next one fell a week later about lunchtime, out side Brown's Factory. The whole office staff were killed outright except for one, a total of seventeen killed and two hunded injured.

Well over a hundred bombs of different types and sizes fell on Walthamstow alone.

When the war ended, I knew that I would see my father once again. I was just twelve and a half when he left and nearly sixteen on his return; it doesn't seem long, but how young people grow in that short time.

Mum received a telegram saying that dad was back in England and had landed at Liverpool docks and had been taken to hospital suffering from ulcers and a touch of malaria. Mum went up by train to Liverpool to see him in hospital and I went and stayed with nan for a few days.

It was a few weeks later when I was in the swimming pool at Leyton baths that a friend of mine came and said, "Your dad's home."

I have never dried and dressed so quick in my life. I dashed home and entered the room. I am sure he did not recognise me at first and then I rushed over to him and we hugged and hugged and had a good cry together.

Jillian Kearns remembers the exploits of her gran's dog

Bobby

I remember the daily journey to the butchers to get what ever was available. I didn't like the butcher as he teased me - it was supposed to be fun. He always pinched my nose with his bent fore finger and middle finger, then pushed his thumb between his fingers and said "Ah there's your nose, I'm going to give it to the little dogs for their dinner!"

That made me cry!

Then one day, we called into the local greengrocer, who it was reported had some kippers. Mother and I had just met gran's dog, Bobby who took himself for walks, so he also came into the greengrocers with us. Mother asked very politely for some kippers, the shopkeeper started a tale of "I'm so very sorry, Connie. If I had some kippers you would have some, but I've jut sold the last packet."

Mum was very disappointed. "Oh dear," says mother, "whatever shall I get now?" Nobody noticed little Bobby, who had slipped into the back of the shop and came out with several pairs of kippers in his mouth!

"That **** little dog." shouted the shopkeeper.

Mother and I chased Bobby home to gran's. Dad and gran had kippers for tea and Bobby was very popular.

Gran had to go to work so when she was out Bobby had to fend for himself. If he wanted chocolate he would pop to the local shop and stand on his hind legs with his paws on the counter where chocolate was served. If he stood to the right he wanted toffee and if he went to the fridge he wanted ice cream. When gran went to the shop to pay for her newspapers, they would say, "Mrs Knight, you owe us for Bobby's sweets, chocolate and ice cream!"

Marjorie Williams recalls how she met her husband

Winnie's Loss

On New Year's Eve 1940 I was nineteen years old and a member of the youth club attached to a small church. We had planned a party and as most of our lads had gone to war, our vicar suggested that we invite some of the soldiers who were billeted in empty properties in the street where our small church hall was situated.

Winnie was told to pass the word around. Alas, only one soldier came – a sergeant. I discovered later that it was his birthday and some of the lads had arranged the date with Winnie. On emerging from the blackout he discovered that she was much taller than he was but he gallantly spent the evening with her.

A couple of weeks later he and I met again at a local dance. In the autumn of 1942 we married while he was on forty-eight hours embarkation leave. Thankfully, he survived the war and we enjoyed almost forty-nine years of happy marriage.

Ernest Wallace was evacuated to Kent from London

And I Still Love Her!

The relationship between my mother and father was very loving. They cared greatly for each other. It was a relationship that endured considerable periods of separation, aggravated by the 1939-45 war years. These bonds, enhanced by laughter, gave stability to my sister and me during those traumatic times.

In 1939 I was thirteen years of age, and at the outbreak of war was evacuated with the school to a town in Kent. This was ostensibly to avoid the anticipated bombing of London. What a laugh! Like a lot of evacuees, I found I had moved into a much higher social strata where tea was served at 3.30 in Wedgwood cups on a silver tray by one of the maids. At 8pm, a four-course meal was served where I had great difficulty in selecting the correct sequence of solid silver cutlery. My table napkin was aligned beside my plate in its special silver ring.

The maid regarded me with a maternal instinct and complained, with a twitching nose, that I needed to change my clothes more frequently. (I wonder why?) The gracious lady of the house decided that the meager billeting allowance, essentially for food only, would be augmented with her own personal allowance for clothing.

Eventually education was restarted by the generous acceptance and sharing by the local grammar school. Their smart straw boaters readily displayed the difference in social standing. These compared with our scruffy cloth caps, which were stuffed into pockets at the slightest pretext.

Air raid sirens and the need to scurry to a shelter frequently interrupted classes. A further interruption would occur when in a mid morning session the headmaster would appear at the class-room door to say that my mother was outside with a parcel of sweets, cakes and clean socks. I was instantly mortified in the presence of my grinning friends, and shriveled before their eyes. "He's got his Mum here again."

Our meetings were tense on my behalf, and her loving eyes didn't see the scowling brat who felt utter humiliation at this cloying maternal gesture. The conversation was usually stilted with very little thanks from me for items, which required so much self-sacrifice from her, in those lean war years. As the air raids intensified so these exasperating meetings were repeated leaving me with mixed feelings of rage, shame and guilt.

In 1943 I left school and the excitement of the air war over Kent skies and returned to London. This was greatly to my mother's wishes as she now had the husband she loved, the son she doted on, and her daughter, restored as a family entity. Alas, this lasted a short time only and in 1944 I volunteered for the Fleet Air Arm for pilot training.

After the softness of earlier years, life in the Navy was certainly more severe, but buffered with humour, it was acceptable. After a period of 'square bashing', I impressed the Board by assuring them that I had joined the Navy to avenge the death of Nelson, and was sent on an educational course to Chelsea Polytechnic to study mathematics and navigation with sixty other potential Naval Aviators.

We slept in rooms close to the Polytechnic and marched in orderly fashion to our lessons every day. It was necessary to maintain some service procedure and roll calls were necessary at the beginnings of morning and afternoon sessions.

By the second week, despite desultory bombings by German nuisance raiders, we had settled in nicely. It was at an afternoon roll call summons, that there we were, thirty hungry Naval cadets waiting for dinner.

"Right, line up, dress by the right, wake up you lot. Atten-chun! Will Cadet Wallace take one pace forward and dismiss. His mother is waiting in the reception with his clean pyjamas."

My humiliation was complete. I shrunk out through a gale of laughter to confront my mother with nostrils flaring and teeth bared. I was certainly not the loving son she wanted. The verbal attack was violent, although I can't remember what I said. She left with tears in her eyes. Within days I had received a letter from my father chastising me for my treatment of her.

By January 1953 I was married and my parents had moved to Scotland. My new wife and I visited their old house, now empty, to see that everything was secure and that there were no burst pipes. At 7.55 the main fuse blew and the house was plunged into darkness. This coincided with the exact moment my mother died in Scotland from a cerebral hemorrhage suffered earlier in the day.

Nine months later my wife gave birth to our son.

I often wonder about reincarnation. I know my mother loved me greatly, but I have condemned such thoughts over the years. Her loss was a great blow, despite her eccentricities. She would have loved the grandchildren. She must have thought that I was so cold and uncaring. It wasn't so. I loved her then as I love her now.

Diana Moyse lived in Roehampton

Who is He?

My brother was a newborn baby when our father was called up. After a few years, father was sent home as he was invalided out of the army. He arrived home and walked down the path. John, my brother, took my hand and said, "Diana, who is that man?" To which I replied, "That's our daddy."

I was six and a half and John was three.

I also remember that we were not evacuated from our home in Roehampton, London but during the blitz our mother took us to stay with my father's family in Newcastle for six weeks. We slept three in a bed. The bed had nits, but we were safe!

Eunice Jones shares an early embarrassment

Nose Bleed

During 1942, my mom stayed up late with me to await the first leave of my sailor boyfriend.

I ran eagerly to the front door to welcome him with a big hug but somehow got my nostril caught on the big hook that supported his kit bag and gas mask and as he walked across the hall I was dragged along with him to the living room.

My nose streaming with blood, my mom retorted, "Silly madam getting so excited, you've caused a nose bleed."

In my eighties, I've still got a split on the inside of my right nostril!

Sheila Stafford recalls life in Devon

Sweets and Lice

I lived with extended family in Paignton. My earliest memories include watching grandad put a latticework of tapes on the windows and the iron fencing from the front garden going. Of being taken in the middle of the night to huddle in the space under the stairs, everyone silent while bombers droned overhead on their way to bomb Plymouth; being terrified by the unearthly wail of the siren.

We used to walk in the lanes around Stoke Gabriel and have picnics on the banks of the Dart. American soldiers stationed nearby would come upon us picnicking, talk with our parents and trudge miles back to camp to return with packets of sweets for my cousin and myself. When their jeeps passed us on our walks they would throw these same sweets to us from the open backs of the vehicle.

A sadder memory is that my cousin and I were farmed out to a distant relative when my uncle's plane was shot down and he contacted TB after days drifting in the sea in an inflatable rescue dinghy. He came home to end his days. He was twenty-nine, my grandmother's youngest son and she never really got over it.

For some of the war, my dad managed an aeroplane factory in Scotland. I remember being lifted into the empty interior of a Spitfire (I think), it was like being in an echoey tin can. He had to tell the workforce – a contingent of fearsome ladies – that they had to have their heads examined for lice. To defuse a probable riot he added "and my wife and daughter will be the first two women to have their heads examined." No doubt the sight of my angelic self did the trick…

Mrs M Leith recalls an incident involving her husband and the law!

Rabbits

My husband was in the RAF and while on leave, he went drinking. When he arrived home he went looking for our pet rabbit. At that time we had an air raid shelter in the street so he went to search there. He was away quite a while and I was getting worried, as it was now 2am. A knock came at the door. I opened it expecting to see my husband. He was there, but accompanied by a policeman, who thought that he was 'taking the mick' – he didn't believe that my husband was walking around in the early hours looking for a rabbit! Eventually, all was sorted, but we never found the rabbit.

Irvin Stewart was posted to Upper Heyford

The Toss of a Coin

In mid 1943, I was a Sergeant Wireless Operator/Air Gunner posted to Upper Heyford, where my colleagues and I met up with twelve pilots. After about a fortnight the twenty-four of us were sent to a satellite aerodrome where we crewed up, one pilot with one Wop/Ag. The pilots, like us, were newly qualified and had been used to flying small aircraft, e.g. Tiger Moths and Ansons. They were there for conversion to Wellingtons prior to going to a heavy conversion unit converting to Lancaster Bombers. As they learned their craft we flew with our pilot doing our own particular work.

The twenty-four of us shared the same hut except for a couple of officers and one particular Tuesday the usual discussion was taking place "What shall we do tonight?"

Stan Schofield said he was going dancing at Banbury Town Hall. This was greeted by raucous shouts of "It's rubbish on Tuesdays, there is no talent there".

Nevertheless, Stan wanted to go so I said I would go with him and off we cycled. After about an hour it was obvious the rest of the lads had been correct, there was precious little talent and Stan said to me "There is only one nice looking girl here" to which I agreed, only to find that we both chose the same one. Stan suggested we toss up to see who should be the one to ask her to dance, and if it looked like he was fixed up, then the other would return to camp. Well he won, asked her to dance, took her for a drink, seemed fixed up, so I returned to camp.

Next day, about 11.30am I was in lessons when we heard a tremendous bang and learned that Stan and his pilot had taken off in a Wellington to do 'circuits and bumps' (take-offs and landings). They reached about 500 feet when both engines failed and the aircraft crashed, killing them both.

I have oft times wondered, would Stan not have been killed if I had won the toss? Not that I would have taken his place, Stan had his pilot and I had mine, but did Stan's life depend on the toss of a coin? It is something I have never forgotten.

Barbara Algar recalls their house sharing agreement

Bed & Breakfast

Prior to the commencement of World War Two my father joined the RAF and became an instructor with the regiment in charge of the Balloon Barrage. As he was already in the forces he was amongst the first to be sent abroad. To supplement our income, my mother opened her home as a 'Bed & Breakfast,' which made her liable to take in army personnel. The army would send round a billeting Sergeant and he would decide how many bedrooms you had spare. He would then proceed to make a two bedroom into a four bedroom with the delivery of four single beds. We ended up having enough room for eight soldiers. Over the next few months we had every nationality you could imagine but my mother took a liking to the Canadians and New Zealand/Australian ex prisoners of war, I think she was so sorry for them. At the time I was resting from the stage for a few months so was able to help her. She gave me strict instructions that if Sergeant King came round to arrange to send the Royal Army Pay Core Boys to billet, I was to tell him she was full. Of course, I let it slip that the ex prisoners had gone that morning and within two hours, eight R.A.P.C. were deposited at the door. The allowance, by the way, was thirty shillings a week (all found).

My father died two years after the war aged forty-two with an illness contracted in the forces. The Air Force gave him a pension of seventeen shillings a week, which I may add, died with him.

"But I always carry a sack of sand in case of incendiaries, constable."

Contemporary Cartoon

Iris Campbell lived with her family in Stoke

Long Distance Love

My Aunt Joan, my mother's younger sister, was twenty years old when she married her sweetheart Edward, in 1941. The marriage was a rushed arrangement when it became clear that Edward would soon be sent overseas to fight in the war. Sure enough, two months after the wedding, Edward found himself on a troop ship bound for North Africa. He wrote regular letters home to Aunt Joan and she showed some of these to my mother when we made our regular Sunday visits to her house for tea.

After Edward had been away for about eighteen months, mum asked Aunt Joan if she was coping on her own, not the first time that she had posed this question. I remember Aunt Joan smiling and saying that she was all right and not to worry about her. I got the impression that she was not missing Edward as much as she used to.

Some time later, perhaps two months or so, I was upstairs in my room one evening and I heard mum and dad talking. I couldn't hear exactly what they were saying but I realised that they were talking about Aunt Joan. I crept quietly out of my bedroom to the top of the landing and listened to what they were saying, hardly daring to breathe. Dad raised his voice at one point and said that 'Somebody had got to say something to her before she got herself a worse reputation.' Mum said that she didn't believe it, to which dad replied, 'Our Ken said he saw Joan with a man going in to her house late on Saturday night. He saw it with his own eyes. What more proof do you need?'

Mum agreed to speak to Joan, so I had a tingling in my stomach the following Sunday as we walked the half mile to Aunt Joan's house. We sat down as usual to tea and cakes and the conversation took its normal course. I made an excuse to go to the toilet, knowing that mum would say something when I was out of the room. I walked out and hid behind the door from where I could hear what was going on. Mum came straight to the point and asked Aunt Joan if she was seeing another man while Edward was away. Aunt Joan denied bringing any men back to the house but she did admit to enjoying herself at the dances in the town. 'I might give them a kiss good night but nothing else.'

Mum was obviously satisfied by this explanation but she did go on to warn Aunt Joan about the dangers of 'getting herself a reputation.'

When I heard that the topic of conversation had moved on I came back in to the room and mum and Aunt Joan carried on as if nothing had been said.

It was left like this until early 1944. Edward had been away since the middle of 1941 and Aunt Joan was clearly not missing him much at all. Suspicions continued but Aunt Joan denied any extra marital goings on. One morning, dad had to go round to Aunt Joan's house to mend a leaking tap in the kitchen. It had snowed overnight and there was a liberal covering all across Stoke and surroundings, including Aunt Joan's front garden. When dad arrived at 8am he opened the garden gate and began to walk up the path. He stopped as he noticed another set of boot marks on the path. One set, going away from the house!

He had caught Aunt Joan red handed and it was a very angry dad who knocked on the door. Aunt Joan apparently burst in to tears and said that she loved the man and was going to go away with him. He turned out to be a 'Yank.'

Aunt Joan and 'Hank the Yank' were the subject of much gossip for a time until the novelty of their relationship wore off and the gossipmongers moved on to someone else.

Hank the Yank landed on Utah beach in Normandy on the 7th June and Aunt Joan was devastated when he left her. So she now had two men writing to her.

In the end, Aunt Joan wrote Edward a 'Dear John' letter. He was heartbroken, as you might expect and never returned to the home that he had shared with Aunt Joan for such a short time.

Hank the Yank survived the war and returned to his home near New York. Aunt Joan, who had remained faithful to him (as far as we know) divorced Edward and became a GI bride in 1947, emigrating to the USA where she still lives a very happy life with her 'Hank' and four little Hanks, (now not so little!)

Postscript: Edward returned from the war and started his own business in the building industry. He prospered and met a lovely girl who he married in 1951. They had two children and led a very happy family life until his death in 1998

Lucy Baruch shares a glimpse of life in Hertfordshire

Sandon

From the outbreak of World War II until 1941, Lydia Rickman wrote from the village of Sandon to her daughter Lucy, who was studying in the United States. Lucy Baruch shares some of the fascinating details from her mother's letters - giving a flavour of what life was like in Sandon in 1940.

1939

September 6: Sandon still has no evacuees.

September 22: We get petrol for seven miles a day.

September 25: We planted another row of lettuces and are going to put cloches on them in the hope they will come to something before the cold stops them growing. Even a leaf or two would be a help, if food gets difficult. Chambers has promised to catch us some rabbits in the wood.

October 19: I enclose the first sign of rationing; this envelope with sugar in it I got at a teashop. Sugar is hard to get.

December 28: We have had the first snow of winter today. It got cold the day after Boxing Day and has been bitterly cold. The rationed things are all one needs: a quarter of a pound of bacon a week hits some people pretty hard, but I find it a convenient lunch dish.

1940

February 13: It snowed hard yesterday morning so I went to Baldock for some needed supplies for fear of being snowed in again. If the frost holds till Saturday it will have been three months below freezing except for one thaw of two days in January, and one of four days last week. Two nephews of Cecil Sale who keep pigs are going to take over our lower field to grow 'roots' to feed them. We aren't allowed to plant grass, and I didn't see how we could manage to cultivate it ourselves for food.

March 1: It is lovely having double daylight saving, so blackout is not until 7pm.

March 31: Sandon Women's Institute had parties for the searchlight men on Friday and Saturday. There are two parties in Sandon parish and half of each came each day. We are asked to let them have hot baths, and I said I would take two on Fridays. I shall be interested to meet some of the men. I gather they were all Territorials in the Royal Engineers. At the tea party yesterday they all seemed about thirty, I should think. It would be a frightfully monotonous job, ten men living crowded together with nothing to do off duty and miles from anywhere.

April 8: It is so cold here the snowdrops show no sign of flowering.

April 9: I had planned to settle down this evening and write a good long letter but since I listened to the 6pm news and heard about Norway and Denmark (being invaded by Germany) my scattered brains just refuse to collect. I have been sitting here by the fire doing nothing at all. It seems too awful to be true. One just cannot bear to think of what it means for us as well as them, too. I expect this is the beginning of the real war.

April 15: Father shot a rabbit one morning and we have had a one-pot meal of it that has been very satisfying and trouble saving.

April 16: It has been snowing this afternoon and the temperature is 34f, and there is a bitter wind. The trees are still completely bare, and no spring flowers yet. It all seems incongruous with daylight till after eight o'clock.

May 31: There are many things I should like to tell you but can't, of course (because of censorship) except the things that are published such as barricaded roads and removed signposts that are outward and visible signs that bring it home to us even in Sandon. Everyone obviously feels grim but everyone one meets goes straight on with the job, though, as someone put it, "all our minds are firing on only three cylinders." People are settling down already to face whatever may happen and just hang on, knowing if they can hang on over this summer Hitler is sunk, even if it takes some time to prove it to him. There is something imperturbable about the British when roused out of their ordinary complacency as now.

June 25: I had about fifteen or twenty from the council cottages practicing with our fruit sprayer (turned stirrup pump) this afternoon. We had a demonstration with practice bombs from the ARP authorities at Hitchin last evening and I was given the job of putting out one of them, and felt much surer of myself after having really done the trick, as did these women this afternoon. I am also having an informal First Aid class for some of the mothers who want to know what to do in case of need.

June 29: I am spending a lot of time and energy helping organise a fire-fighting group among the council cottage women. The sergeant of the searchlight company came to arrange hot baths this week. Their hours are rather odd now as they have to sleep in the mornings, so baths have to be available in the afternoon - not easy to arrange. There is no medical service of any kind available, so I can't think what would happen if any jettisoned bombs should strike Sandon. However, the mothers now have certain rudiments of knowledge and some of them also simple stocks of requisites for dealing with burns etc. They hope to have a stirrup pump of their own in time, only they are hard to get now, everyone having just wakened up at once to the possibility of needing one.

July 16: The Air Raid Precautions arrangements here continue to be unsatisfactory beyond belief, but are better than at one time. I haven't got hold YET of a stirrup pump for the council cottages but have seen that they have some requisites in case of fire or bomb there, and have tried to help them learn a little about first aid, knowing almost nothing myself. They are a nice intelligent lot.

July 25: I was flabbergasted when I got to Tewin (having heard rumours only of the raid in that part) to find that our friends had borne the brunt of it. One incendiary fell in the end of their garden, within two feet of the seat and between them and the house next door, and five high explosives between them and the village green. One bomb fell on the metalled road and destroyed all the water pipes and electricity and telephone cables etc under it. Windows were broken in cottages nearby but not a single person was even scratched. It was a perfectly incredible escape. She said it was terrifying beyond words to hear the thing roaring towards you 'sowing' bombs which you heard bursting after their screaming fall. But now, after seeing what the chances are of them missing one, she has got a confidence she never expected to have and has entirely lost the sense of nervous apprehension it is difficult to avoid having at the prospect of air raids. They have only the scar on their lawn to show for it. The bombs didn't even scorch the garden bench or seat. The German radio broadcast the next day that they had bombed the nearby 'city' (Welwyn Garden City) so presumably they were aiming for that but their aim certainly wasn't very good.

September 8: I heard on the nine o'clock news that London was being raided (and there was much activity of planes and searchlights about here). They said fires were started along the Thames in words from which I deduced it was the gas plant at Becton.

When I went to bed I was aghast to see a great red glow due south. I hoped it was only Becton, but today I realise from the papers it was the Surrey Docks as well, and all that crowded district around them is, I suppose, laid waste. It just makes one sick to even think of it. And tonight, I suppose, they will repeat it and kill hundreds more, and our bombers will be doing the same in Germany.

September 29: The things one hears about London are just so awful that one dare not think about them. I wonder whether you get anything in America except the ballyhoo about how brave everyone is. Of course they are, but the conditions are evidently indescribable confusion, in which the people, not the government, have created what order they wanted.

November 11: Blackout at 5.40pm makes a long evening, but I am thankful they decided to keep the clocks at summertime all winter. We have had no very near bombs lately, but the unexploded ones all over the place are a nuisance. The night Coventry was bombed we had a constant procession of planes overhead from dusk to dawn. Their drone pervades one's sleep and every time one woke up, there they were. No bombs near us so I realised they were on a big expedition to the Midlands. I think the first lot must have gone home before the last lot got over, for they seemed to be going both ways at once, but very high up. Of course we are straight on their route from Germany over Holland to the Midlands.

December 5: (from London) I am dumbfounded at how little damage there is. John Lewis's is of course mostly gone, the C & A Modes is entirely gutted. There is a gap at the corner of Davies Street, the corner house being gone. There is a crater being filled in, in front of Daniel Neal's (Portman Square) and another at the corner of Duke Street and Oxford Street. Tottenham Court Road is still closed off and so is the upper part of Bond Street. There are blank windows every here and there along the streets and some buildings, I know, have been hit but don't show it in front. So of course there is more damage than shows on the surface, but that is what a cursory look around shows.

December 16: For the first time since the war began I am finding blanks in the simple menu I usually live on. Cheese is very difficult to get and Stilton (at three shillings a pound) was literally the only cheese Selfridges had in stock last week. I bought a large chunk and shared it with the Evans's when I got back as they also go in for cheeses and fruit and nuts instead of desserts.

There are no dried fruits of any sort to be had and no marmalade anywhere. Selfridges are sold out of tinned fruit but one can still get it in smaller shops. Sweets have completely disappeared in all forms from small shops but I got a stock at Selfridges so as to have some to hand out at Christmas. I also got a pound of crystallised ginger for a Christmas present. Chocolate you can get only if you happen to get in on the day the shop gets its monthly ration from Cadbury's.

Bananas are off the map, so are lemons and a very few oranges are being distributed. Dates and figs, usually a standby at this time of year, and also raisins, are not to be had. Tomatoes are still to be got, not very good, and 1/6d a pound. I managed to get a couple of pounds of onions before the shortage got so acute they were not to be had at all, and am using these very sparingly for flavouring only. I have written all this at length so you can get a picture of what the shipping crisis means to such a family as us. In short, it isn't bad yet at all for us, but is on the verge of being unpleasant, though not serious.

The Fat Ration

The 1940s - Month by Month

1941

January
- Amy Johnson was killed when the 'plane that she was delivering for the RAF crashed in to the Thames Estuary

February
- The first German 'Afrika Korps' troops arrived in North Africa

March
- Women were encouraged to register for war work, replacing the men that had joined the forces
- The Lend-Lease agreement was signed

April
- Income tax was raised to 50% to help finance the war
- Hitler conquered Yugoslavia

May
- The German battleship Bismarck was sunk in the North Atlantic
- Rudolf Hess landed in Scotland, bringing an offer of peace from Hitler
- A Gloster-Whittle E28/39, Britain's first jet propelled 'plane, took to the air

June
- Hitler invaded Russia opening up the Eastern Front, probably the turning point in the war.
- Clothing rationing was introduced

July
- The Germans bombed Moscow
- Coal rationing was introduced

August
- Britain and the USA signed the Atlantic Charter

September
- Jews in occupied countries were ordered to wear a yellow Star of David

October
- German forces reached Moscow

November
- The aircraft carrier Ark Royal was sunk by an Italian U boat

December
- The Japanese bombed the US naval fleet at Pearl Harbour, precipitating the USA's entry in to the war
- Britain declared war on Japan

====================

The War at Home

Miss P Strickland grew up in London

Tarpaulins and Tate & Lyle

We lived next door to a London hospital and every night I worried about it getting a direct hit. Every night my mother would wake us up when the warning siren sounded and we went down to the street air raid shelter in our pyjamas. We could never get to sleep again because of all the adults talking. One day when we got out of the shelter, we could see that all of the houses across the road were just a mass of rubble. Very few people had glass windows, as these would be blown out every other night, so they were boarded up. The roof of our house was blown off at the same time and it was fitted with a large tarpaulin weighed down with bricks attached to the edges. These used to bang against the wall when it was windy.

Mum worked in the nearby dairy, cutting up ounces of butter and lard and weighing up ounces of tea and sugar for the milkman to take on his rounds. Everything was rationed. One morning her friend didn't turn up for work and after an hour, mum went to find her. Her friend's house was a pile of rubble. She waited while the rescue workers dug out her friend and her husband. They finally managed to get the husband out alive. He had been repatriated as he was wounded fighting the Japanese. He was in tears, he said that he had had to listen to his wife screaming because her glasses had been blown into her eyes and he could not reach her. She was dead when the rescue workers found her.

On one occasion, the Tate and Lyle sugar factory was bombed. It was next to the Thames and it took a week for the firemen to put the blaze out, the river was covered in burning sugar. This also gave the German bombers a good view of that part of London!

A family in Australia with the same surname as ours, used to send us food parcels. But they always included a bar of soap, so much of the food tasted of soap. Powdered egg was very useful, making delicious omelettes and pancakes.

Practically every street in London celebrated VE Day and VJ Day. Afterwards, you could see the holes in the roads where the bonfires had been!

John Rogers moved from Sutton Coldfield to Swansea

A Hell of a Bang

I attended Bishop Vesey's Grammar School in Sutton Coldfield, the third oldest grammar school in the country, founded in 1527. In October 1940, the school governors decreed that when the All Clear was sounded after midnight, school would start one hour later than normal, at 10am. More than once, when you were in your classroom after morning prayers at 9am, quite a few pupils were absent. Just before 10am they would arrive in the classroom.

"Where have you been boy?" asked the teacher.

"Oh, please sir, the All Clear didn't go off until after midnight."

Quite often an area would have the All Clear ten to fifteen minutes later than another area and the teachers could not dispute that.

At the end of July 1945 I went to live in Swansea and at midnight on August 8th 1945 all the ships off the Mumbles Head in Swansea Bay put their lights on and sounded their hooters – it was VJ Day, the end of the War. The following weekend, we had a fireworks celebration in our road. One of the organisers had three naval rockets. He fixed two loops on his high garden wall so that he could place the rockets in them one at a time. We had about a forty-minute display, naval rocket number one, then more fireworks, naval rocket number two, more fireworks then finally, naval rocket number three. Naval rocket number one and three exploded beautifully, very high up. Naval rocket number two went up as high but did not explode. Instead, it turned back to come racing back to the road. I shot in behind my garden gate; other people were crouched behind gates and walls. A few seconds later, a HELL OF A BANG! You could hear the sewer pipes rattling under the road. Nobody was injured but several were frightened!

John Milne spent the war years in and around Hamilton

Processed Cheese and The Queen Elizabeth

When the bombing started, Dad joined the ARP in Hamilton where we lived. During the blitz on Glasgow, Dad would get a phone call before the sirens went and go off in the car. We didn't have an Anderson shelter, but stayed in the centre of the house away from the windows. They were covered with a coarse net stuck on with wallpaper paste to prevent flying glass in the event of blast. From our front window we could see parachute flares slowly dropping like fairy lights in the sky. Bombs exploding far away made a strange sound. Not a bang, more a crump, like running over a plastic bottle.

My most vivid memory of the blitz was the white face of my great aunt Mollie, as seen through the glass of our front door. She had come to seek rest and shelter from the bombing. She and great uncle George lived in a first floor tenement flat just over the wall from Fairfield's Shipyard. The worst part of the raids for them was not the bombing, but the guns of the ships in the basin. Every time an enemy plane appeared they would open up a barrage of fire. The concussion from this was so great that every pane of glass in the house was shattered, along with their nerves. So they came to live with us.

I don't remember ever being hungry. I had no great liking for meat or sweets so didn't miss them. Contemporary newsreels of the time show very few fat people. One would refer to the well-fed Americans as being a bit soft, but they did send us food parcels. We had relatives who were naturalized Americans, living in New Jersey. They regularly sent us food and it was with great excitement that we unwrapped each item; many of them new and strange, like processed cheese and bitter cooking chocolate. At one point we talked of moving to the safety of the States, but I think the fact that the King and Queen remained, influenced the decision to stay and fight it out. In hindsight, I couldn't see dad doing anything else.

One year a holiday was spent at Dunoon, just down river from the defensive boom across the Clyde. The boom nets were to prevent enemy submarines from reaching the large number of merchant vessels moored at the tail o' the bank, waiting to go in convoy. One day, people were running out of the hotel and pointing. Just coming in to view, was the great, grey-painted mass of the Queen Elizabeth moving up the Clyde towards the boom and safety. Everyone just stood silently and waited until she was safely through. It was quite usual at that time for the larger and faster ships to cross the Atlantic on their own and not in convoy.

Uncle Rob was Chief Officer on one of the Anchor Line vessels that did this, relying on speed and surprise to avoid the German U-boats. He had a sudden promotion on the eve of D-day when the Captain of the Empire Mace fell off the boat deck and broke his collarbone. He had to take over at a few hours notice, bringing ship and crew through that memorable time unscathed. He was mentioned in dispatches for his efforts. He told us afterwards that his ship was at the head of a line heading for Gold beach. Over the bow was the coast of occupied France and behind there were ships as far as the eye could see.

After the landings he was granted some leave and took it about as far away from the sea as he could get, at a little croft called Badnedin, in the hills four miles north of Nethybridge.

Rachel Noble also has reason to remember the war years in Scotland

D-Day Babies

My husband was in the RAF when my baby was due in 1944, so I went to stay with my mother in Dundee. One afternoon I lay down on the bed for a rest. It was very hot and I was getting near my time. I lay facing the wide-open window and suddenly I heard a rat-a-tat sound. Almost simultaneously, a very low flying aircraft went past the window and I could clearly see the swastikas. It was all over so quickly and I just lay there listening to a neighbour calling to someone about it, so I knew I hadn't imagined it!

A few days later, my daughter was born on the 3rd of June, three days before D-Day. My husband was given three days compassionate leave to come and see us. The only leave that was allowed at that time was compassionate because we all knew that something very big was about to happen.

On the 6th June, while my husband was sitting with me in the ward, the nurse made a very dramatic entrance. She was a tall, very stout woman and she stood by the door with a newborn baby in each arm (one of which was my daughter). She announced that we had 'sent an armada across the channel' as per the official announcement. She then proceeded with all the details that had been given out.

My husband's jaw dropped! He was so disappointed to have to listen to this momentous news secondhand, as he had been hugging the radio for the past few days. I don't know how he managed to tear himself away from the house to come down to the nursing home – no transistors to carry about then!

Ruth King worked in Earl's Court

Fire Watching

I was working in the dental practice in Earls Court in the 1940s. Although I say it myself, folk were wonderful in those days. Patients kept their appointments, even if it meant they had to lie on the floor in the middle of treatments, or go down to the basement where we developed the X-Rays. Earls Court suffered severe bombing and when I came out of the station I was barred from going down Earl's Court Road until I informed the policeman on duty that I did have a dental practice at number 302, then I was escorted to it!

One thing did distress me, when I left in the evening to return home and go back to the station, was to see the platform full with mothers and children settling down for the night with rugs and blankets to keep themselves warm. I had to walk on the extreme edge of the platform to get round them all. I still have my tin hat up on a shelf in the garage from my fire watching days. My sister and I did our fire watching in Pinner where the family lived at that time. Our watch was 2-4 in the morning, and several times we were told "You young ladies shouldn't be out at this time!"

The war years, although sad and grim, were full of camaraderie and friendliness. We were all one big family suffering together and we wanted to help one another.

Mr R Francklin lived in East Sussex

The Family Next Door

Next door to us was a family of five – parents, two sons and a daughter. The two sons were Territorials and were called up soon after the war started. During the Dunkirk evacuation, news was received that one son had been killed and the other was missing. Three months later during the Battle of Britain a flight of German bombers flew over and one detached itself and I suddenly saw small, silver, egg shaped objects dropping down. Standing mesmerised my father sent me indoors, saying they were bombs. A stick of bombs dropped across the town. The first bomb was apparently aimed at the station or a level crossing and it landed some three hundred yards away. A cloud of smoke rose from a building and the daughter next door was creaming hysterically that it was her grandmother's house. Everyone tried to pacify her but the truth was that her gran had been killed. A most tragic family - today all three names are on the town's war memorial.

Nora Wilson recalls an incident in Batley

Wreckage and Life Savings

Before his call-up my uncle Longley worked for my dad and one night he took the van home to Batley. That night Batley and Dewsbury were bombed. The next morning Longley rang my dad to say that the van had been bombed. It had received a direct hit. It had been parked in the cul-de-sac; the edging stones were still roughly in place, but no van. There was a church nearby and it was rumoured that aeroplane wreckage had been found under the wall of the church. My dad, who had gone over and Longley went to see it. There was a policeman on guard duty and dad told him "That's no aeroplane- that's my van engine."

The policeman's responded to this, "Well if that's so I'm not standing guard no more" and off he went.

I was in Batley during that raid. I had not been well and I went to my grandma and grandad for a few days. When the sirens went my grandad took us up to a neighbour's house. He wanted to go to my auntie Nora's to see that she and my cousins were all right. Her husband was in the forces. It was a perfect night for a bombing raid as it was brilliant moonlight. Mum and dad, back in Shipley, heard that the raid was in the Batley and Dewsbury areas and, of course, were anxious about my grandparents and myself. So dad, after seeing about his van, came to take me back home.

First we went to see another uncle - Tommy - who was an Air Raid Warden. Near where he lived a bomb had fallen in the middle of a row of terrace houses. We stood behind a barricade at the bottom of the fields where the houses were. People kept asking Tommy to go to their house to fetch their savings from their homes. Perhaps from a tin box under the sink, etc. Tommy made several trips up to the houses on such missions. The bomb was an unexploded one and he really took a risk as it could have exploded at any time.

Aphra Marshall recalls teenage years in London

The Doctor's House

In the late 1980s my son and daughter-in-law took me to see the old Edwardian house in South London, where I had lived in the 1940s. A large eight-bedroomed doctor's house it was the focus of my father's practice and the source of consultation for his patients, their refuge in times of trouble and hard work for me and my family keeping open house at all times of the day and night for those in need. We shared the local drama of shattered windows, fallen ceilings and fine plaster work broken beyond repair by overhead German bombers and later by the uncertain destinations of the doodlebugs followed by the shock of V2s crashing near the Crystal Palace. My sister and I used to climb out on to the balcony at the top of the house and watch the glow of the London docks burning in the distance.

I can hear to this day the thunder of gunfire from the emplacements in the nearby golf course, the scream of falling bombs and on more than one occasion the sight of crashing German aircraft as they fell in a ghastly burning fireball onto the streets nearby. I can still remember the feeling of pity for a young pilot trapped in such an aircraft. It made no difference that he was the enemy. Whilst we hid under the stairs for protection or tried to shelter in our overcrowded indoor steel shelter with a terrified dog in our midst, we listened to the windows shivering splinters of glass all over the blankets covering the shelter and the floors. We made jokes about the endless clearing up Hitler made us do. Afterwards, we were just thankful that when the All Clear was sounded, we were still in one piece and would have time to shovel up the fallen plasterwork into a wheelbarrow, brush up the endless shards of glass, cover the windows with tarred brown paper to keep the house weatherproof and have the place tidy and ready for the next surgery.

One by one my siblings went to war until I and my mother and aunt kept house for my father who worked all day and did Duty Doctor at the Warden's Post at night. One wall of the big house had to be propped up by a huge wooden buttress to prevent it collapsing and to keep the doctor's house in working order. People came and went at all hours of the day: fugitives from the 'occupied countries' in Europe would call, in a desperate search for news of relatives, friends who might be on the patients list. Sometimes they too had been a victim of war and tragically killed in the local raids. A pitiful sight these political refugees made, some of whom carried only a cardboard box containing their possessions with no home, no money and nowhere to go.

One family of three elderly ladies arrived at our house after a night's bombing raid having lost their home and all their possessions except for their tame parrot, which had been saved from falling debris by its cage placed under the stairs. We gave them a home 'for a while' which turned out to be seven years since it took them that long to have government compensation for losing their house. More people in the house meant more rations to share and we ate a little better in those spartan times.

When the buses were bombed or the roads too badly damaged to use I would cycle three miles to my convent school in West Croydon. One sunny morning as I cycled along the empty main road after a night's bombing raid I met a German 'plane swooping down over the highway machine-gunning the street. I could see the pilot's face as he swept the 'plane towards me riding alone on my bike and people shouting from the houses for me to 'take cover.' I was angry, I'd had no sleep under the stairs, I was fed up with shovelling broken plaster work out of the house and totally fed up with the Germans so, I kept on pedalling with bullets hopping off the road beside me. The gods were kind to me and I was unharmed and arrived at school to take my end-of-term exams. A great part of the school had shattered plaster walls, with broken glass everywhere, doors which hung crazily and freezing cold winds blew through the vacant windows. Still the nuns appeared clean, tidy and disciplined and ready to supervise our exams in the candlelit gloom of the cellars.

After all those years, I looked at the old house, which brought back so many memories. It was now turned into eight flats and the garden into a car park, where flowers had bloomed amongst the vegetables which grew so inadequately in that harsh clay soil. I felt a twinge of fellowship with a mortally injured building now so plain and unloved. As a family we were amongst the lucky ones in that we all survived the war and my parents, now long dead, rejoiced in our homecoming.

Mabel Johnson movingly recalls waiting for her husband to return to Oxfordshire

The Girl at the Window

It is early spring 1943 in Yorkshire, my husband Bill and I are newly married and I am preparing to join Bill who is stationed with a Photographic Reconnaissance Unit (PRU) at RAF Benson in South Oxfordshire.

Bill was flying the blue painted Spitfires of 541 Squadron that were fitted with cameras instead of guns and with extra petrol tanks in the wings. These modifications allowed the planes to fly over and photograph most of Germany and the German occupied continent, unarmed and always alone.

Bill had found us accommodation in a farmhouse on rising ground overlooking the airfield in the delightful village of Ewelme, from our front sitting room window I could watch the Spitfires taking off and landing. The village was an idyllic rural treasure and we cycled and walked in the glorious countryside around, a favourite place was Shillingford, where we punted on the River Thames. The local KCB cafe (Keep the Countryside Beautiful) in Benson village was frequented by the RAF, we often enjoyed coffee or a light meal there. We also went into Wallingford to shop and go to the pictures. Always returning with pleasure to Ewelme, it was where we made our first home together.

Nevertheless, the danger of Bill not returning from an operation over enemy territory was always present and we knew our lives could change drastically in a matter of minutes.

Whitsuntide fell late in the year 1943, Whit Sunday was June 13th and we were due to go on leave the next day. I had our suitcases packed and Bill's uniform pressed, we were really looking forward to a short break with our families in distant Yorkshire. The weatherman had predicted clear weather over the weekend and Bill was flying on Saturday and knew he would be flying at first light on Sunday too, taking advantage of the clear skies.

On Saturday evening we took a walk around the village; charmed by all we saw, the village street with its old houses and cottages, the ivy covered pub and the church of St Mary, where we leaned over the wall and talked with anticipation of our coming leave. Wandering home we passed the village war memorial, seeing it there by the roadside, carrying its messages of past sadness sent a shiver through me.

We were up on Whit Sunday at 4.30am, Bill only wanted a bowl of cornflakes for breakfast and we had tea together. I watched as Bill put on his battle dress and checked his top pocket to make sure he had my silk stocking with him. Unarmed PRU pilots on a sortie had to be especially alert, turning and twisting their heads constantly to spot an attacking enemy fighter plane. Months earlier, Bill had asked me for a silk stocking to wrap around his neck as a protection from the chafing of his shirt collar. In the first rays of dawn we walked down the farmhouse steps and Bill picked up his bike that he always left leaning against the wall and we walked down to the iron gate that was half way down the driveway. We opened the gate and Bill kissed me goodbye. He got on his bike and pedalled to the road that led to the airfield. The last glimpse I had was of him bending over the handlebars with my school scarf wound round his neck. Slowly I turned back to the sleeping house and went upstairs to bed.

I awoke to the sound of Merlin engines coming through the open bedroom window, I realized I must be getting up if the planes were returning. I kept running to the window to lean out as each Spitfire came by, they always flew low over the field at the back of the house. I could see the pilot, but could not recognize them. I didn't count the Spitfires, it would not have done me much good if I had. I didn't know how many had gone out or even if I had awakened as the first one returned.

I went downstairs to prepare breakfast. As we were leaving the next morning I decided to eat our whole weekly bacon ration - two rashers - along with lots of mushrooms. Bill used to pick mushrooms at the dispersal while he was waiting to fly. Time passed and Bill didn't come home, so I decided he was staying in the mess for an 'operational meal' with his friends and I thought it best if I started to think about lunch. We had two lamb chops - our meat ration - so I turned my attention to them and the vegetables.

Although I was trying to act as if all was normal, I was really thinking of little else except the fact that Bill wasn't home yet. I spent my time by the front living room window, looking out over the airfield on which all the landing activity had now ceased. Turning my eyes often to the iron gate on the driveway and hoping to see Bill pushing through the gate on his way to the farmhouse door.

While I was in the kitchen talking to my landlady, suddenly there was a loud knock on the open front door, it seemed to echo down the stone hall. We both must have turned a little pale at this sound, but when she went to answer the door I could hear voices talking for quite a little while. I thought to myself that the caller did not want me or they would not have spent so much time talking on the doorstep. However, shortly I heard footsteps coming down the hallway towards the kitchen door. Then I was really afraid.

Into the kitchen walked Bill's Squadron Leader and Flight Lieutenant. I knew why they were there, I cannot remember exactly what was said, I don't know that it was necessary for words, they must have expressed sorrow that Bill had not returned. I do remember hiding my face behind the door for a moment to calm myself. I took them into our sitting room and we sat around the fireplace.

They then told me that although Bill had failed to return from his sortie they did at least know what had happened to him. Apparently the radio operators employed to listen constantly to all enemy transmissions had picked up a message that the German pilot was sending back to his base. He was reporting that he had shot down a Spitfire over the Dutch Coast. As 541 Squadron was the only one flying Spitfires that morning we knew it had to be Bill. We even knew the exact time and the exact place, the only thing the German pilot did not say was whether or not the pilot had baled out of the damaged plane.

Having to come and give me such news must have been difficult for them, I was conscious of this. Normally letters would be sent to families of missing airmen; this was probably easier than having to look into my face and give me the news. As we sat and talked together a thought flashed through my mind, I probably said the most naive thing they had ever heard. I said "If that was the time that Bill was shot down - then I am sure he must be alright - I don't think that Bill could have died while I was sleeping peacefully upstairs." I don't suppose they really had much faith in this theory, but it eased my mind and made me stronger to face all that had to be done now I was alone.

I didn't cry, I felt giving way to tears would make everyone around me feel helpless and uncomfortable, after all this was happening to so many of us. Before they left they asked for all of Bill's airforce clothes, I went up to our bedroom and emptied the drawers of everything, including the things that were in the suitcases ready for our leave, along with Bill's newly pressed uniform. It was a strange feeling, handing over things that had only a few hours ago been a part of our lives. Bill was gone and almost every vestige of him had gone as well.

I cycled down to the phone box in the village to let our families know what had happened, it was all so unreal. The day was beautiful; a typical summer afternoon in rural England, a tea in the garden day, and here I was breaking to them as gently and hopefully as I could, the most dreadful news of our loved one.

I returned alone to Yorkshire the next day.

I had been home in Doncaster for three weeks and one Sunday afternoon when we were all at tea, a lady called at the house. We did not know her, but she introduced herself and said she lived in the next road and thought she may have news for me.

A German propaganda station used to broadcast in English. The announcer was the detested Nazi sympathizer derisively called Lord Haw Haw by the general public. To encourage people to listen to the broadcasts, they would give names of prisoners of war, one or two at each broadcast. We had never listened at home and even though I wanted news so badly we still had not tuned in - it would have been foolish - if I had not heard Bill's name I would have been more heart-sore. But the lady said she was used to listening and she said that Bill's name had been given, also my name and address. She also told us that the announcer had stated that a message from Bill would be read at a later broadcast that evening. I sat at the table and started to cry - I think it was the relief that after all, Bill was most probably alive. Bill would have carried no papers on a flight, certainly no letters or envelopes that had my name and Doncaster address on them. We phoned around to other family members to let them know that there may be a message from Bill later in the evening.

I don't think we had ever sat around the radio listening so attentively before. We heard the usual propaganda and at the end of the broadcast they read Bill's message. It was very short, saying he was safe and unhurt and that I was to carry on bottling gooseberries. Only Bill would have known about this, I had picked the gooseberries in the Ewelme farmhouse garden and bottled them one or two jars at a time.

Several weeks after this broadcast I did get a postcard from Bill, it was the one that had been read over the radio, it was lovely to see his handwriting. Apparently a Red Cross worker who came to Bill in Amsterdam prison asked him to write a card home. Thinking this may have been a ploy to make him reveal what he had been doing over Germany that morning, all he mentioned was the gooseberries, knowing that it was a very meaningful phrase to me.

During the weeks that followed the broadcast I received over eighty letters from all over the UK and even one from an amateur radio operator in Newfoundland who had also heard the broadcast. I answered all their letters, as I was most appreciative of their kindness, especially as they were all awaiting news of missing loved ones themselves.

Bill was a POW in Stalag Luft VI in Lithuania until the Spring of 1945. As the Russian Army advanced westwards the camp was moved to Poland and finally to Fallingbostel near Hanover. As the invading Allied Forces advanced further into Germany the camp was moved again, this time to the east. During the march, in April 1945, Bill and three companions walked away from the guards and escaped back to the Allied lines. Although Bill's clothing at this time consisted of badly worn bits of uniform, he did retain his few personal possessions, including my silk stocking; it gives me pleasure to still have it today. Bill was flown back to England in a couple of days and we were together again. Almost a month later we celebrated VE Day, together.

Alastair Barclay recalls the war years in Stewarton

Memories of Stewarton

Stewarton is a small Scottish town, south of Glasgow. On the morning that War broke out, the broadcast was hardly over when a rumour spread around the town that a German bomber had crashed in a field at Clerkland Farm. Half the population immediately flocked up the Dunlop road to witness this spectacle, only to discover that it was an unfortunate weekend flier in a small plane, which had run out of fuel. Thus Stewarton entered the war...

For the first week the schools were closed but so too were the places of entertainment. But there was plenty to do and everyone was scurrying around making black-outs, filling sandbags, billeting and looking after evacuees, registering or volunteering for the forces, and generally adopting the patriotic attitude that war seems to produce in this country.

The evacuation scheme had commenced on the previous Friday when a large contingent of children, some accompanied by mothers, had arrived in town from Glasgow. After a weekend however, many of them returned to the city as 'there was nothing to do but stare at the green fields.' Most of those who persevered lasted but a few weeks more until there was only the odd child left.

In the following months, civilians were encouraged to join one of the voluntary organisations such as the Red Cross, ARP, Fire Service, WVS, etc. In 1940 after Dunkirk, the Local Defence Volunteers were formed. At the outset they were something of a laughing stock as they had no proper uniforms or arms, and actually went on guard carrying sticks for rifles; in fact some wags named them "the fireside sodjers."

In due course however, the name was altered to Home Guard, the men were issued with real army uniforms, rifles and other equipment, and after training they became first class part time soldiers, with local headquarters at the Drill Hall.

In 1941 the real army came to town when camps were established in the district. To cater for the army off duty a Church of Scotland canteen was opened and this proved to be a first class refuge and home-from-home for the soldiers. The ladies and girls of the town performed wonders in providing tea, sandwiches, rolls, cakes, etc. all at extremely reasonable charges. I'm informed that they even washed and darned the lads' socks on occasion. In an average year, 150,000 rolls, 7,000 loaves and large quantities of tea, coffee, etc. were sold and in the post office section, 41,000 letters were posted. One ex-serviceman who was stationed in the town for a spell, Mr Joe Gilmartin, informed me that of the canteens he visited all over Britain, not one could compare with the warmth of welcome, friendly atmosphere and exceptional value for money he experienced in the Stewarton canteen - praise indeed!

Not only were the troops well provided for in the canteen, but the townspeople opened their doors to them, offering hospitality and friendship in homely surroundings. To misquote Churchill, "never was so much done for so many, by so many."

Wartime radio was one of the main morale boosters, and some of the programmes bring nostalgic memories for the tremendous pleasure and laughter they brought in those troubled times (as Godfrey Winn might say). One of the most popular shows was called 'Happidrome' - a kind of Coronation Street with laughs and featured 'We three', namely 'Enoch, Ramsbottom and me.' Another big favourite was the American styled 'Hi Gang' starring Bebe Daniels, Vic Oliver and Ben Lyon. Other programmes were 'Garrison Theatre', in which Jack Warner made his name and 'Old Town Hall' with Clay (penny on the drum) Keyes. But the radio programme with the biggest following was 'Itma', starring the unforgettable Tommy Handley. Remember the odd characters he met each week like Mrs Mopp, Colonel Chinstrap and Claude and Cecil?

The swing era was now at its height and the jerky syncopated dance music of the thirties had developed into the smooth and swinging sound made famous by the great Glenn Miller Orchestra. The top British band was Geraldo's Orchestra broadcasting about six times a week all during the war years, and other leading bands were those of Oscar Rabin, the RAF Squadronaires and Victor Sylvester, while Joe Loss became uncrowned king of Green's Playhouse in Glasgow.

Stewarton was a real swinging town during the war as there were socials, dances, concerts, whist drives and other sprees every other night of the week. Occasionally at those functions something unforeseen, due to the wartime conditions, might occur. At one particular dance held in the Institute Hall, the dancers were 'hooching' their merry way through 'a drops o' brandy in the wee sma' hours.' Suddenly, the band stopped playing and the lights were dimmed. Amid the confusion a voice from somewhere announced - "Yis'l hiv tae stoap noo - the sireen's jist went"!

Immediately, the First Aid personnel present rushed to their post at the Old Rifle Range, feeling comparatively fresh and ready for action, to be joined shortly by their non-dancing colleagues looking drawn, unshaven and browned off!

Stewarton had a very distinguished visitor in 1942 when on Thursday 15th October - a dull drizzly day - King George VI came to town to inspect the troops, prior to their embarking for the North African campaign. The visit was kept extremely hush-hush and nobody knew much about it until the very last minute. The schoolchildren were then given a half-holiday to welcome the VIP and everyone expected a top ranking army officer. It was only when the King stepped out of his car and began to walk along Lainshaw Street that the secret was revealed.

When the war ended in 1945, demobilisation was immediately set in motion. Soon, all the Jimmys and the Jocks began to trickle home, once more "to sleep in their own little rooms again," just as Vera Lynn had predicted.

In Stewarton, the town council inaugurated a welcome home fund. Subsequently, on demobilisation each man and woman who had served in the forces or merchant navy and the next of kin of those who did not return, received the sum of twelve pounds; it was a very fine gesture indeed. Altogether, a total of £5,112 was distributed, with a balance of £242 left over for memorial maintenance.

It all happened a long time ago and while no one wishes to live in the past it is quite pleasurable, just occasionally, to look back and remember.

Robert Burns put it this way:
" Still o'er these scenes my memory wakes,
And fondly broods with miser care,
Time but th' impression stronger makes,
As streams their channels deeper wear."

Stewarton Home Guard

Mrs A Howarth's family lived in Paddington

Blue Pencil

As you can see from the date on the following letter, written by my father, it must have been a particularly cold winter in 1940. We lived in Paddington, and my father worked for Charringtons Coal Merchants.

I find it amusing that he used the term 'blue pencil' instead of a swear word! I believe this came from censorship of letters during the war.

The letter was written to his mother-in-law (my grandmother) who lived in Little Missenden, Bucks.

My Dear Mum,

Many thanks for your letter, and glad to hear you are keeping OK. We are in a nice mess over coal in London, as there have not been any trucks arriving at the various coal wharves owing to severe weather. Horses have not been able to work all week, so people without coal have had to come and fetch it in prams, taxicabs and also carry it. Everyone is rationed to two cwt a week because of the shortage, but we have not been able to deliver it. The lorries that we have got on are being used for the big contracts such as hospitals and munitions factories and they have had to work for the last three Sundays, although none of us has had to go in. We just give them the orders for coke and they have to go Becton Gas Works near Dagenham to get it, as there is no coke in London. Still you can't help laughing.

We had half a ton in last week, because I could see what was going to happen. Our blue pencil telephone is ringing from morning to night by customers asking when they are going to get their two cwt and all we can say is that there is 'Nothing to Report'. We sold out of coal on Saturday, every blue pencil nob, and I didn't get finished until three o'clock. Our manager is breaking down under the strain and worry - he is like Hitler – can't sleep at night. Our wharf clerk, James, had to go for another medical exam on Monday and they have passed him Grade 2. I expect he will go in about a week's time - so he told us last Wednesday that he was going to get married on Saturday by special license. Our manager had a blue fit when he asked for Saturday and Monday off. He didn't mind him having Saturday off but blue pencil having Monday off as well.

After a bull and cow he let him have it. Actually, James only got married so as to get the allowance for a wife. His wife is going to work while he is in the Army and save up the allowance for him until the war is over.

Well this weather has given me the hump. We have not been outside four walls since we last came home from Missenden.

Ted Humphreys grew up in Watford

Memories of Wartime

I was nine years old when the war started in 1939. When the first air raid warning sounded I was playing with my friend in Oxhey Park, near Watford. We took refuge in a slit trench that had been dug by the Home Guard in anticipation of combating the German hordes if they should invade. When nothing happened we went home to tea.

My main memories of that time were of watching German planes flying overhead, picked out by searchlights. Of standing in the front garden at night, wearing my dad's steel helmet and hearing a 'whoosh' of a piece of anti aircraft shrapnel that went by my head, far too close for comfort!

Dad was in the Home Guard. He was exempt from the call-up as he owned a grocery shop. As dad owned a motor bike he became a Home Guard dispatch rider, complete with some type of fibre crash helmet. He kept his Sten gun in the wardrobe and I used to take it apart to clean it.

We slept every night in the cellar of a near neighbour: The Misses Thomas. One night we heard a roaring noise as a bomb passed overhead. I am told that this so upset us all that mum & dad decided to move us to North Wales. My father could not come with us as he had the grocery shop to run. We went to Betws-y-Coed, but before we could find a cottage to rent we stayed with a Mrs Jones at the base of an enormous slate tip. The first meal that Mrs Jones gave us was very salty porridge that we could not eat and we very quietly had to tip it into the stream that ran at the side of the cottage! Dulwich College had evacuated to a large hotel in the village and I attended as a 'day boy'. My sister went to the local school.

I remember that we went to the local circus and that when a big box was opened in the circus ring, a large lion ran out. There was no cage and the trainer had to grab the chain that was around the beast's neck and loop it over a stake that had been driven into the ground!

When we returned to Oxhey later in the war I was sent to Harrow High School. The Headmaster was Mr Thompson who took us around the area in a large open top car. His father-in-law used to watch on the roof for the doodlebugs and he was supposed to ring a bell when he saw one coming our way. Often there was a big bang when one hit the ground and then he would ring the bell!

Rosemary Mary Somerville recalls riding in Windsor Great Park

Romany

I was about ten years old and, with my younger sister, riding Romany, our pony, in Windsor Great Park when we suddenly heard a tremendously loud noise and realised there was a doodlebug overhead. They used to stop and go silent for a few minutes before they hit their target.

We were very near the Copper Horse, which commands a panoramic view, and could see this thing over us very clearly. It suddenly stopped just short of us and we knew it would land somewhere in the Park and were worried what the pony would do when it landed. So I dismounted and we both lay down on the ground (not under trees) and held on tightly to Romany's reins. He was delighted to be given a chance to eat some grass. There was a crash and an ear splitting explosion and the doodlebug landed on Windsor Racecourse. We saw it all. Romany never even looked up - just continued eating. I remounted and turned for home to meet our mother cycling furiously, quite sure that we had all been killed.

My father was in the Royal Observer Corps and sat on the Round Tower in Windsor Castle spotting German bombers and my mother ran the local canteen for soldiers.

It all seems a long time ago now.

Geoff Darby spent the war years in Huddersfield

Trek Carts and Bevin Boys

In 1940 we started losing some of our schoolteachers in to the forces. Our front lawn was dug up and we planted potatoes. We scouts were asked to go round the local mills and houses in Huddersfield with the 'Trek Cart' to collect waste paper and cardboard for the war effort. Air raids began in January 1941. Sandbags were delivered to homes for incendiary bombs and I attended FireWatchers' lectures. We were shown the type of bombs to expect and we had a section on war gases. I became a Fire Watcher and had pictures given to me of all the German bombers so we could recognise their 'planes.

The following year I began work in the school holidays delivering the mail. I was quite lucky to deliver near the large firework factory, which was now making and testing parachute flares. I spent part of my time picking up the used parachutes for mother to make in to large handkerchiefs!

My sister attended Hull University and was asked under the State scheme to study Aeronautical Engineering and moved on to military aircraft design.

In August 1943 I left school and started my first job at the reservoirs of Huddersfield. The Pioneer Corps camped around the perimeter installing and operating large smoke canisters to conceal the reservoir. I was loaned to the government – we had invented the 'bouncing bomb' and I was assisting with surveying and with the installation of anti dive bomb nets around the reservoir.

In 1944 I was, under conscription, sent to a miner's hostel to train as a coal miner – one of the Bevin Boys.

We managed for food, just. The only time we really had problems was when I began to eat more with working on the coalface. Food for sandwiches was scarce. We made many concoctions at home with wartime recipe books. We used the British Restaurant in Huddersfield and the one in Leeds sometimes to get a hot meal – it assisted with the food rationing.

We coped on clothing coupons. Mother made clothing up from old curtains for my sister. The milkman, one of a large family gave me some useful old clothing to wear in the pit.

One spin off from the blackout meant we could clearly see the night sky and we learnt the name of, and where to find the different constellations in the sky. In those days we seemed to see an amazing number of shooting stars.

Bryan Jones lived in London during the war years

Recollections

As a small boy, I tried to talk to my grandfather about what had happened to him when he was in France during the First World War. He, like so many thousands of others involved in that conflict, having been disabled, disfigured, maimed and abandoned (by a 'grateful' country), was reluctant to dwell on the grisly detail of the trenches of Passchendaele and the Somme.

My grandfather's interest was in the Battle of Britain. Up in the sky, where he could witness the Royal Air Force giving the Boche a damned good thrashing and sending them back to Berlin, Hermann Goering and Mr Adolf 'Bloody' Hitler. Their tails scorched and flaming remnants of their twisted swastikas stuffed up their fundaments. In bloody rout!

On many occasions, I sat on top of the air raid shelter with my grandfather out in the family garden, watching the likes of Douglas Bader and Sailor Milan knocking the hell out of Heinkels, Junkers and Messerschmidt 109s. My hero became exultant. Every single victory reported on the wireless by the BBC or in a newspaper was greeted with the war cry "UP YOURS ADOLF!"

My grandfather was almost stone deaf. His life had been saved by a medical orderly using a field dressing to push his brains back into his skull. He had been delivering messages between allied lines of communication when his horse had been cut from under him by a mortar shell. He was left for dead in No Man's Land for sixteen hours or so, the horse having been vaporised and obliterated.

Although I do not know how long he was in hospital, he returned a physical and mental wreck, to many people an unsightly and ugly monster.

To me he was grandad, in my eyes the hero. I idolised him. He was brave to the point of stupidity, firstly by defying my grandmother and secondly by refusing to vacate his bed in favour of the air raid shelter. He quite rightly pointed out that any bomb landing within the area of his bedroom and consequently likely to disturb his sleep (due to his deafness) was going to send the shelter and all who sailed in her to kingdom come!

This is the stuff of legend and from it emerged my mother. The most beautiful creature alive, I saw her fleetingly in those early days of the war, emerging from my bed dazed after an interrupted night's sleep in the shelter or coal cellar. She would hug me, kiss me and enjoin me to be a good boy and do as I was told. She would crawl into my still warm bed after a night of working in the local munitions factory and I would be led away by my grandmother and told "not to make a noise" for fear of waking the sleeping worker.

I missed her so much during the day, often snuggling up to her outdoor coat, to seek out her scent from the lining or sleeve. I could not wait for her to get out of bed and after a brief hour or so and a hurried meal, she would be off back to work. I could only look forward to the weekends, when we could be together and she would take me to the wonderful escapism of the local picture palace.

Prior to this she accompanied my father around England to be close to him during his various postings as a sergeant gunner in the Royal Artillery. I, of course, was dragged along with her. She would not have 'her baby' farmed out as an evacuee to strangers.

Folkestone, Lowestoft, Portsmouth, Southampton and Plymouth plus several other east and southern port towns became our temporary homes. This inevitably brought us into confrontation with the "bleedin' Germans" and several near misses. In Plymouth, we were bombed out completely and had to move house and, when eventually my father was posted abroad, she decided to return to London - just in time for the Blitz!

We commuted between my two grandmothers who lived in Walthamstow and Stepney respectively. One being close to the main London reservoirs and the other next to the London docks! Air raids and dodging bombs became a family preoccupation.

At one time, much to my delight, the nearby school was hit and, on another, a row of shops butting onto the back yard of our house went up, showering the adjacent gardens with boiled sweets and sausages.

In Stepney, another near miss. On a visit to dad's family home we stopped off at one of the pubs. Dad was on leave and fancied a pint. Mum was in the off-license getting gran her 'little drop of gin' and I was in the loo after the hour-long ride on a 661 trolley bus from Walthamstow. Suddenly, we heard the whine of an air raid siren. Mum grabbed me and after a short debate, dragged the Old Man away from his pint! All three of us fled up the road to number 42, rushing through the ever-open door, along the passage, out into the back garden and down the steps of the Anderson shelter, with a quick hello to family members forgathered, just in time to shut the door. At this point came a devastating explosion! A German V2 rocket had landed on the pub that we had so recently vacated; it was a direct hit.

The devastation was total, leaving a crater fifty yards across! Not one brick was left standing on another. Every family in Longnor Road (except ours) lost a member!

Pat Jones spent her childhood in Stoke

Milky Way and Moonlight

I lived in Alsager, Stoke-on-Trent, with my younger cousin. We were used to finding bomb-craters in the surrounding fields. We lived between Radway Green munitions factory and Crewe station. One day I arrived home from primary school to find a hole in the roof, a missing chimney stack, all the electrical sockets and switches hanging loose on the walls and the 'hanging' chain, the only remains of the mirror over the fireplace. Had we been bombed? No. It was a thunderbolt, which had created havoc to three or four houses in the main road!

Our blackout curtains were embroidered with beautiful designs of lupins and hollyhocks by my aunt. Also, she always gave us a slice of 'Milky Way' each night before we went to bed. I remember the thrill of receiving a present of half crown savings stamps when we had a birthday! That was our only present.

When the air raid siren sounded, I was carried down the stairs half asleep and I recall seeing the moonlight throwing a coloured pattern on the wall through the stained glass in the front door. This I believe, was the reason for years later, of a recurring dream where I flew downstairs and saw this pattern of colour. During the air raids, I lay head to tail with my cousin in a camp bed in the cellar, listening to my uncle's model steam trains running around the cellar and under the bed!

Janice Aves lived in London and Spratton during the war

Childhood Memories of Wartime London

We lived in a terraced house in Tooting and in the front room was a Morrison shelter. It was made up like a bed and during the night bombing raids, the family would all sleep together in the 'cage.' One afternoon there was a raid and the windows were blown in and on the opposite wall, shards of glass were embedded into the wall like daggers, and the whole room was smothered in glass pieces. After that, all of our windows were covered in green mesh, which would stop the windows from shattering, but it did make the house quite dark. This meshing was also used to cover the windows on the trams and buses.

My father was not accepted into the active service as he had been born with a slightly crippled foot and therefore was deemed to be unfit for action. He always felt cheated over this as he would have liked to sign up to 'do his bit.' So he joined the Home Guard. Thereafter, he was the one to clear bombsites and put webbing on the windows after he had finished work.

I can remember at night the blackout was total. There were no street lamps, so walking home in the dark was very difficult. Several times we entered a house a few doors along thinking it was ours. The key fitted all the houses in that row. Same landlord, same key! Nobody needed to lock their door, London was a safe place apart from the enemy above.

There was a very sad time when my uncle Lewis was killed at Monte Casino, Italy. He was just in his middle twenties. When the bombing over London became very bad in 1944, I was evacuated to the village of Spratton, in Northamptonshire. My mother had just given birth to my sister, so she also came with the baby. When we first arrived we were shown into a big mansion type house, called The Grange. It was very derelict and dirty and had previously been occupied by soldiers. (Polish, I think). The large rooms were filled with bunk beds. I slept on top and my mum and baby sister slept at the bottom. There were so many people there, and it was so noisy. During the night there was a lot of screaming and running about going on as bats were flying all around the house and over our heads. I must say I was very frightened at that point. In the morning, my mother was very distressed and walking along the road carrying the baby and me tagging along, she was quietly crying. A lady stopped us and took us back to her house for a cup of tea. She was so kind to us. The next day she had found a house for us to live in with a family in Spratton. It was a little thatched cottage, one of four, with tiny windows. Sometimes the 'Hunt' would pass by. Men in red jackets, horses and barking dogs - quite a spectacle for a little London girl. We stayed with the family for about a year and returned to London while the bombing was still going on, but my mother was so homesick as my father could only visit us very occasionally.

Maurice Darling lived in North West London

Don't 'Roll out the Barrel'

My first memory was going to a paper shop in Kilburn High Road, in London, on a Sunday morning with my sister and cousin to get the papers and seeing a traffic bollard knocked flat. I realise now it was the result of the blackout, but I asked my cousin, "Is that what a bomb does?" Later, I realised that bombs did more than that. Where we lived in Kilburn, over a shop next to the Black Lion, had no shelter so we crouched at the bottom of the stairs during raids. We later moved to Cricklewood with an Andersen Shelter in the garden, my memory of that is of damp and the smell of wet earth. Dad was working at the nearby Handly Page Aircraft Factory; he spent many days away.

Working at different airfields repairing bombers that arrived back in England shot up after bombing raids, he told me later how, as the planes landed, they had to wait until the injured and many times dead airmen were taken out of the planes before they could start their patching up.

At school we had shelters in the playground. At the time we thought we were safe, but all these shelters were was just a brick affair with a chemical toilet in them. We had two of them, one in the boys playground and one in the girls, there was also one under the school in the storage area. It was only after the war finished that I realised why my two sisters and I were in different shelters - if one of the shelters had been hit only one of us would have been a casualty. We spent our time singing at the tops of our voices, of course this was great for us, usually we were told to be quiet. We could sing any song we liked, but not 'Roll out the Barrel.' Our Headmaster, Mr Meckiff, would not allow that, I suppose he was teetotal.

The war was dragging on but nobody I knew thought we would lose. Then came the V1s and later the V2 rockets. Before, when the siren warned that the German bombers were about, we had time to get in the shelter. These were a different kettle of fish. At night you could see the fire out of their engine and during the day you could see them plainly, but as long as you could hear the noise of the engine you knew you were safe. Then one day, something happened that I remember plainly to this day. It was round about midday, I was in the garden with my younger sister. Mum was also in the garden when a V1 came over the railway line behind our house. It was the lowest I had ever seen one. Mum screamed at me to get in the shelter, she grabbed my younger sister. The engine cut out and I saw it just miss the Express Dairy chimney and then down it came; there was the usual explosion. I was out of the front door like a flash. Mum was following, calling on me to get in the shelter. The bomb had landed in Ivy Road, just off Cricklewood Broadway. When I got there, they were pulling people out of the wreckage of the houses that had been hit. They were putting bits of curtain and oilcloth over them, but the thing I remember most and it's stayed with me all these years, was a little girl who was wandering about crying. A policeman picked her up. She was covered in white powder, I suppose it was from the ceiling plaster. A woman asked the policeman where the little girl had come from and offered to take her. I heard the policeman say, "She will be OK with me, she was just wandering about."

I have often wondered about that little girl. Were the people being laid out on the pavement her parents? Was she now an orphan? I found out later that ten people had been killed and the Officer of Health for Willesden had been awarded the George Cross for burrowing into the debris to give a blood transfusion to a trapped person.

Mike Golding also grew up in Hawkhurst

Bomb Alley

Hawkhurst is situated on the Kent and Sussex border, north of Hastings. I was six at the outbreak of the war and for the first few months we did not know what to expect. My first memories are of the German planes going over on their way to London. Hawkhurst was in the area known as Bomb Alley as we were on the direct route from Europe to London.

As the Germans' main object was to destroy our airfields there was a lot of action in the air above us. In September 1940 my family went Hop Picking, a normal local summer job to earn a few pounds to supplement the allowance my mother received from the army as my father was in the RASC, serving overseas.

Seeing the Battle of Britain from the ground was something that has always remained with me, seeing the dogfights with the German fighters trying to protect their bombers. Having seen this live it seemed to take place much slower than depicted in any film I have seen about this event.

During the whole of the war I can only remember being frightened once and that was when we saw a German bale out of his plane when it was shot down and I thought that the Germans were invading.

When the night raids started on London this was one of the dangerous times for us. Many of the German bombers either did not reach London or did not drop all their bombs so to lighten their load to get home faster they dropped their bombs anywhere and that is when we had most damage in the village. We lived in a bungalow and one night a bomb dropped near us, it blew off the chimneystack and part of the roof. The first thing I knew about it was my grandfather knocking on our bedroom window asking if we were all right. I had slept though the whole thing. After that we were issued with a Morrison Shelter.

The doodlebugs were the next thing we had to contend with. These were directed to London but as we were in Bomb Alley they went over us on the way to the capital. All around us were gun sites, mainly Beaufors, to shoot them down or try to knock them off course and that was when they came down around us. The local paper used to publish a map each week to show which parish had had most V1s down in their area. The RAF also used to chase them, either to shoot them down or to fly beside them and tip their wings and make them crash. They developed a plane to do this called the 'Clipped Wing Spitfire.'

One day I was out with my brother John and a friend collecting mushrooms. A doodlebug was tipped by a Spitfire and was heading for the field we were in, we ran toward a riverbank hoping we would be safe. The pilot of the Spitfire must have seen us as he fired at the doodlebug, knocked it off course and it exploded two fields away. That was the nearest I came to being a wartime casualty.

One day my friend and I were watching a doodlebug being chased by two planes. Our planes could fly just a little faster than the V1, but on this day this thing came past them all and fired at the V1. I thought that if this is another German rocket we are doomed as they will never catch it. But it was one of ours; it was the first time the Meteor had been put into service and the first time we had seen one.

Prior to D-Day we had many troops in tented sites around the village. The biggest being the field where the council built an estate after the war, of which we were the first to move to in 1947. A lot of the work there was done by German prisoners of war who had either stayed behind or were waiting to be sent home.

D-Day I will always remember because of the number of planes and gliders that flew over that day, it seemed to be from dawn to dusk and for the next few weeks there were various regiments camped in the village some for only a week at a time.

My memories after the war seem dull compared with what we had been through but one that stands out is watching the South Coast Air Race. This took place from Hurn airport in Hampshire around the coast and finished at Herne Bay in Kent. This is where I saw the Brabazon, an eight-engine airliner, which never went into service.

Mike Golding's father crossing to France (pre Dunkirk)

Sheila Chugg recalls working at Fairford

Train Journeys

I was employed as a booking clerk at Fairford Great Western Railway Station. On weekends, a certain number of troops were allowed time away. There was a large GI camp nearby and on that particular morning they were queuing for tickets. One soldier approached me at the ticket window with a "Round trip to Lunnon, ma'am."

I took his money and gave him a ticket, continuing to serve the rest. It was almost time for departure when he rushed back to the window and said "Say ma'am, I wanted to go to Lunnon not Pad-in-ton." After some explaining he just managed to get into a carriage, before the train departed!

My work mate and I were just fifteen years old and we witnessed from our office windows, planes from the nearby RAF station leaving on raids. In the early mornings we would see them return, some damaged. On a couple of occasions they crashed on landing and inevitably there were casualties, which necessitated bodies to be dispatched by train, on their last journey to their homes. I think we grew up very fast as we witnessed the sad spectacle of young men's coffins being loaded from the platform onto the train. This memory has never left us and we often recall those brave young men.

Joyce Williams lived in Leyton

The Friendly GI

In 1944 I was a nineteen year old working in a Post Office in Leyton, Essex. One day, a black GI came into the office – he was friendly, I was not busy and we chatted for quite a few minutes. Now I had certainly never met or spoken to a black man before and had rarely seen one (the only experience was The Black and White Minstrels —and they were white men painted black.)

In the evening, I was rather dismayed to find this black GI waiting for me (I already had a steady boyfriend.) However, he walked me almost home; my mother would have had a shock if she saw me with a black man.

As we walked, the GI said,"I would never be allowed to do this in my country. I wouldn't be able to walk or talk to a white girl."

I had never thought about racism, it had never entered in to my life!

I said goodbye to the GI and I never heard or saw him again. I honestly don't think he had any designs on me – he just wanted to be able to write home and say he had walked with and talked to a white girl!

Dorothy Bass lived in Middlesex

Helping the War Effort

I lived at home with my parents in a three-bedroomed house. One morning an Army sergeant visited us. He asked my mother how many rooms we had vacant. One bedroom (my brother's, who had been called up) and our Sitting Room. We were told that two soldiers would be occupying these rooms. When they were moved on we had the Air Force. Then the ATS towards the end of the war.

Our road in Alperton was very friendly and all helped with the war effort in housing Our Boys. All the pubs had music and dancing in between air raids. At weekends my friends and I visited London, particularly the Hammersmith Palais and shows in the theatres. The sirens aften sounded but the shows carried on.

My brother was at Dunkirk and he was on the Lancastria when it was bombed and sank - he survived. He was also in the D-Day campaign. My future husband, who I was going out with at the time was captured and was a POW in Germany.

Overall, I think we were very lucky to all survive.

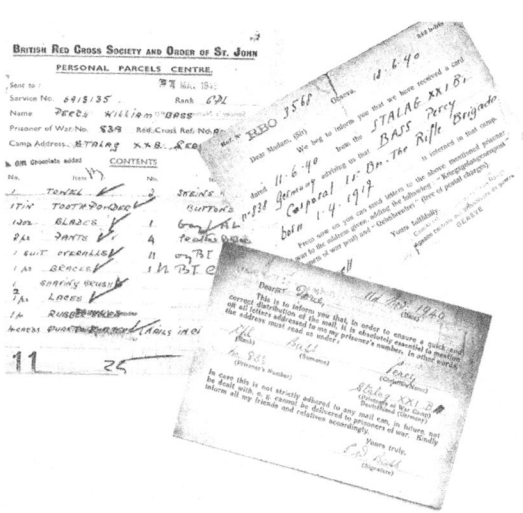

Dorothy's future husband – a Prisoner of War

Fred Lacy recalls his training near Bristol

Hullavington

Enemy raids on Bristol and the surrounding countryside were a feature of my short time at the Hullavington Airfield from June to September 1940. Night flying would sometimes be enlivened by the vivid glare of fires from as far away as Bristol and the nearer presence of enemy aircraft would be signalled on the airfield by the dowsing of the flarepath. This did not always go to plan. During an enemy raid in August, one of my colleagues, engaged on dual night landings in an Anson trainer, landed just as the lights went out and was immediately abandoned in mid field by his terrified instructor, who ran off to crouch beneath the airfield boundary hedge. My friend was able to taxi in the dark to dispersal and switch off. We received this tale with glee, as the instructor was an unpleasant bullying type of individual -I had him as well - and his demeanour towards us all was subsequently somewhat mollified. To be fair, we heard that some of the instructors had participated with the AEF earlier in 1940 in France and their nerves were possibly a bit 'shot.'

Our course comprised some twenty ex RAFVR Sergeant u/t pilots plus a few Army officers who had volunteered, still in their particular uniforms, to train as aircrew. For those of us from the prewar RAFVR, Hullavington provided our first experience as members of a Sergeants' Mess. Whilst at that stage of the war the food was of high standard, we were not impressed by the reception we received from the permanent members, most of whom had worked hard and for many years to gain their 'stripes.' We of course had been made up to NCO rank immediately upon joining the VR, although this exalted rank was denied any subsequent post-mobilisation volunteers.

In consequence of the somewhat chilly atmosphere in the mess, most of us elected to visit the local hostelries off camp on free evenings. It was necessary to 'book out' at the guardroom, one's name being recorded in a large book by one of the duty service policemen. The guard room window was walled up with sandbags, with just a narrow strip through which one shouted to the scribe who could not see one's rank. On one particular evening I bawled "Ser'nt LACY" and in response to "Oo?" from the SP, shouted "LACY! - L - A - C - Y" and went on my way with my friends. On return, it by now dark, one had to enter the guardroom by way of two doors, like an airlock and pronounce one's rank and name. This was duly struck by the scribe from the above-mentioned book containing the names of those who had earlier left camp. Any names left over at the end of the evening might have belonged to those AWOL or worse, having been involved in a local air raid.

To my amazement on the occasion referred to above the scribe was unable to locate my name. I was ordered to await the arrival of the Orderly Officer. Upon the arrival of the officer, the book was again searched for "LACY" to no avail and I was ordered to remain until all names had been struck through, the officer meanwhile retiring to the comfort of his mess. Finally, at 0130 hours, the evening's list was all struck through barring one name - "LAC (Leading Aircraftman) WYE." "That's me", I yelled "SERGEANT LACY – LACY. Recalled once more from the Officers' Mess, the Orderly Office reproved me in no uncertain terms for not having clearly stated my rank and name on booking out earlier!

All in all, however, I enjoyed my training at Hullavington. Once solo, we flew many exercises in our forgiving Ansons. One such exercise required aircraft to take off in pairs and attempt to photograph each other with a camera gun from the aircraft turret. Two pilots were in each aircraft and took turns to fly and 'shoot' at the other plane. This at first was not an easy exercise at, as briefed, 1,000ft, because of turbulence on those hot sunny days, so a close friend and I agreed that calmer air at height would surely ease our task! He and I usually arranged to fly together and I'm afraid we customarily bullied the pair in the other aircraft to be sure to meet us at 6,000ft over Swindon! Our photographs were rated top of the course with excellent marks.

This was the epic time of the 'Battle of Britain.' Some of our course would fly off to Kent in the hope of seeing something of the battle! The innocence and ignorance of youth!

I well remember my very first Anson flight, which was piloted by a charismatic Irish instructor - Flight Sergeant Boyd. There were two of us student pilots on board and Boyd flew to Savemake forest for his piece de resistance. This involved very low flying above the long straight forest clearances and turning at the end of them whilst gripping the control column between his knees, and signalling a left or right turn with outstretched arm like a motorist. At the same time he pulled back one throttle sharply with the other hand to 'honk' the undercarriage warning horn! My colleague and I fell about laughing! Ah, happy, innocent days!

Jean Macpherson waited for her brother to return to London

Aircraft

When the war started I worked in a guesthouse opposite my home. On the day that war broke out all of the guests were at church. I sat at the bottom of the front stairs to listen to the radio and heard that we were now at war. I went out of the front door to call over to my older brother who was waiting for the news – we did not have a radio in our house. The news was also broken to the church congregation. My brother had been interested in aeroplanes since he was very young and was greatly excited about joining the RAF.

In 1942 both our lives changed. My brother went to London to join the airforce. I followed him later to take up a post that I had been offered, working as a nanny for the children of a Harley St doctor. We lived in Hampstead and being young, the bombs didn't really worry me.

My brother always came back to London for forty-eight hour leaves and we had good times. He loved music and we went to the theatre a lot and the pictures; the organ used to come up at the interval and we all had sheet music to sing to.

It all came to an end in 1944. We were both going to be home at the same time but he had one more operation to do. He was a Sergeant and about to become an officer at the time. I had been at home less than an hour, with my coat still on when the post came with several letters from my brother. There was also a telegram to say that the crew and plane that he was flying were missing. They flew Halifax planes and went out alone. They dropped arms and spies over France and to the underground in Norway and Sweden. They were over the latter that night and to this day my dear brother is missing. I'll never forget my mother's quiet sorrow.

I refused to return to London without my brother and joined the Land Army. I married a lovely man in 1946 and we called our son after his uncle.

Joan Lloyd-Davies enjoyed her time in Aldershot

Memoirs of a Nonentity

World War Two had started; Hitler and Goering's merry men were busily re-arranging the map of London night after night and we were forced to spend time in that most luxurious of apartments - the Anderson shelter. We shared this shelter with a neighbour and her rather 'dishy' son (he and I were then at the tender age of eighteen and our 'bolt hole' was, to us rather romantic). Southall, where we lived was considered a 'bomb alley', and I lost quite a number of school and college chums during that very dangerous period.

Meanwhile, World War 2½ was being waged within our home. My brother flatly refused to eat his ration of margarine, and my mother gave in to him and he had our entire butter ration; this caused such animosity between my brother and me that we actually came to blows. One particular fisticuffs was so intense that it made my mother ill. I was beginning to realise that I was on a losing battle as he was a *very* strong fourteen year old. I also realised that it was totally unfair to mother, so the next day I went to the Recruitment Office to offer my services for King and Country. It was disappointing to find that there was no place in the WRENS so I had to forego the thought of wearing that attractive uniform. There was no chance of anything to do with the sea. It was the same tale with the WAAFS for they also had all the girls they wanted, so it had to be the ATS. Very shortly after this interview, the call up papers arrived and I was to meet on a London railway station. There were hosts of us young girls ready to board the train for the north. My destination was Glencorse Camp, Penicuik, near Edinburgh. We were packed like sardines on this train with bodies crowding the compartments and corridors; another girl and I hit on the idea of climbing onto the luggage racks above the seats which proved to be good as we had a reasonably comfortable journey and managed to snatch some sleep.

We arrived at the training camp after a long tedious journey, but we were not allowed to go and rest, as straightaway there was office procedure and queuing at the QM stores to receive our Army issue. Most of us enjoyed the training and our huts were quite comfortable and there was plenty of good food. My only bad experience at Glencorse Camp was when we had to go into the gas chamber with our gas masks on. After a while we were told to remove the masks so that we experienced what it would be like enhaling gas. I let the side down because I flaked out and had to be taken outside for resuscitation. We did a lot of 'square bashing' and drilling, lots of lectures, and lots of jabs. We also discovered that the myths about the Scots being mean were totally untrue. How kind the people were to us, wherever we went, in cafes, on buses, they insisted on paying for us because we were in uniform and serving King and Country. We even had invitations to their homes. In fact, their generosity was unbounding. We had great thrills parading along the streets, with a Drum and Fife Band at our head, accompanied by the cheers from the passers-by. How proud we felt! After this rigorous training we eagerly scanned Part I orders to see where our destinations were to be. Several of us were posted to Parsons Barracks, Aldershot, which was not too far from my home.

First impressions of Aldershot were that it was dull and drab, but we soon discovered that it was not so, for there were so many exciting things to do in our leisure time - sport, cinema, dances (any amount of them), cycling and more. There was wonderful country around where we could go for walks. We were lodged in Nisssen huts dormitory fashion of about twelve girls; attached was a small room, which housed our sergeant. We were quite a mixture, from the girl with the posh voice (she used to say "gel" and "orf") to the one who had been 'on the game', but we all got on so well - the camaraderie was there.

I joined the concert party with a song and dance routine, but eventually had a chance to become part of an Adagio duo with a wonderful male dancer who had been a member of the Diagalev Ballet. His regular girl partner met with an accident and he needed someone to replace her. With the concert party we travelled all over southern and SE Command doing variety and even pantomime. Also in London we did 'Stage Door Canteen' at the time when the doodlebugs were at their height.

I applied to become a PTI as I had always been active in all kinds of sport, and was accepted. Courses at Devizes and Guildford followed, and I was lucky enough to come out of the course with a Distinction pass. These were early days for female PTIs and whereas the Army chaps automatically had sergeant's stripes at the end of their course, we had to be content with a solitary stripe. Another 'beef' about this was that although we were entitled to the Cross Swords badge, we were never allowed to <u>wear</u> it. However it was an enjoyable job, albeit part-time; it gave me some time out from the office routine, as there were netball, hockey and volleyball matches to arrange as well as the gym classes and cross-country running.

You must excuse my lyrical description of Parsons Barracks, but I honestly believe those years were some of the happiest times of my life.

As D-Day approached however, it did affect our high spirits, when one day we would see a heavy massing of troops, then the next day they were gone. Very sad.

As soon as the War was over, I went abroad with 'Stars in Battledress'; came back and did a film stunt, pantomime, variety shows in the provinces and eventually became a Windmill Girl!

Mrs J Turner recalls her time in the Forces, initially in Portsmouth

Battery Powered

When the war started I was an eighteen-year-old private posted to Hilsea College, Portsmouth. My job was in the quartermaster's office in the barracks. In the early days, I recall seeing cat fights over us before the bombing started in earnest. One afternoon I actually heard Lord Haw Haw on the radio from Germany saying that "There is no need to take up the tram lines in North End, we will do it for you."

The next day they did just that, spot on target. A huge bombing raid on Portsmouth, not far from us.

Early 1940 was an edgy time. One Saturday evening our college was overrun by armed sailors (much to the girls' delight). The following morning I pretended I had work to do at the barracks so made my way totally alone along the road where there was complete silence. A lovely sunny day but no birdsong or dogs barking and no people. Scary. Once in the barracks, a heavily armed sailor met me. They were everywhere.

The bombing from then on was intense - after work and food we were in the shelter. After some months we were posted to Leicester, living in requisitioned private houses. We heard droves of German aircraft night after night going to bomb Coventry. I saw the devastation myself, poor people. Leicester did not escape attack and there was loss of life. I was trapped in the cellar of the house I was living in when a land mine exploded nearby.

In 1941 I was transferred to a Heavy Ack Ack outfit. I was now a sergeant major, at twenty-one years of age. I met my battery at Oswestry before moving off to Liverpool. Near the docks there is Bootle. I saw what the bombing had done. Streets upon streets of what were once terraced houses razed to the ground. Devastation as far as you could see - the death toll must have been horrendous!

Late in 1942 I was married and posted to Netley, near Southampton. At one point I was ordered to Hayling Island to look at a possible campsite. Once again, I was in a requisitioned house and every day a squad of royal marine commandos exercised outside my house. One Sunday I decided to visit my parents, so I set off to the station with my escort in tow. Only to find no trains running on Sundays. The squad waited for me to emerge but I couldn't face the humiliation so I hid until they marched away. I got a lift by a Wren to Havant. She wasn't very happy and remained silent the whole way. This was probably due to a sailor I knew asking her to take me - perhaps it was off her course. Arriving back at Havant station late that evening posed a problem. How was I to get to my house, a long walk? The London train pulled in, with hoards of inebriated sailors and waiting for them were several lorries and in charge was a CPO. I asked him for a lift and he was happy to oblige so off we went; the driver, with me, a huge bunch of hydrangeas and the CPO crammed into the cab with taunts and banging from the back. I was taken all the way to my house and I was so grateful.

I was discharged in November 1943 expecting a baby, to start a completely different life. I was standing on a tiny platform in a small country station on my way to civvy street but still in uniform, when the siren sounded. The other person with me was a naval captain and he ordered me to "bloody well get under cover." I have taken orders and given them, but didn't expect my last one to come from the Navy! I didn't move.

Once home, I encountered shortages especially with fruit. Spam was a welcome American addition and thanks to our marvellous Land Army and 'dig for victory' campaign, we managed. The cinemas were open, lovely teashops and tea dances and a few evening dances and the inevitable whist drives. Also pubs stayed open.

The night of the day when my daughter was born in April 1944, Bournemouth experienced a huge incendiary attack. The bombs and gunfire shook the nursing home I was in and it was just like old times. The cinema opposite where I used to live received a direct hit and was totally destroyed, the film showing was 'Hell's a Poppin'.'

Apart from the dreadful injuries and loss of life this about sums it up.

Barry Thorpe moved to Bletchley

Bletchley

From 1942-1944 my cousin, grandmother, aunts and myself went to live away from London to a small village near Bletchley. My mother and my two aunts all worked for the Foreign Office at Bletchley Park (where the Enigma code was broken). My cousin Graham and I had no idea where our mothers and aunt went each day, as they never said a word about their jobs. One event I remember is my mother coming into my bedroom at possibly ten-o-clock one night and saying, "We've sunk the Sharnhorst." I believe this was a big morale-booster for the staff at Bletchley Park and she wanted to share the elation with me.

One exciting event I remember is Graham and me going into the field at the bottom of our garden and meeting up with Canadian and US Army personnel. They gave us chewing gum and chocolate, which was something we just never had in 1943. There were trucks and also tanks around - I suppose they could have been part of the D-Day invasion force.

My father came home from the Air Force one day and gave me a model Lancaster bomber he had made. It was about eighteen inches long, carved in wood and the underside was a duck egg blue with bomb doors and four model bombs underneath. All the windows were made of Perspex, which was used in real aircraft. I took this 'plane to school and was the envy of all my friends. My father was only with us for a few days and then went back to being a wireless operator on Beaufighters.

Doreen Gale spent the war years working in London

De Gaulle and the Min of Ag

I went to work for the Ministry of Agriculture in Whitehall. When women were called up they refused to release me so I worked all over London - Smith Square, Whitehall, Soho Square and others. I did one night a week first aid in Whitehall and one night a week as a Westminster casualty warden. I did two years as an ordinary warden and three as a casualty warden. The area our post covered was Northumberland Avenue along the Embankment to Waterloo Bridge across Parliament Square and the back of Horse Guards Parade and under Admiralty Arch to Trafalgar Square. Downing Street was in the middle of our section.

We worked in the office all day and went on duty at 6pm. If no alerts, we went to bed at midnight but during alerts we were out and about. Three hours on the embankment to see if anything fell in the river or banks. Sometimes we didn't get to bed until 3.30am and we had to be up at 7am and at work by 9am working until 5 or 6pm. Then face a journey home. When it was a weekend we did a 24-hour shift. I often did Christmas Day duty so older men could be home with their families. Christmas lunch was provided by

Westminster and I remember that for several years, as I walked down Charing Cross Road and across Trafalgar Square after lunch, I saw no cars or transport of any description.

I also belonged to the Women's Home Defence and learned to fire a rifle and deal with Mills bombs. The worst incident I had to attend was the bomb that fell on the Guard's Chapel towards the end of the war. Many were killed or badly injured. I had been on duty overnight and was going home but we were called to the scene.

I only saw Churchill twice in the war years but was far more familiar with De Gaulle. He worked at the War Office next to the Ministry of Agriculture and we seemed to go to lunch at the same time - in the end he used to raise his hand in a sort of salute to me.

I remember at the Ministry dealing with letters for small pig keepers when they had to join a club to get food for their pigs. I had to read the letters and put 1, 2, 3, 4 or 5 on them for stock letters to be sent by temporary staff. I was confused to get odd letters on religion and a bit uncertain about them. We sorted it out - our letters were addressed to the S P K - Whitehall but in Whitehall Place was the Society for the Promulgation of Christian Knowledge. They were equally confused at receiving letters on pigs. After this, we had a meeting three times a week to exchange letters!

Mary Singleton was a nurse in Weston-super-Mare

Nursing in Weston

In February 1942 I enrolled in the Civil Nursing Reserve and did two weeks basic training at Bristol Royal Infirmary. We were posted to Kewstoke Emergency Hospital at Sand Bay, near Weston-super-Mare. It was the peacetime convalescent home of the Birmingham Hospital Saturday Fund. When we rang the bell we were taken to a ward and told to undress. They thought we were patients! We were billeted in cottages on the seafront. Feather beds and no gas or electricity. We had not been issued with tin hats so used saucepans in an emergency. TB was common then and there were TB wards for children and adults, also wards for sick soldiers. The operating theatre was always on the ground floor in wartime, as it was thought safer. There was no lift, so we had to carry the patients up and down stairs - we had no training for this. That summer, soldiers were billeted in marquees on the beach lawns, which may have had something to do with the air raids on Weston-super-Mare, which were totally unexpected. Some of the injured were brought to Kewstoke. The mood in Weston was sombre. The list of casualties was pinned up outside the Town Hall.

We received £4 a month in pay; the sisters received £8. As a vegetarian, I was always hungry. We could not buy rationed foods but we could get buns, rolls and for some reason prune tarts! Fish and chips were never rationed which was a blessing to many. There were 'warship weeks' and 'wings for victory' weeks and the nurses put on plays at the Winter Gardens in aid of these. No radio or TV was available to us and we didn't buy newspapers (paper was rationed) but the war news was of great interest to us. Every household gathered each evening to hear the 9pm news on the radio.

My friend Barbara and I decided to return to the Bristol Royal Infirmary to take three years training to become state registered nurses. We came in for many more air raids in Bristol. Our pay was reduced to £2.60 a month so although there were cafes we couldn't patronise them. We had to supply our own black shoes and stockings. The training was very strict, which we did not appreciate at the time, but were glad of later.

The war became a way of life, as birthday succeeded birthday. It was bleak but all we knew. Coffee was not popular then and was never rationed - nor was cocoa. Soon, the Yanks began to appear in the streets of Bristol. The American army practised segregation in those days and certain pubs were allocated to white troops and black troops. Armed MPs roamed the streets, shouting into Bristol buses if they felt inclined. There were a lot of street fights. The trouble was that local girls often preferred the black Yanks and this caused the white Yanks to lose their cool. The Yanks from the southern states had a liking for blonde girls. Two of my friends were sometimes chased through the streets - scary! It was not long before a crop of mixed race children began to appear - and they could not be explained away. The Sisters of Mercy in Redland took many of them in. I saw about fifty cots in a dormitory and the smell was terrible. I think the nuns meant well, but they obviously couldn't cope with the numbers.

Eileen Yeldham helped to defend our shores at Sheerness

Radar

During the war, I was in 628 Mixed Heavy Anti Aircraft Battery - Royal Artillery. There were six of us girls in a team who were on a clifftop in the Thames estuary at Sheerness - so we were kept very busy hoping to keep enemy planes from London.

To operate the radar, firstly the diesel engine had to be cranked up by hand to produce electricity to power the *transmitter*. This would be dealt with by two girls and the increased power passed to the *receiver*, where we dealt with it as soon as a plane came within range. Our information was then passed to the gun emplacement where girls were working on a *predictor*, which as the name suggests was able to pass range etc on to the 3.7 gun just a couple of yards away and fired by men who were in the Royal Artillery. So radar was not just dealt with by the RAF or WAAF!

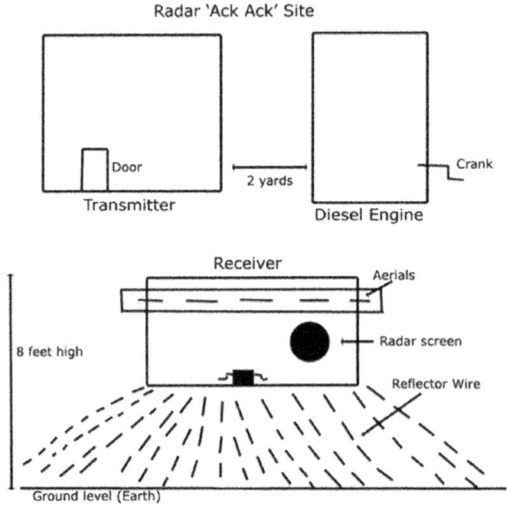

The Radar Setup

Joe Rider was posted to the West Country

Searchlights

I well remember sitting at the breakfast table on the morning of Tuesday 9th January 1940 when the postman delivered a small brown OHMS envelope addressed to me. It contained my calling-up notice. My mother was out of the room at that moment so father said "Don't tell your mother until she has finished her breakfast."

And so on the following Monday, at the age of nearly twenty-two, I set off by train to Taunton for three months initial training in a Royal Artillery S.L. Regiment. When I told a colleague at work (he was an 'old soldier' in every sense of the expression, having been through the Boer War and WWI without a scratch) he said, "You know what S.L. stands for? It's Scrubbing Lavatories!" Actually it was a Searchlight Regiment.

At the end of the training period no searchlight site was ready to which we could be deployed so the next two months were spent at various locations in Cornwall. It was at the Recreation Ground in Camborne that I received my only 'war wound' - a badly sprained ankle. I had been ordered to play football as recreational training when someone else's foot landed on mine. I spent several weeks hobbling around with the help of two brooms, which I was given to use as crutches. At the time we were billeted in the Camborne Drill Hall and one night there was an invasion scare. All the men were ordered out on patrol to look out for German paratroops, armed only with pick-axe handles.

Most of my army service was spent in Hampshire, Wilts and Dorset and I had a very 'cushy' time compared to many others in the services. It was not until November 1944 that I went overseas to serve in the Army of Occupation in France, Belgium, Holland and finally Germany.

I recall too, the winter of 1947, which was exceedingly cold. My place of work was in London, just behind Liverpool Street Station. The windows were boarded up due to war damage and the only heating anywhere near my desk was a tiny gas radiator. I wore my army leather jerkin and mittens but my hands were so cold that I could hardly hold a pen.

Eileen Kelly grew up in Birmingham

Bundles of Socks

In 1940, Birmingham had six weeks of nightly bombing. Every evening the sirens would sound then the familiar sound of the German bombers – for bombs to light up the area, then the crash of bombs, anti-aircraft guns and finally the all-clear. Then, a few hours later, a repeat performance. I remember the sad sight of women with babies and small, tired children queuing up at the entrance to a communal air-raid shelter. Every morning there were gaps in the streets and news of some familiar faces gone for ever. It was easier to walk to the town to work – two or three miles – than to take a tram, which might not be able to get through.

In the telephone exchange where I was employed, girls worked shifts, the last one finishing at 8pm when men took over. If an air-raid warning sounded whilst we were on duty, a few were directed to a special room to take emergency calls and the rest went to a shelter under the building. I never went to the shelter. I used to skip out and walk home to be with my mother who was often alone when my dad was on duty in the power station. He was an electrical engineer in charge. The night of the Coventry raid the usual warnings came in to the telephone exchange. By a series of lights changing colour, we on the switchboards knew when German planes were coming via Hull. As they got nearer, green lights changed to amber. Then, when they were approaching Birmingham the lights changed to red. This particular night the red light did not show. We knew the planes were not far away but it was only when I went back the next morning for the 8am shift that we found there was no communication with Coventry. There were calls piling up for Coventry numbers but no means of contacting Coventry. That was why Birmingham had a night off. The next night we were back to 'normal.' I remember 'Lord Haw Haw's' voice on the radio saying that "Birmingham would be Coventryised!"

Birmingham factories were targeted with some dire results. There was a bomb aimed at Telephone House which had a white roof, but it missed. I was in the town one night when a land mine skimmed over a line of trams at the terminus and then demolished a hotel. The trams all lit up and then their electricity was cut off. My dad brought me home a firebomb that landed on his desk in the power station on my birthday. Life in those days was unreal.

I got called up and chose the WRENS but recruiting was closed for three months so I went in the Land Army. I was based in Warwickshire so I could get home occasionally for a weekend. I used to go back early on a Monday morning on the train. Train stations were sad places where uniformed men and tearful women were saying goodbye. All was darkness on the train and at passing stations. The Station Masters called out the name of the station when we stopped. I used to have about a mile to walk to the farm in the dark but somehow the sound of an owl hooting or the cry of a fox made life seem normal. Reading about food ships being sunk in the Atlantic made me feel that I was doing some good, helping to grow food. As time went on, food rations were rather frugal but when ever I went home for a weekend I was able to take some eggs and at Christmas, a chicken. In those days chicken was a luxury and the egg ration was one egg each per month. I also saved sugar from my ration as I did not put it in tea or coffee. I took it with damsons which were prolific on the farm, so that my mother could make jam. There was no fresh fruit in Birmingham because there was no-one to pick it and get it to town. Fruit lay rotting on the ground. Most of the farm workers had been called up into the forces. I worked the fields with a horse called Tich and sometimes with a tractor. It was hard work but very rewarding.

We had Italian prisoners 'helping' on the farm. Actually, they helped themselves to willow branches and made baskets, which they sold. But they were likeable lads. They didn't want war and were not anti-British. In fact, they were there on VE day and they joined us in a celebration. One of them, named Rafael, wanted to marry me and take me to live on his father's farm in Italy. He used to sing to me as I was milking the cows – he had a lovely voice but I wasn't about to get swept off my feet. The Italians went and then German prisoners came. They were very different. No singing, no smiles and behind them, a Polish soldier with a gun. I wouldn't have married one of them!

However, my Land Army days came to an abrupt end with the news that my father was dying and my mother was alone with him. Both my brothers were in the army, one sister a nurse, the other married with her husband in the army and a young baby to look after. So, instead of finishing my time in the Land Army and getting a free college course in horticulture, I had to get a compassionate discharge and go back to office work in Birmingham. After my dad died I could not leave my mother so I stayed 'til she died nine years later.

It was 1947 when my dad died and we had just had the worst of winters. It snowed on New Year's Day and kept snowing and freezing until April. There was no coal and we had coal fires then – no central heating. We kept dad warm with hot water bottles because the bedroom was freezing.

Food was very short. Clothing coupons could be used up on one coat. All other clothes had to be constantly mended. We made skirts out of curtains and blouses out of parachute silk. There were sometimes bargain bundles of stockings or socks 'off ration.' We queued up to get these, only to find that the bundles were composed of stockings without feet or one twice as long as its mate! Nothing wearable, but we had to laugh.

Many parents had seen their children evacuated and family life disrupted by the war. Sons and husbands who had fought and survived wanted to get back to some sort of stability. Thousands had been killed at home and many were disabled. Picking up the pieces was not easy but there was a great sense of relief, as families were re-united, mixed with grief for those whose lives were over. There was LIGHT! After many years of blackout, the sight of lights shining from windows was wonderful. The voice of Vera Lynn had lifted us all during the dark years and now the songs were a source of hope. She and many others did so much to keep everyone's spirits up; the awful discoveries of the gas chambers and mass graves were coming to light. So much evil causing so much misery.

I think the whole future of Europe – maybe the world – depended on the 1940s.

John Bennett was billeted in Ponders End

Four's a Crowd

As eighteen-year-old engineering cadets, four of us were billeted in a small terrace house in Ponders End, Middx, with our landlady and teenage daughter. Four of us were in a small double bedroom such that the beds almost touched. It was difficult to get through the hall as there were four full army kits, four rifles and four bicycles to impede passage. The six of us had our evening meals (usually rabbit) around the metal Morrison table shelter. When the siren sounded at night we all slept under the same Morrison table. Two of us were banished to the Anderson shelter in the garden; I will not go into why.

At that age I remember we had no fear and it was not unusual for the trolley bus to rock from bomb blasts on the way to the cinema in Edmonton and for the lights inside the cinema to flicker for the same reason. It was difficult to see where one was through the small lozenge of clear glass in the windows. On foot we used to pick up pieces of shrapnel which used to clatter on the ground, taking care to let the jagged pieces cool first.

One night the ceiling came down on me, I spat out the dust from my mouth and went to sleep again. I was woken by our landlady who nearly had a fit!

Dennis Devier served near King's Cross

Home Guards and Blueberry Hill

In 1940, I joined the RAFVR and whilst waiting for call-up, I joined the Home Guard. Our headquarters was just off King's Cross Road, a quarter of a mile from the main station. That area was heavily bombed at that time. I soon found myself a corporal Browning gunner, although our main task was attending bombed houses & digging out the occupants.

One night, a land mine exploded behind our HQ. We all went to see what we could do. We worked right through the night, removing the rubble from the collapsed house. We could hear tapping below, which urged us on. We could also smell gas. About 5am we reached the family in the cellar, to find that they'd been overcome by the leaking gas main. That was tragic & hit us hard.

Next, I was on night patrol, passing Mount Pleasant post office, when I heard a bomber coming from the direction of Ludgate Circus. As the bombs dropped, I knew the next one was mine. I threw myself flat and will never forget that my feet were drumming in terror. The bomb landed only twenty yards away and lifted me up bodily. I was lucky, because it landed on the fire station (empty, all out fighting fires). This took all the blast and I was unhurt. The last of the stick exploded a hundred yards further on. I got to the house that had been hit and dug a woman and her daughter out. They were shocked but not badly hurt. I took them to the Royal Free hospital. My biggest dismay was, on returning to the site, to find that where the chemist shop windows had been blown in, the goods had been looted.

It was a grim time, so we formed a band. My father & I played finger-style 'G' banjos. Jack played the guitar, Tim, the clarinet and Dorothy (our leader) played the piano. A motley collection, but we made good music! Thus commenced the Saturday dance in the school hall. At first, we charged 3d for entrance. This was raised to sixpence then a shilling in an effort to stem the crowds that attended. It was amazing that, with bombs falling all around, so many people came to dance.

Quite often, when we playing, there would be a call – "Browning gunners up!" We would down our instruments & race up to the roof, collecting our guns on the way. We were called to try & shoot out the flares dropped by the bombers as they targeted King's Cross main railway station.

Dorothy was an excellent pianist and always managed to get us the sheet music of the latest numbers. My abiding memory was 'Blueberry Hill.'

Eve Fielder had a memorable incident whilst pregnant in Salisbury

Ma'am

I am now living in a flat, which in the 40s was part of our local Infirmary. In August 1942 I was awaiting the birth of my first baby. My husband Fred and I were married in November 1940 and he was on active service with the local regiment, the 'Wilts.' As I was returning home one day from the town centre, there suddenly appeared from behind the cathedral a low flying aircraft, which then came up Fisherton Street machine guns open. I looked up and saw the cross on the wings and a swastika on the tail and couldn't believe my eyes. I actually saw him unload his bomb, aiming towards the gasometer which he machine gunned and caused a fire but the bomb came down over the railway lines. Next thing, I was pulled to the ground, finding myself covered by two American soldiers.

"Are you OK ma'am?" they said.

I replied, "Thank you, yes and I only live up the road and wanted to get home."

Next thing 'Jerry' came back down the street and I was this time hustled down into the men's toilets by two British soldiers.

"You alright miss?" they said.

I replied indignantly, "Ma'am if you don't mind." They laughed.

That was Friday August 14th and Rosemary was born on Monday August 17th, a beautiful baby and we were both doing well!

Doris Parr recalls the Yanks

Yanks and Tinned Chicken

In about 1943, the 8th American Army/Air Force arrived down our way. Jeeps and lorries, and young men in odd uniforms to us, were seen everywhere, especially at the cinema and dances. They had unusual names like Hank, Chuck, Lou and Wayne. My mother and several older women from our road worked in the evenings at the US camp, in the canteen. Glamorous GIs called for them in jeeps and lorries, while us girls waved them off, rather enviously. No young girls were employed in the evenings at that particular camp. Most evenings, our mother brought home delicious doughnuts. They were quite different from those in our bakers' shops - crisp and with a hole through. We waited up for our mother to come home, hoping for a doughnut to eat with our cocoa. We were not often disappointed. Just before Christmas 1944, the Yanks proved their worth, when a nearby munitions factory was bombed and set on fire. The fire trapped many girls and older men, and there were a good many casualties. The Yanks turned up to assist the Fire Brigade, Police and Air Raid Wardens, in the rescue.

Christmas was not a great time of jollification by 1944. The shops were rather bare by then, and had no decorations, balloons, tinsel or coloured baubles. Toys were rather scarce, and so was paper, which affected books and cards. My mother made an 'Austerity' Christmas Pudding, using carrots, a bit of our precious sugar ration, grey war flour, which was very nutritious, and a little bit of dried fruit and egg. We were lucky enough to have relatives in the United States. They sent several food parcels to us, which were more than welcome. They contained tins of lovely creamy white cooking fat, tins of fruit and even butter. Once they even sent a whole chicken in a tin! We were amazed at the chicken. From these parcels came our first tea bags, and Yvonne and me sat foolishly undoing each packet, to tip the tea into the caddy, having never seen such things before. I once sent my aunt and two cousins in the US a letter telling them a few things about our everyday life, to interest them. I can't remember what I wrote, but I must have let out a few secrets as the letter was returned by the censor, with a stern warning not to write about such secrets again. I may have mentioned the barbed wire that was positioned around our coastline, in case of an invasion. I had no idea this was a secret, I thought the whole world knew about it.

In our small town, living near to us, was a man who was known as the 'conchie,' being a conscientious objector to war. The local children called him names, and we treated him terribly. My dad said he should be shot, and at that time, I suppose we all agreed. It is only now, long after those days, that I realise he must have been a strong and brave person to stand by his beliefs and live through the war in one small town, jeered at and shunned by many. He must have had a family I suppose; I never bothered to find out.

Alan Everson was a cub in Croydon

Croydon Airport

By the spring of 1940 many of the children who had been evacuated six months earlier were returning home, so the authorities decided to re-open our school. Just one teacher had returned and as the children were of varying ages it was arranged that each age group would attend for just one hour a day. This was an excellent arrangement from my point of view and my best friend Bob Stanley and I took full advantage of this happy state of affairs!

Our cub pack, the 64th Croydon, had also re-started and if the weather was fine we would meet on the large green opposite Croydon airport, which by this time was an RAF fighter station. One such occasion was on Thursday 15th August. We were all playing rounders when we stopped to stare at a large aircraft flying low over the rooftops. With total disbelief we noted the black cross of its German markings and as we stared as though hypnotised a large cylinder shape dropped from beneath its fusilage. In complete horror we stood transfixed to the spot like statues as the bomb fell on to one of the nearby houses and with a tremendous explosion, sent a large column of thick jet black smoke high into the air.

The sight of more aircraft following the first one galvanised us into action. We raced across the green and flattened ourselves against an open wire and wooden chestnut paling fence bordering some allotments. Just what protection this offered is debatable, but lying flat against something, however flimsy, was the instinctive reaction of a bunch of very frightened boys with their equally frightened cub mistress.

As we lay there watching the bombs falling all around, with more and more columns of dense black smoke rising high into the clear blue sky, one of the boys shouted that our bright yellow and black bordered scarves could easily be seen by the German pilots. So, with one accord we all whipped them off and hid them under our bodies. Looking back, Bob Stanley and I often laugh at this somewhat comic reaction, but we were only nine or ten years old and it seemed perfectly logical at the time.

When there seemed to be a lull in the attack our Akela led us, running as fast as we could, to the nearest house. As we piled in through the door the air raid siren sounded its warning note, better late than never I suppose. Whilst we were huddled in their back room we heard machine gun fire, whether from our own fighters or the German bombers we neither knew or cared, the very sound scared the wits out of us. When the raid was over and the All Clear sounded my father appeared at the door, having been making frantic enquiries as to our whereabouts, and escorted some of us home.

We quickly learned that one house in our own road had received a direct hit, killing one of our school friends. We stood in stunned silence as we stared in disbelief at the spot where his house had stood just a short time earlier. Semi-detached like all the rest, it looked as though a giant knife had sliced the pair in half. The sight of a fireplace surrounded by floral bedroom wallpaper set high up on the dividing wall looked somewhat bizarre and that, together with a staircase leading nowhere was all that remained of what had so recently been his home. Within an hour or so our road was completely blocked by hordes of sightseers who came on foot and bicycle to gape at the bomb damage, severely hindering the work of the rescue services.

That night we elected to sleep in our Anderson shelter and as we settled down in our bunk beds we heard one of our neighbours singing lustily to her young children. The one song I clearly remember was 'The Minstrel Boy' the first two lines of which were:

"The Minstrel Boy to the war has gone, in the ranks of death you'll find him."

A very strange choice we thought, scarcely calculated to cheer them all up!

Bob Turrell had a near miss in Folkestone

Too Close for Comfort

In 1941 I was fourteen and worked as a yard boy for a local building firm in Folkestone.

Getting to work one morning after an air raid the previous night, the foreman told me to go and look to see what damage had been done. I made my way on my bike to the east end of the town, riding along Radnor Bridge Rd I saw in a turning off to my left a house with no front to it like a dolls house with the front open.

I went up to the house and sat at the kerb looking round for the name of the road (Lennard Rd) to tell the foreman.

Riding back to Radnor Bridge Rd there was a huge explosion with bricks and dust thrown into the air.

Soldiers came running towards me. I stopped one and asked what it was. He said that it was an unexploded bomb and they had been expecting it to go up at any time.

A good fairy must have been looking after me that day but it was still too close for comfort.

Mrs W Ferris also had a narrow escape in South London

Soot and Silk

I lived in South London during the war and the early air raids were frightening for us. I was twenty years old and scared stiff so my sister and I brought the mattress off our bed and put it under the stairs in the hallway to sleep on. To keep my insides steadier I slept in my 'roll on' corselet for some time.

By 1943 I had married and during a serious raid my husband and I were in the front sitting room and we stood as close up in a corner as we could, a 'plane was so close. There was a huge explosion and all the glass from the bay window came right across the room and the blast through the house brought the linoleum floor covering up in large wrinkles. We dashed in to the kitchen/dining room where my mother was having a cup of tea before going to bed. The soot from the fireplace had covered her and the jam tarts completely. It was such a shock but we all burst out laughing – it was such a relief that nobody was hurt.

Because of clothing and household linens all being on coupons, it had to be make and mend very often. The sides of sheets, worn out in the middle, were made into boxer shorts for men. At times we were able to buy second-hand silk parachutes and these could be made in to slips and French knickers for ladies.

Strangely, after the first winter's raids one became philosophical. My son was born in September 1944 and in the early morning of that day the first rocket fell in South Norwood; I could have done without that! You didn't hear it arriving, just a terrific explosion. Of course, it wasn't until sometime later that we were told what it was.

Joyce O'Shea remembers the war years in Greenford

Doodlebugs

One late evening in 1940 an incendiary bomb dropped on to the middle of our road. Our next door neighbour who was an ARP warden rushed out in his pyjamas, tin hat on his head, carrying his bucket of sand, a broom and a shovel. He threw the sand on to the bomb and then without thinking started to sweep it up and his broom caught fire. I was watching out of my bedroom window and had to have a little giggle. His wife rushed out with another bucket of sand and put the fire out, then she had a go at her husband because he had grabbed her best broom. They made it up later and he bought her a new broom. Incidentally, the lady in question had a life-size nude statue in her back garden and on Mondays she used to drape her fur coat around it as my mum hung out the washing – my mum was rather old fashioned!

My father-in-law was the only person injured when a doodlebug was dropped on Glaxo, in Greenford. He was burnt from the top of his head down his back, legs and one arm. Two of his fingers were fused together. He had a steel plate put in his head, which was permanent and he lost half an ear. After weeks of salt baths and a lot of determination, he recovered and eventually returned to work. Much later we visited Glaxo and were shown a huge piece of shrapnel and a video showing the damage done on that night. We were quite amazed when the voiceover said that nobody was hurt. When we questioned this we were told that the video was produced based on information in Glaxo's magazine at the time and the report didn't highlight the injuries so as not affect morale. We were quite upset to think that my father-in-law's injuries were not properly reported!

Vera Walton recalls her first sight of a doodlebug over Petts Wood

Norah

It was summer 1944. In our Petts Wood, Kent semi, my husband and I, our two-year-old Alasdair and my student sister Norah were asleep in our beds. After a relatively peaceful series of nights we were awakened by the air raid warning.

I was surprised when Ken said firmly, "Take Alasdair to the shelter." We alerted Norah, who peered under the blackout curtain and saw an aircraft with a flame coming from its tail.

"It's alright Ken," she called, "It's one of ours. It's got its lights on."

It was, of course, a doodlebug, the first that we had heard.

Ken, a professional civil servant at the War office had some foreknowledge of them which was why he was insistent that we should shelter.

Norah is still liable to be teased about her naïve remark!

Edith Higgins worked in Hull

Elastoplast

In 1941 I was seventeen years old and lived on the outskirts of Hull near the village of Cottingham. The Lancashire Fusiliers were stationed there and I was friendly with one of the soldiers. One particular night we went to the cinema and whilst in there, we had an air raid. A bomb dropped opposite the cinema and the whole building shook. We were told to stay where we were but I wanted to get home to my mum and my sister, so we sneaked out. We ran for over a mile, stopping for breath in doorways. Whilst in one doorway, the flash of a gun went off and we saw that we were at the door of a Funeral Directors! However, on we went, searchlights going, bombs dropping, guns flashing and eventually got home just in time to hear the All Clear!

I worked in a factory during the war making Elastoplast dressings. During one of the raids, the factory was bombed. Fortunately nobody was working at the time so the only casualty was the night-watchman who sadly, was killed.

There were yellow gauze dressings strung around like streamers all over the factory. Elastoplast strewn everywhere. The machines were badly damaged and a lot of work had to be done to clear up. Some of the girls were kept behind to do the work and the rest of us were sent home. We got a week off work but I would rather have been paid!

On another occasion, in the middle of the night the air raid siren sounded. Mum was the first to get up, followed by my sister. I however, woke up and then went back to sleep again. My mother called me and I answered and nodded off. After several attempts my mother shouted that if I didn't get up at once she would drag me downstairs. Undaunted, I finally got out of bed dragging my eiderdown behind me and saying "I don't know what an earth all the fuss is about!" By this time Mum was in a fit state to murder me, although she didn't want the bombs to hurt me! "Hull is on fire" she shouted "and madam doesn't know what on earth all the fuss is about! Look out of the window." This I did, to see that Hull really was on fire. However, mum made my sister and I along with herself, sit behind the settee with our backs to the wall. We didn't go in the shelter that night as it was bitterly cold. There we were sat on the floor behind the settee with cushions on our heads! My sister and I were full of giggles, poor mum was so worried and afraid. The cushions of course, were to protect us from flying glass should windows be blown out, very wise and thoughtful of my mother, but we made a remark that cushions wouldn't stop the bombs and set us giggling again. How thoughtless we were, not thinking of mum.

Although Hull was bombed very badly nothing was heard of it. There was never any news on the radio only that a town in the North East had been bombed and yet there was the largest loss of life per population of any town in England.

Maurice Rudge recalls the bombing of Bristol

The Bombing of Bristol

It was Good Friday night, April 11th 1941. Mother was shaking me, "Come on," she said, "The siren's gone. Down to the shelter." It was just before 10pm and I could not have been in bed for very long. This had been a regular occurrence during the last few months. Down the garden we trundled - mother, me and brothers George and Roy. We all had our allocated carrying duties, me with a few pillows, brothers with blankets and mother following on with a box with all the important papers such as ration books, insurance policies, a few old photos, birth and marriage certificates and anything important that she could think of. Father was on nights at the aeroplane works at Patchway.

The Anderson shelter consisted of six pieces of very heavy gauge corrugated iron with each sheet about six feet tall and curving in at the top to form a tunnel shape. These were bolted together at the top with half-inch bolts and a front and back of the same material added. A front entrance consisted of a two feet by three feet gap. The whole lot was buried, for about half its height, in the ground and the earth extracted from the hole was placed on the top of the shelter to protect it from bomb splinters. It was the householder's responsibility to build a blast wall to cover the entrance. Ours consisted of a big box shape, some two feet thick four feet wide and six feet high, also filled with earth from the garden.

The inside measurement of the shelter was six feet by four feet six inches so you can tell that it was a bit of a squeeze. One of the early faults with this type of shelter was that when it rained it would partly fill with water, so quite few times I had to bail it out with a bucket. The council overcame this problem by concreting a three-inch shelf to the inside, halfway up to ground level. This proved invaluable as a six feet by two feet frame was issued with wire mesh to make a bed frame. This rested on the concrete ledge with a bed made up, which was sufficient for us boys to try and get some sleep. Mother had an old armchair.

This particular Good Friday night turned out to be one of the heaviest raids that we had up to then. I do not think that any area of Bristol escaped that night. It was reported that one hundred and eighty had been killed and one hundred and forty six seriously injured.

The All Clear siren sounded at about 4am so it was back to bed again. During the night we would constantly hear bombs whistling overhead and land with a crunch, shaking the ground. The noisiest thing, that frightened us the most, was the mobile Bofors gun that seemed to stop up the street and let off a few rounds. I think the objective was to keep them on the move so that they would not be on a fixed site that could be put out of action by the bombing.

Castle Street, Bristol before the blitz

Castle Street, Bristol after the blitz in 1940

Peter Rook witnessed a very serious incident at Pembroke

Terror in the Early Hours

We arrived at Pembroke Dock in July 1940 and settled in very quickly. The weather was fantastic and I enjoyed exploring the area and watching the flying boats and seaplanes. Pembroke Dock was indeed a pleasant town and I enjoyed the swimming at the nearby Bay of Freshwater and above all the friendship of local children.

On Monday 19th August 1940 the peace of Pembroke Dock was shattered. Three German aircraft attacked the Admiralty oil tanks at Llanreath and set off a vicious fire that raged for three weeks, ultimately destroying eleven of the seventeen tanks which meant a loss of some thirty-three million gallons of valuable fuel for the RAF base. It was a very hot sultry afternoon when suddenly there was an almighty explosion. I went out into the street and a while later the air raid warning sounded and when it died away, silence returned. Then I saw a large column of thick black smoke rising up, which within a very short time drifted over the town and sometimes seemed to turn day into night. The acrid smell of burning oil permeated everywhere and it wasn't long before the countryside around the town was covered with a thin film of oil, even garden vegetables were covered.

Within a few days there were some six hundred and fifty firemen fighting the fire, most of them were drafted in from places as far away as Birmingham, Bristol, Gloucester and, closer to home, Cardiff. They worked long hours and I remember their dishevelled appearance after long hours fighting the fire. Many of them suffered severe burns and I remember women taking them sheets, presumably for bandages and first aid. These very brave firemen were fighting a fire, the like of which they had never encountered before. Five members of the Cardiff Brigade were killed and thirty-eight other firemen were seriously injured.

One Sunday in August, we were having lunch when we heard the sound of an aircraft, we went out into the garden in time to see a large plane approaching the pall of smoke. My father said, "Its OK, its one of ours." I told him that I thought it was a Flying Pencil (Dornier Bomber) and within seconds we saw a stick of six bombs leave the aircraft which then disappeared behind the smoke. A few seconds later there were six terrific explosions. Some few minutes later the siren sounded. During the afternoon on this day mother, father, my sister and I went up to Barrack Hill to see the fire, there was a crowd of people there and hundreds of fire hoses extending from the fire down to Llanreath beach. It was like a Bank Holiday, unbelievable. How the firemen were able to endure the colossal heat I will never know, they looked so tiny against the giant pall of smoke. There was a high moat round the tanks and I guess this was built to protect the town should such a disaster actually happen. It was an unforgettable and awesome sight with massive flames and huge plumes of thick black smoke billowing out and black bubbling oil pouring over the edges of some of the tanks like giant saucepans boiling over.

A few days later I had gone to play with other children in a house at the top end of Lewis Street, where a number of army families were housed. We were playing with model seaplanes in a bath of water when the siren sounded. I immediately collected a small tin of syrup I had bought for my mother and ran hell for leather to get home. I was about halfway down the street when the roar of aircraft engines suddenly came from behind. Next the earth shattering noise of bullets striking the road no more than about two feet away from me. I looked up as I ran and saw a German Junkers 88 being chased by a Hurricane. Both planes were so low that they were very close to rooftop level. What is still so vivid in my mind is the image of the pilot and the bomb aimer behind him. I could see their faces and their brown leather helmets. As the Junkers 88 headed towards the harbour it climbed away with the Hurricane hard on its tail still firing its guns. I think the bullets that landed near me were not aimed at me, I think it was the Hurricane's bullets aimed at the German plane.

Sunday 1st September 1940, became a night indelibly imprinted on my mind. I remember a red flash; I do not remember an explosion, that must have rendered me unconscious. When I recovered I found myself tangled in a sheet and partly buried in rubble. I had no idea how long I had been there but it was now the early hours of Monday 2nd September. The deafening noise of exploding bombs, aircraft engines and looking up at the stars, remain with me to this day. I was dazed and bruised and I can only say that it was as though I was having a terrible nightmare. I was alone and very frightened, choking dust and smoke and the familiar smell of coal gas adding to my fear. I also remember that rubble was still falling on me from the wall dividing our house from the pub next door. I remember the reassuring sight of my father and an army lance corporal arriving. I saw that the bedroom door was closed then, suddenly, it burst open and my mother rushed through it and crashed on to the rubble below. Amazingly she did not break any bones, she was, however, very badly bruised. The noise of the raid continued and it was only possible to communicate by shouting. My father was climbing over the rubble looking for my sister, he was very distressed and emotional, and kept repeating, "I can't find her, where is she." I can still re-live the haunting sound of his voice and I have no doubt he was thinking that she had been killed. The bedroom in which we had been sleeping was totally destroyed, along with the ground floor kitchen. Amid all the confusion and pandemonium I also have the abiding memory of poor Miss Jenkins, standing at the open doorway through which my mother had fallen, continuously shouting, "Mrs Rook, Mrs Rook." She was in a terrible state. In the confusion I remember mention being made by someone that there was a serious risk that the pub wall would collapse and there was also the strong smell of gas. My father eventually found my sister and incredibly she was wrapped in her mattress and even more remarkable was that she was still asleep! An army lance corporal wrapped me in a blanket; I was only wearing a vest, and took me out into the street. He and other soldiers and ARP wardens then brought my parents, my sister and Miss Jenkins out. We were taken to the home of the street ARP warden, Mr Dyke, and we spent the rest of the night in his front room. I do not remember how much longer the raid continued, but eventually the All Clear sounded. Apparently what had happened was that a stick of bombs had been dropped at right angles to Lewis Street. The first bomb exploded above street level, the second one made a direct hit on the bedroom and kitchen of our house and a third one dropped at the top of our garden.

The following morning, the street was littered with debris and there were a few people viewing the results of the raid. I remember looking through the hole that was once the front room window and seeing my wristwatch on the mantelpiece, it was given to me by my parents on my tenth birthday. I wanted to go in and get it but I was not allowed to. It was never recovered.

I was cold, frightened and, I think, in deep shock. We were standing there like refugees, no home, no clothes, totally dejected. I remember my father talking to a short man with grey hair and a moustache, who had stepped out of the crowd. In fact he was Mr Tom Kenniford, a farmer from Cosheston, just a few miles out of town. He offered us accommodation and the next thing I remember was that we had this large room at his farmhouse. We were cramped for space but it was warm and comfortable. Thus began our new life on a farm.

I would like to place on record, a tribute to the Kenniford family for their generosity and kindness. Also to those who rescued us and Mr and Mrs Dyke who took a homeless family into their home for the night and to other people in Pembroke Dock who were very kind and friendly.

I would also like to thank Mr Vernon Scott, author of 'Inferno 1940', for allowing me to use statistics and figures relating to the fire and the Blitz on Pembroke Dock.

Pat Collins worked as a Wren in Portsmouth

Portsmouth Dockyard

During the war, I was a Wren in Portsmouth working in the naval dockyard. We passed signals from officers on shore, by telephone, to ships and submarines that were coming and going in the harbour. We worked at night it was very dark, of course. During the many air raids we moved to an underground office and passed signals from one area of the docks to another – what was burning and where help was needed.

Surprisingly few bombs actually dropped on the docks but lots fell on Southsea Shopping Centre and Commercial Road. One night we were working underground as usual during an air raid when I heard a huge noise very closeby, but no bang. The room seemed to move. In 1999, two unexploded bombs were dug up in exactly that area. I am sure that one of those was the bomb that I heard.

One Christmas Day we cycled past one of the dock gates. The night before, a bomb had dropped on to the small houses there and I remember seeing strands of silver tinsel in amongst all of the rubble.

Soon after the French capitulated, two French Cruisers came in to the harbour. The British went on board and took all of the French sailors off. They were given the choice of joining the Free French or being sent back to France. Those that chose the latter option were taken out to Spithead on an old paddle steamer and told to take themselves home - it was a very old boat!

After the invasion of Europe in June 1944, many of the bodies and casualties came back to Portsmouth. One boat, which was full of bodies, was towed back from France backwards. The workers who had to work on the boat were given double time because of the unpleasant conditions.

We lived on basic rations but we had plenty of milk and concentrated Orange Juice because of my baby. My daughter drank loads of the Orange Juice and it rotted her milk teeth – her second set were OK though. We didn't know anyone in the Black Market so couldn't get hold of any 'extras.' My mother in law regularly gave an egg to her Pekinese dog and I couldn't get one for my daughter!

The 1940s - Month by Month

1942

January

- Japanese forces captured the Philippines

February

- Singapore fell to the Japanese
- The Japanese bombed the northern Australian city of Darwin
- Call-up was extended to single women aged 20 and 21

March

- British commandos raided the Nazi U-boat base at St Nazaire

April

- Malta was awarded the George Cross
- Princess Elizabeth registered for war service

May

- In the North African desert, Rommel's Afrika corps began a major offensive against the Allies

June

- Tobruk fell to Rommel's forces, with 25,000 Allied soldiers being taken prisoner

July

- Sweets were rationed
- The battle in North Africa began to swing in favour of the Allies following the battle of El Alamein, which the German forces failed to take

August

- The Duke of Kent died in an air crash
- General Montgomery was appointed commander of the Eight Army in North Africa
- The German siege of Stalingrad began
- The 'Bouncing Bomb' was patented

September

- Many of the Jews in the Warsaw ghetto were slaughtered or sent to concentration camps

October

- General Montgomery launched a massive offensive against the German Afrika Corps at El Alemein

November

- Montgomery's forces broke through Rommel's defences, forcing him to retreat
- Russian troops regained the initiative at Stalingrad

December

- The Beveridge Report, which laid the foundations for the Welfare State was published
- The first controlled nuclear chain reaction took place in Chicago University

=================

Childhood

Pat Barham lived in Kent

Battle of Britain Sunday

One beautiful morning in 1940, I went out into the garden and heard a sound like the distant rolling of drums. I thought it might be an air raid over Dover but dad said it might well be heavy artillery, as he had heard on the wireless that the Germans had broken through, over-running Holland and Belgium. It seemed unreal to be standing in a garden full of apple blossom and lilac, listening to the sounds of a terrible battle.

The situation soon became all too real for us, as the news came in of the retreat from Dunkirk and the capitulation of France. It became evident that Hitler intended to invade England and preparations were made. Tank traps were placed across the roads to the coast and in large fields, farmers put up big posts to hinder the landing of troop-carriers. Signposts were taken down and the names of railway stations, etc were removed. Church bells were silenced as they were only to be used to give warning of the invasion. Dad began to hoard a small quantity of food, mostly in tins, which we could take with us if we became refugees. It was all rather frightening but I never saw any sign of panic and never heard anyone express a doubt of our winning in the end.

All that summer there was fighting overhead as Hitler bombed the harbours and airfields. My youngest brother had been nervous of thunder as a child and when nearby Detling airfield was attacked my mother thoughtfully called upstairs to him, "Don't worry darling, it isn't thunder, it's only bombs!"

It all came to a head on Sunday 15th September 1940 when Dad, Brian and I were walking to Bedgebury Forest. There had been a massive attack that morning, further east, but that afternoon we suddenly saw a huge array of bombers, flying in formation, wave upon wave, with a fighter escort. They were fairly high and we couldn't distinguish much of what was going on but our fighters were obviously attacking and we could hear the cackle of machine guns and the high-pitched note of 'planes diving.

Suddenly, a big German bomber appeared low in front of us and eight or nine men baled out. The aircraft was too low when the last man jumped and his parachute did not open. His body was later found in Hawkhurst churchyard. The 'plane went on, just skimming the trees and crashed a few miles away.

Then we heard the screaming engine of a Spitfire out of control and diving towards us. Nobody jumped out and it burst in to flames halfway down. I felt sick. It crashed and exploded somewhere in the forest and a tall column of smoke appeared.

As we made our way home, we felt that we had seen something momentous and in fact it was the turning point of the war and the day now commemorated as Battle of Britain Sunday.

When dogfights had taken place during the day, my brothers and I got on our bikes in the evenings and scoured the countryside for souvenirs such as spent cannon-shells, bits of twisted fuselage, etc. We eventually held a small exhibition of these finds, charging 2d or 3d to view, in aid of the Spitfire fund. Our contribution of six shillings was duly noted in the columns of the Daily Telegraph.

Sheila Darzi recalls living in Blackburn

High Tea and Iron Rations

My memories are cameos rather than ongoing. Obviously, there was the deprivation, but what you have never had, you never miss. My mother traded sugar for butter and tried to entice me to eat the weekly egg, which I frequently refused. We seemed to eat very well.

So, what do I remember?

Going to school with my gas mask bouncing on my bottom. The sensation and smell of wearing it, and sucking in as hard as possible!

Always having my identity disk round my neck.

Being told I must not speak to the many evacuees at my school because they were dirty (typical example of NON-toleration) and subsequently getting into dreadful trouble when I came home in a nit-filled beret after 'they' had taken mine! Then being plastered in potassium permanganate.

Being aware that my father and uncle – wholesale fruit and vegetable merchants, occasionally came back with half a side of pork hidden under boxes of damsons from some Westmoreland farmer. I found the concept of them doing 'something bad' rather puzzling because they were god-fearing and totally honest.

Going to the British Restaurant for a lunch with my mother, in the way that kids today would pop into McDonalds. We ate out quite a lot, considering. But it was usually 'high tea' with baked beans or a boiled egg and cake.

My father was a very important factor in my young life. Because he was doing 'essential work' he had to turn down his place in the Irish Guards. He was in his late thirties but this did not prevent his twin brother from being called up.

Central to our lives was my father's fire watching and Home Guard. He was rarely home, leaving for work at 6am until around 5pm. Then off to the Home Guard or an overnight Fire Watch above a bakery where the cockroaches scuttled in hundreds on top of the tissue covering the cakes.

My father took the Home Guard very seriously and complained when my mother did her best to give him a nutritious packed meal each Sunday for 'manoeuvres', claiming that he was supposed to be on 'iron rations.' One day, she thought she would get her own back. So, he sat down for his lunch one raw day and amused the rest of the platoon whilst they watched him take off layers and layers of paper. At last he found two cream crackers with a note saying, "Enjoy your iron rations, soldier boy!"

For some reason, his uniform was kept on the back of my bedroom door. I remember the feel and the smell of damp khaki.

Our family had a holiday bungalow on Morecambe Bay near Silverdale, and we spent a lot of time there. I vividly remember seeing the bombs being dropped on Barrow's shipyards across the bay, where we felt as if we were in another world.

In 1947, my father had an accident with a swing door and nearly lost a finger. No-one went to Casualty then. He sought out the nearest doctor who happened to be Indian. There were two in Blackburn at that time. It must be remembered that even in the forties, a substantial number of young men from South Asia came to Blackburn to learn about the cotton industry. Anyway, the treatment was so good, that we all registered with him. My mother had a chronic illness so we saw him twice a week. At the age of nine, I knew where Amritsar was!

Eileen Smith grew up in Liverpool

The Green Vestments

We lived in a grand house with a garden at the back, a proper bathroom (which was never used), a cellar with a gigantic black range for heating water (never used), and many other rooms scattered over three floors.

I don't know whom this house belonged to or how we got there. My parents had been bombed out of their previous place and this may explain why inside there was almost no furniture whatsoever. My dad slept on the ground floor and I slept on the third floor.

Our family was unusual. My father, a widower with adult children including twins Mary and Joseph, married his housekeeper, my mother, when he was fifty-six. I was born when she was forty and he was seventy-two and blind. I had two older sisters, one of whom was permanently fostered by the Bewleys of Chester, tobacco importers and retailers. My mother also had a son, Bertie.

At night my dad would bathe me with Zambuc soap in a tin bath by a fire, the sole heating in the house. He had a record player with a horn and he loved Paul Robeson singing 'Ole Man River.' He also sang sad songs. 'Don't go down in the mines, dad'; 'The little boy that Santa Claus forgot' and 'T'was only a bird in a gilded cage.' I sensed that he was thinking of my mother when he sang that song but he never said anything.

Liverpool by now was getting bombed. I had a gasmask. Dried egg powder was being delivered and food was rationed. Sometimes I had a spoon of cod liver oil (horrible) or a little Parish's Food for iron and if my nose got blocked, margarine was rubbed on it to loosen the tubes.

On my first day at school the teacher asked me my dad's name. I said "Ike", short for Isaac. Everyone called my dad "Ike." She said it couldn't possibly be that. I had to think quickly on my feet. The King was called George. That must be an acceptable name and so I told her "George." (An accurate choice for on my birth certificate he is listed as George Isaac). My teacher said to the teacher adjacent to her "This is Teresa Smith's sister." The second teacher replied, "She is not as good looking as her sister. Her eyes are too close together." When I got home I climbed on to a chair to look in the mirror and see how close my eyes were.

I had fleas. The school nurse put yellow Oil of Sarafas on my head and purple Oil of Gentian Violets on the scabs around my mouth. I was not the only one to wear these colours or smell so strongly. It was a Roman Catholic school. I learnt to read from The Beacon Readers, recite the tables, and understand pints and quarts. The subject that really hit home though was religion. Heaven and Hell were very real as was the fact that really good people called Saints got 'visions.' I was very very afraid of all this. At night my only prayer was "Please God don't send me a vision."

The cane was ever ready. I got it on both hands for talking. Additionally my mother who was Catholic was often absent from home. Hence I didn't always go to Mass on Sundays. This was a sin and the very worst kind of sin. One Monday the headmistress said, "Put your hands up all those who went to Mass yesterday." I hadn't gone but I sensed that she was in a bad mood so I put my hand up (a lie). She asked me the colour of the priest's vestments and I said "Green." It was the wrong answer and I got the cane. My dad who was not a Catholic took me to Mass every Sunday thereafter and gave me a penny for the collection. He would deliver me and wait outside.

I sat next to a boy named Tommy Carter. At Christmas the Juniors put on a Nativity Play and the Infants had to pay two pence to see this play. My dad did not have the money to give me and Tommy Carter couldn't bring it either. Come the day, my class trouped off to the hall but Tommy Carter and I could not go. We stayed alone at our desk and for the first time I realised that even amongst the poor, some are poorer than the rest. This was my first experience of shame. I felt terrible shame because no money made us different in a negative way.

Socially, Liverpool was vibrant and tribal. Catholics were strongly trained to avoid Protestants. The Catholics would have their religious processions in honour of the Virgin Mary or the Sacred Heart and the Protestants would have their Orange marches. Fights, usually alcohol fuelled, would erupt at some point in all this. Then there was the market, known as Paddy's Market. Lots of Pakistanis had stalls there but there was no mixing.

On one of these stalls there was a wondrous golliwog with large looped earrings. I was with my dad. I yearned for this golliwog. My dad did not have the money. He moved on. I lingered. I saw an opportunity and stole the Golly. I caught up with my dad. He knew somehow that I had this toy. He took me and Golly back to the stall, handed it over and gave me a hard smack on the legs. An American offered to buy it for me. My dad refused and when we got out of sight he hit me again. Everyone got hit in those days especially women and children. I was quite old before I learnt that hitting women and children wasn't normal.

There was also a well-established West Indian community; the Chinese were running laundries and the Jewish community lived their lives in their sector. No one mixed. Everyone stayed in his or her 'gang.' Even in the Public washrooms where women went to do their washing or pay for a bath, no one mixed.

Once I was smacked with regard to my dad, his blindness and money. The school had asked us to bring money for the Blind. When I told my dad, he said that he was blind and nobody gave him any money. I reported the conversation to the teacher and someone had been round to the house before I returned in the evening. My dad was livid. Another wallop! The lesson of that wallop was that you did not repeat anything that happened indoors to anyone outside.

My mother came and went. She usually came when she was in trouble of some sort or another. She would sit beneath the gas mantle with newspaper on her head and then go to hospital or Lytham St. Anne's for convalescence. Nobody liked her. I just found her embarrassing. When I was very small she took me to Woolworths and left me there. I was taken to a Children's home in Mount Pleasant. Another time she tried to sell me to an Australian woman. Then she hit me on the head with a poker. I slid down the wall to the floor. She got the priest, I went to hospital. My hair was shaved off and I was in a room on my own for ages. I was then moved to a ward and we had school in this hospital. The Protestants sat in front and made crosses from silver paper. The Catholics sat at the back and looked at scrapbooks. I returned to school hairless and wearing a red pixie hood. Miss Millar told me to take it off but I wouldn't. My teacher said something to Miss Millar who left me alone after that.

My dad died in February 1945. As soon as I saw his body I knew my dad had gone. I knew inside myself that my life was going to change. My safety had gone. My security had vanished. I went alone to his coffin in his bedroom, lifted the handkerchief over his face and gazed at this skeleton. I felt afraid of everything.

Christine Goodhugh spent some of the war years in London

The Union Jack

My father was a regular soldier and was sent to Malta in April 1939 when I was just fifteen months old. Due to the subsequent outbreak of World War Two he remained on Malta until April 1944, so I did not know my father until I was six years old. It must have been strange for him too, to meet a little girl, having missed all my early years. When my father was posted to Woolwich, shortly after his return to the UK, my mother decided to go with him in spite of the V1s, as they had been separated for so long. We stayed at the old Union Jack hostel near Waterloo until somewhere suitably cheap could be found to rent and a school could be found for me. I remember how exciting I found the underground with so many people, the deep rumbles of the approaching trains and that peculiar oily, dusty smell and wafts of warm air. Our stay was cut short as no suitable digs could be found and one night a bomb flattened a church near the Union Jack - too dangerous, my parents thought, so my mother and I returned to Durrington in Wiltshire, back with my grandparents. That fateful night of the bomb we had all duly trooped to the shelter when I remembered I had left my teddy bear in the room at the Union Jack. Before I could be restrained, I dashed back into the building and came back triumphantly clutching him. Strangely, I felt no fear for myself, I just didn't want my beloved teddy to be left all alone. My poor mother was horrified and I had a severe reprimand!

Valerie Simpson lived near Wolverhampton

Sunday Walks and Bonfires

We lived on a smallholding opposite the church in Wombourne, a quiet village then, five miles south of Wolverhampton. My mum kept a general shop, which was part of our house. The ration books drove her mad! Dad worked for grandad on his rented farm and for his war effort was a special constable. The war didn't affect us too much, we could hear air raid sirens in the towns and had a few evacuees. We marched half a mile both ways from school to the Women's Institute for dinners, which came in big tins. I remember metal fences being removed. It was very exciting when a German 'plane crashed in the water works by the canal. That week it was the Sunday walk after evensong to see the parachute hanging in a tree. The night that always seemed most important to me was when a stray bomb was dropped on a lovely house killing the Spanish nursemaid. A man on patrol duty across the valley had shrapnel pierce his leg. The first aid people applied a tourniquet but sorry to say it was not released every so often and the leg was amputated. Dad was on duty at the police station that night and his dog, Janny sneaked after him. She wasn't seen until next day when she arrived with all her feet bleeding. The bomb dropped three quarters of a mile from the police station and we never found out what happened but afterwards she was frightened of loud noises.

Grandad died suddenly in 1943, across the yard in the lav. He was taken on a hay cart drawn by his carthorses to the church for his funeral.

A huge bonfire was built on the recreation ground to celebrate VJ Day, the real end of the war. The night before the event someone set fire to it and it blazed away. Next day there was a mad scramble round to construct another one. It was rumoured that Tom, the husband of another aunt, was the villain, having visited all six of our pubs to celebrate his demob. He was a very bitter man, like so many after the war.

Mavis Grant lived in Ilford

Chocolate

I was a child of ten during the blitz living in Ilford, which suffered the bombing to a high degree. Then, as now, I love chocolate. The monthly ration was eight ounces. I ate mine up all at once on the first day – just in case I was killed!

We were asked to Dig for Victory and fertiliser was in short supply. Seeing a pile of horse manure in the road, mother and a neighbour dashed out with bucket and shovel.

"That's mine," said neighbour.

"I was first," mother replied.

"That was the Co-op horse – you have the United Dairies" the neighbour triumphantly countered.

Five lads all about five years older than me that I knew were killed and when at last VE day arrived, I remember sobbing for a long time before joining the celebrating crowds in Trafalgar Square.

Sheila Brown moved to Somerset

Washdays and School Dinners

I was about six or seven when I moved with my mother and father to a stone cottage deep in a village in the Blackdown Hills, Somerset, about eight miles from the nearest town. It was just after the war ended in 1946.

The cottage was adjoined to a farmhouse and the farmyard ran along the rear of our back garden. A huge lean-to was fixed to the side of our cottage that served as a garage, accommodated an outhouse and an outside toilet, all underneath a galvanised roof. The outhouse had a large square brick surround in a corner situated by a window. In the top was a large wooden cover and underneath was a huge iron tub sunk into the brickwork. At the base of the surround was an iron door and a cavity where sticks and coal could be laid in readiness for washday.

I can remember my mother starting at dawn on Monday mornings, filling the tub with water drawn from the cold tap; the water had to be heated in a large pan on the range. She lit the firewood beneath and waited for the water to boil so she could do the 'wash' with her trusty blue bag and Sunlight soap.

A huge mangle stood nearby and a scrubbing board. I was the one who turned the large wheel on the mangle when the time came for the water to be wrung from the washing.

My father ran a business from the cottage. He had a car and trailer and went to the rubbish tips collecting the dirty jam jars, sauce bottles etc, and any other glassware that could be recycled.

This was transported home and tipped on to the outhouse floor where I had to soak all the labels off in a big bath of water. When the mud and grime was all off and the logo for the Ministry of Food (MF) could be clearly seen, the glassware was then sold. Back to the Ministry, I suppose.

This was a thriving business, we lived quite well and had a telephone and headed notepaper plus other things, so for just after the war, we weren't doing too bad.

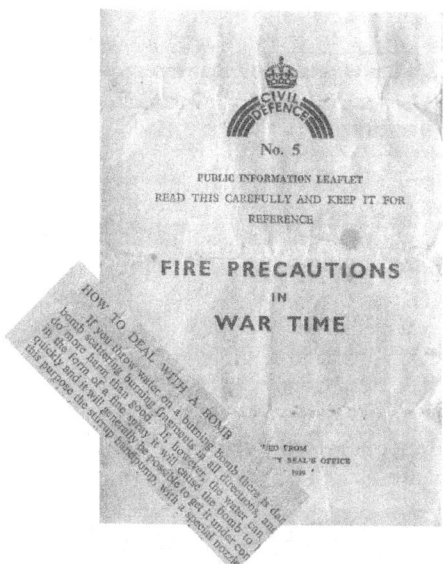

Fire Precautions

Brian Sewell spent his youth in Norwich

Bombs and Bulls

We lived in a roughly oblong shaped cul de sac in Norwich, with terraced houses. A bomb hit one, so the others began to lean in an unsafe manner so we were sent to my granny's about a mile away. We stayed with her until she had an incendiary bomb through the roof, so off we went again to my dad's parents where the houses were already slums by today's standards (shared toilets). Life was OK for a while with my sister and myself at school and mum doing wartime work (my dad was away in the army) when a paint factory nearby was hit by several bombs and yes, the poor old slums got shook up!

So off we went again to a farm, this time about seven miles from Norwich. Peace! Perfect peace, new school and all was well there until the local council repaired our house and we returned 'home' again after our boarding out.

Both during and after the war, we attended Saturday morning cinema. The entrance price could be adjusted by going to a certain cinema, The Theatre Deluxe in Norwich, now long gone. For one 2lb jam jar and one 1lb jam jar you were allowed in. Alternatively, the entrance price was a rabbit skin!

The jam jars were purloined from the back yard of the Norwich Co-op and the rabbit skin was from our mum's endeavours to supplement the inadequate meat ration.

One other Saturday morning pursuit was cattle herding. A gang of boys would meet the cattle train at a small station about two and a half miles from Norwich. We helped to off load the cattle trucks then herd the cattle up the main road with boys strung out on the sides. A lead bull, with a ring and trailing rope from his nose, was in front and the farmer took up the rear. We were the watchdogs to prevent any cattle making off down the side streets, though they did seem more subdued when led by the bull. Once safely penned on the market we then roamed about all the other attractions that made up the huge expanse in the centre of Norwich. Horses, cattle, sheep, calves, goats, all manner of fowl, pigs, rabbits, you name it, it was there.

We later returned to our farmer for payment and the possibility of more work and for all the long day our reward was 2/- (10p today!)

Sheep were something totally different as once offloaded from the trucks they would just take off scattering in all directions – you really earned your money then!

Barry Ledgard lived in Bradford

Bananas and Bonfires

The main difference to my young life as a result of the War was that the sweeties which were in plentiful supply prior to 1940 suddenly disappeared from the face of the earth, and I was mystified to see the all sweet shops with completely bare shop windows and interiors. As the 40s developed I never ceased to wonder how the sweet shop owners made a living when they had nothing to sell!

I lived in a 'back to back' house up a passage from the cobbled street. As the war developed, we knew that Bradford was on an almost direct flight path for the heavy bombers coming from Europe to bomb Lancashire's heavy industries and the Liverpool docks. Sheffield's steel works were also nearby and we were overflown by German pilots looking for Sheffield who had gone a few miles astray.

Bradford was not a particular target for the Germans, but we did suffer bombing and severe fire damage a few times when German bomber pilots, frustrated because of heavy cloud cover over their targets, dumped their bombs more or less anywhere on their way back home. Quite a few times Bradford and district was that 'anywhere'!

We were occasionally cheered, when an German aircraft which had been shot down was towed into the City centre, to give us visible evidence that 'we were winning the war.' I was more cheered, as a child, by the sonorous, deep and inspiring voice of Winston Churchill reassuring me that we would achieve victory at the end of the day.

A family down the street had a relative who worked on the docks in Hull, and one day they received a bunch of bananas, which was triumphantly borne aloft up and down the street. In common with most of the other children I had no recollection of what a banana was. I was permitted to see one consumed by its proud owner, and have a sniff of it as he ate it, which stirred my memory of a long forgotten aroma. I was given the skin which I took home to my mother in triumph and was very disappointed to see her cast in into the dustbin with a muttered comment that I didn't catch!

In May 1945, I came home from school to learn that the Germans had capitulated at last, and it was with great pride that I climbed on top of our outside toilet and fastened a union jack to a metal spar. The flag remained there awaiting the victory over Japan, which was expected to follow fairly quickly.

The street party celebrations were mind blowing to the youngsters, as mums dredged up from hidden cupboards many foodstuff delights, saved for such an occasion. Trestle tables were erected down the middle of nearly every street in the city, covered with table cloths, and then filled just before we left school with jellies, custard, sandwiches, pies, buns and cakes. Every street seemed to vie with others to produce the best for their children. We had a great time and ate until we almost burst, to the delight of the mothers who watched over their brood with the lines of stress, fear and worry almost visibly fading from their now cheerful and smiling faces.

James Gunn grew up near Hampstead Heath

The Town & Country Kids

Father called us The Town and Country Kids, because we lived in a little house on Hampstead Heath, that sprawl of heathland, woods and ponds which runs in a great curve across outer North London from Finchley Rd to Kentish Town.

Our dad spent his entire working life there as a park keeper come forest ranger, one of eleven men living with their families in a cluster of flats and houses on the Heath.

There were nine children in these families, with ages ranging from eight to fourteen. We called ourselves the Kenwood Rangers after the Kenwood Estate, an enclosed area of the most beautiful gardens and parkland forming the very heart of the Heath. A magnificent Adam country house dominates Kenwood, which once belonged to Lord Mansfield.

In that far off golden summer of 1940, we found our way via a fire escape on to the roof of Lord Mansfield's country house where we formed a highly illegal camp among the great chimney stacks. We could see St Pauls, Tower Bridge, Big Ben and on clear days, the North Downs.

The Battle of Britain was a daily show for our benefit – the ranks of Dorniers, Junkers and Heinkels droning up the Thames valley, the Spitfires and Hurricanes wheeling among the vapour trails, with the accompanying faint rattle of machine gun fire. Then losing interest as only children can, we would descend to scuffle for conkers in the fallen leaves while young men just a few years older than ourselves, fought and died far above our uncaring heads.

In late September the Luftwaffe turned to night raids. The Big House was closed, the art treasures put in storage with the few remaining pieces of furniture shrouded with white dust covers. The House stood silent and empty, but the Kenwood Rangers gained entrance through a basement window and unbeknown to our parents, Lord Mansfield's great house became our adventure playground. We played murder, sardines and hide and seek. While the elderly caretaker brewed up his tea in the Lodge, we flitted about the moonlit corridors until we were sent scurrying for home across the lawns and along the ancient avenues of elms and limes with the sirens howling their warning overhead. The sky split with searchlights and starred with flares and shell bursts. The thump and crack from the gun battery on Primrose Hill with the crump of the first bombs of the night and the first fires beginning to glow on the eastern horizon in the direction of the docks.

Within four years I was on active service in Egypt and Palestine. There are many traumatic memories of those times but none as clear and vivid in my mind as our adventures in The Big House in 1940.

Mr P Evered lived in Somerset

Who Would Buy a Farm?

At the start of the war I was in Minehead hospital with double pneumonia. I was in the men's ward as the children's ward was thought to be too noisy for me. My bed was below a window, which was quite large and shaped like a church window. I could see the sky and a wall of the Methodist church. One day a workman came and put sandbags up in front of the window. I can see him now looking down on me and saying, "There's a poor little boy." From thereon I only had a small patch of sky – it was like looking up a tunnel.

I can remember how I went with my parents down to Porlock Wier to see a Junkers 88 that came down in Porlock Bay. All we could see was the body and tail of the plane as that was as far as the soldiers would let us go.

When they built the Pillboxes they used to roof them to look like a real house with painted windows to complete the camouflage. As children we used to play in the sandbag emplacements.

My father had a small farm and one of his fields was next to an American camp. While they were there our hedges used to have little white sacks hanging from them. Of course, today's children would know all about them but in our day sex education was not given to us children. We were told, "Nice people don't talk about such things."

At the outbreak of the war, my parents and others were shocked that people were buying farms to put their sons in as farming was a reserved occupation and so they were able to keep them from being called up. You see, before the war you could have given away these farms, as the only farms that sold were those that had a milk round.

Horse drawn implements - *By Ministry of Information Photo Division Photographer [Public domain]*

Mrs Dennett lived in Poole

The Wrong Week!

In about 1940 when I was about four or five, I had a small operation on my parent's kitchen table. It was to remove a type of growth on my gum. Even now I can still remember the chloroform going over my mouth and screaming the place down.

Also when I was about seven, I broke my elbow – apparently a simple greenstick fracture – easy for a child to do. I was in hospital for two weeks! The first ward was one where my mother could visit a short time each day – don't think she would have though, as I had a new brother! The second ward where I spent the following week was only visiting every other Sunday afternoon! Unfortunately, I was in the wrong week! Luckily our neighbour was a nurse in that ward so I did get news from home, also a treat now and again.

Mrs B Halton grew up during the war in the North West

Tin Baths and Clogs

When the war ended dad began work at the Royal Ordinance Munitions factory. My mum worked in a mill weaving material. I remember watching her cut patterns out of material then sew it on her Singer sewing machine. I was amazed to see a dress being made for me. I was told to take notice – that way I would learn!

Sunday was the best day of the week. Mum would spend all day in the kitchen cooking things like boiled tongue, jam roly poly pudding, apple and custard pies and other fancy goods. Sunday tea was a treat for us all.

By this time I had a younger brother to play with and if it was fine, we would play football, cricket and other outdoor games on the playing field. When it was time we would go home tired and dirty from play. A large tin bath that was hung up outside was put in front of a roaring fire and filled with hot water. We each took it in turn to get in then when we were all done we had hot buttered toast done on the fire before going to bed for some much needed sleep, to do it all again the next day.

All the neighbours knew my mum. If someone was ill or had just passed away then they would send for Little Mary, for she knew just what to do. Mum would bath them and lay them out. Till one death came knocking on our door; my dad was just thirty-six when he died.

Winters were very cold; we had ice on the inside of the windows. I remember we'd breath on them to melt the ice and outside there were icicles hanging from the window ledge. We'd brake one off and suck it. I always wore clogs that my mother made. She nailed irons on the bottom of them, great for sliding on ice and making sparks. When it was bedtime because it was cold we would take an oven shelf wrapped in a blanket to bed with us - the oven was part of the fireplace then.

Archie Beggs remembers growing up near Birkenhead

Sam Bosh and Church Steeples

I was born in 1928 in the small town of Moreton near Birkenhead, referred to in the area as either 'Bucket Town' being a reference to its sanitary system or alternatively 'Debtors Retreat', it being conveniently isolated by flooded dirt roads which discouraged creditors and bailiffs.

In those times it was quite normal for figures to be observed in the dusk engaged in loading the family possessions on to handcarts. 'Doing a flitting' was the term, the evening before the rent-man was due.

The war did not affect things a lot at first. Jackie Beeton, a local 'bad lad', was called up and to our amazement returned on his first leave with three stripes on his sleeve. It subsequently transpired that he had stolen a sergeant's tunic to come home and swank.

Rations were meagre but adequate and often we suspected it was horsemeat not lamb we were supplied with but as the amount was so small it did not matter a lot. Being permanently hungry we felt the cold in winter keenly. There was food around - the black marketeers did well and Churchill did not look undernourished. A sensation was caused one day at school when a pupil produced a banana - everyone crowded round to look at it, his brother had brought it from abroad.

I attended secondary school at New Brighton, four miles away. By this time Britain was expecting an invasion and the whole coastline was protected by barbed wire and concrete tank obstacles, pill boxes and minefields and with six airfields around the area the variety of aircraft gave us great interest. There were many forced landings and not a few crashes.

The bombing itself had surprisingly little effect on us children, we visited all the bomb craters and demolished houses with simple curiosity not realising the tragedy and horror that lay behind. Living out at Moreton we did not receive many bombs, and we spent many nights freezing in the brick built air-raid shelter in the back garden, listening to the enemy planes above. These could be easily recognised from ours as they de-synchronised their engines to foil our sound locators and it gave them a rhythmic buzz like someone sawing plywood.

One freezing night we stayed by the minute fire in our living room - father, mother, myself and little sister when the air-raid sirens went - we heard Jerry above and then there was a whizz and a tremendous bang. The shock wave sent a cloud of soot and smoke down the chimney. Then the reversal of pressure sucked all the blackout screens from the windows. I remember shouting "the lights, the lights" for it was an offence to show any light in the blackout and we all scrambled under the kitchen table.

What had actually happened was that two bombs had been dropped - one in the next road and one a dozen houses away which tragically hit the reinforced concrete roof of the shelter killing Mrs Barrie and her eleven year old daughter June instantly. Poor Mr Barrie was on ARP duty and had to come home to the scene of desolation.

As children we accepted things without question, either you got blown up or you lived, none of us ever needed counselling.

My secondary school at New Brighton was staffed by a mixed bag of masters, some back from retirement, some a little eccentric. The maths master was a Victorian gentleman type who had been an officer in India and possibly an excess of curry had left him a bit irascible. When I submitted my results of simultaneous equations he hurled the exercise book on the floor with the shout "all bosh and piffle son", hence his nickname 'Sam Bosh'. Despite his manner we all respected him.

The Spanish master had a violent temper and would throw your book out of the window. Another master who had been seconded from a Catholic school and whom I suspect was a product of the Christian Brothers upbringing was a right sadist. He had the practice of creeping up behind any pupil who had offended in any way and administering a vicious slap on the back of his head with the remark "you've had your little joke now I'll have mine."

During the whole of my school days I learnt little except how to measure the height of a church steeple, (something about the shadow) very useful! The most interesting experiment we did was carried out in the temporary absence of the master by one Gibson, when in the furtherance of scientific knowledge urinated copiously into the red hot forge thus simulating ammonia production and a gas attack.

Transport to school was by either a Guy utility bus with wooden seats and an engine that rattled like a cement mixer, a vehicle of great discomfort, or a normal bus running on gas produced on a trailer. These were not fast, being just able to overtake a horse and cart - if it was loaded, and when confronted by the moderate hill that lay on route would often expire half way up. We all prayed devoutly that it would remain at rest but after time for the gas to generate it would eventually get into motion. We all lost faith in the power of prayer!

Toward the end of the war all the school kids were promised a great treat - some town in America was sending us a present each. To children who had not had any palatable sweets for years, speculation ran rife, anticipation rose to fever pitch as the day approached and at last we were given our parcels. When opened they revealed to be a pair of hairbrushes - admittedly of good quality. I looked at mine sadly and thought of the opinion expressed on my school reports 'could do better'.

John Wood-Cowling recalls life in Glasgow

Johnny

Here is the life of a ten-year-old boy in 1946-47; we will call him Johnny.

His father managed to get himself killed in Norway in 1940, a sailor. Johnny could not remember what he looked like. His mother had long gone, there was a rumour that she was in America. He lived with his aunt, seven of them in two rooms in a tenement, one sink, a small grate, outside toilet, shared by thirty-six people! It froze in the winter so you used the park, the women poured buckets of piss in the gutter.

Folk talk about the good old days - a Bobby gave you a cuff on the ear. Nothing could be further from the truth and Johnny and his pals could run like hares. Thieving was not considered a crime in these circles, you simply took it from people, big shops, anybody better off than you, in fact it was a sort of welfare state. Robin Hood was a hero. Johnny specialised in gas meters, they were situated in wash-houses shared by everybody in the tenement. All you needed was a paint scraper to ease the gap on top of the oblong cash box; a lever to rip it open, 'Bob's your uncle.' Only the landlord suffered - he deserved it. Big shops were a doddle, your mate created a diversion, you took your pick of the counter. Woolworths was a favourite.

Johnny lived in appalling poverty, yet he would buy a comic for two pence - it introduced him to a world he could only dream about. These comics had funny names Hotspur, Wizard, etc. They always had four stories. Strang the Terrible was a favourite, he ran around Africa in a loincloth, he had a club over his shoulder and muscles Johnny never new existed. Strang was always braining lions, elephants and natives with the club. The natives were always cannibals; not much wonder we were racists!

The second story was Cannonball kid, a super footballer. A typical drawing was Cannonball kicking a goal, the ball hits the goalkeeper in the stomach and both the goalkeeper and the ball go through the back of the net. We lapped it up. Some guys thought it was for real, Johnny's pal thought he played for Glasgow Rangers or should have. The third story was about Smith of the Lower Third, a public schoolboy and his teacher, a half-wit called Mr Smugg. This was a world Johnny would never enter. The stories were about getting one over on Mr Smugg. Smith was a fag to a nasty senior boy, a fag round our way is for smoking, who knows maybe it was the same sort of thing in the public school. Johnny missed the point. A rich uncle was always sending Smith a five-shilling postal order; Johnny would have sold his sister for an uncle like that! The stories were tripe, I think the moral was 'behave yourself like Smith and you might make it' – on your bike!

The fourth story was some half-wit doing his National Service in the Army. Unlike any normal guy in our street he loves it. The series lasted two boring months, telling us how he loves cleaning his kit, stripping down Bren guns he becomes a crackshot with a rifle, he loves long marches in Dartmoor - freezing, soaking, it toughens him up. I don't know where he is coming from, he should try our street. And the sequel to the yarn - he signs up for twenty years. What a mug.

Johnny is sitting on the stair head staring at the gutter, watches a low life collecting cigarette ends in the gutter. Johnny thinks guys like that let the tone of the neighbourhood down, he decides to kick him when he passes. The Protestant Minister arrives, glares at Johnny - he knows he is a Catholic. "Move you", says the man of God, he goes up the stairs. Johnny notices the dreep on his nose, he lets it drop six inches then sniffs it up. "Dirty prody bastard," Johnny thinks, "why doesn't he use his sleeve!" The Minister's name is the Reverend Gunn, needless to say he bawls and shouts fire and brimstone, the guys call him Tommy Gun. Ten minutes later Johnny's pal comes down. "Is that the Minister visiting your mother?"

"Yeah" his pal replies. "He gave her some wee cardboard envelopes on a string. She has to put two pence a week in the envelopes and he will collect them next month. Having trouble heating the Manse."

Johnny Christ! He should be giving you lot money the bloody old swine. The Reverend liked his food - he died choked on a chicken bone. Nobody on our street mourned - they had never eaten chicken.

One Sunday, Johnny and his pal were sitting on the stair head in Scotland on a Sunday. In those days you were not allowed to do anything not even kick a ball, something to do with a miserable old bastard called John Knox who kicked the bucket hundreds of years ago. To the Protestants he was some sort of hero. I'm not in the fan club; give me Roy Rogers any time. His pal's sister came down the stairs all dressed up with a shawl, black skirt, and black stockings? A closer look - no stockings.

"You two can come with me to the Kirk."

Johnny gives her a shocked look - no me, I kick with my left foot.

"I know you do you wee rat. Go to your Chapel and confess your sins, you have plenty to confess about."

Johnny is taken aback at this rude remark, however he consoles himself that she is secretly in love with him! Johnny and his pal reluctantly go, fill in an hour. Johnny enters the Kirk for the first and last time. Jesus! What a cold dour place. They sit on a pew; the Church is packed. Johnny thinks the Reverend Gunn is a better preacher than he thought he was, or they are terrified of him. Gunn kicks off with they are all going to hell if they do not mend their ways. Johnny could have written the script. The way the congregation is lapping it up, Johnny thinks the wee commie on his street is right, this brand of religion is the opium of the masses. Finally, the Minister says we will sing hymn eighteen, All Things Bright and Beautiful, just like our street! After the song, an Elder of the Kirk, a face that would crack a mirror, passes a blue velvet bag with two wooden handles down the aisle. A fat smelly woman elbows Johnny and passes him the bag. She must be on the black market to be that fat Johnny thinks. He puts his hand in the bag and pulls out a handful of pennies he nudges his pal. "I didn't know they paid you to come here, we will come back next Sunday." His pal's sister said "Put it back you wee Fenian, you're giving me a red neck."

"Oh well," Johnny thinks, "nice try."

Ann Davis did not have a happy childhood

Scrumping

At the beginning of the war my two sisters and I were put on a train in the Guard's van to a children's home, the board outside said 'Home for waifs and strays.' I can remember always being hungry, we used to go scrumping and stuff the apples down our navy blue knickers. We used to eat lots of things from the woods, like sorrel leaves, crab apples, red berries off the hawthorn tree, blackberries and beechnuts and many more things! It was a hard life, I am still affected by it. We had no love or affection shown to us, I remember falling off the garden swing once and hurting myself rather badly but no one bothered we just had to get on with it! We had 2p a week pocket money which was taken away if we were naughty. I was locked in the cellar once for being 'naughty' - it was pitch black as it was being used for an air-raid shelter. To this day I suffer with claustrophobia which has affected me all my life, unable to go on a plane, train or even a coach, I can however drive which enables me to get about!

Fred Harket lived in London

The Bombsite

I called for my mate Terry just like many other days. As usual he was not ready and I had to sit on his outside doorstep and wait for him. He eventually emerged, his hair neatly brushed down with a neat side parting, he was wearing his corduroy lumber jacket, grey flannel short trousers, grey socks drawn up to his knees and black plimsoll shoes. I was dressed the same but my mum would not let me have plimsolls, instead I had leather sandals with a strap and a buckle, I always wanted plimsolls but mum said they were bad for the feet.

"What we gonner do?" he said.

"Go to the bomb site," I replied.

We went to the bombsite nearly every day. We were seven years old, free spirits, no police, no social workers, no school, we could do as we liked. Our bombsite was along the road, it was where three houses had stood before a bomb had flattened them to the ground about two years earlier. There were three bombsites in our road. Luckily, despite his best efforts, Hitler and his huge war machine had not been able to hit our house. Of the three bombsites, ours was the best. It was bounded by a brick wall to the rear, an Emergency Water Supply Tank (E.W.S.) to the left and a derelict house to the right. There was only a small frontage on to the public road so the area was well concealed.

When we arrived, our gang of friends - Tich, the two Ernies, Buster, Billy and Bonar - were already there. They were all busy, lighting little fires, building camps, digging holes. When they saw us we all said, "Wotcher" and we joined in the general activity.

Later that day a rumour had started that the Whately gang, from a bombsite down the road, were going to attack sometime in the afternoon. Panic all round.

The Whately gang had a reputation, they were generally older and bigger than us and sometimes they would attack with broom sticks, using dustbin lids as shields. We started to make barricades with old bricks, pieces of floor boards and sheets of corrugated iron. All of these things were readily available on the bombsite. We collected stones and small handsize pieces of bricks. We made small piles of this ammunition along the flank wall of the house under the graffiti saying "WOT NO FAGS." We practiced our aim on tin cans and old pieces of glass bottles. I was getting pretty scared. The big boys discussed strategy. Should they hold out from the barricades or go out to meet them in the road, falling back to the barricades if they proved too tough? Tich was posted as look out by the side of the water tank.

We grew increasingly nervous and an unusual quietness developed. Then, suddenly out of the blue, some one shouted "GET DOWN" and we all fell flat to the ground. An almighty explosion shook the ground. A German V2 rocket had landed several hundred yards away. I lay with my face down against the dirty ground of the bombsite, the air was full of smoke, debris, pieces of shattered glass, clouds of dust, chimney stacks toppled, the blast was tremendous. I was terrified. I looked up and saw Terry was OK. When the air finally cleared, I got up and ran as fast as I could over layers of broken glass, fragments of tiles and slates which looked like a mosaic over the pavements and road, I ran back to my mum.

Later we learnt that the German V2 rocket had fallen from the sky without any warning, on Melbourne Grove, a nearby residential area. A large number of people were killed and injured, whole terraces of houses were flattened. It was a disaster.

Our little war with the Whately gang never did take place due to the intervention of Adolf Hitler's weapon of terror.

Duncan Hamman recalls his youth near Manchester

A Kids Eye View of the War

I would be about seven years of age when the war started. The only thing I remember about it was when my mother suddenly started crying while listening to the news on the radio. I think this must have been the announcement by the Prime Minister that war had been declared. I started crying too as I thought the Germans would come round to our house and start killing us right away.

Just as the war started the British Government decided to send many hundreds of children over to Canada to escape the bombs. Mum put our names down on the list but we were not included on the first boatload. A German submarine torpedoed the first boat and it was terrible as out of the hundreds of children on board only about eight or ten survived. Needless to say our names were quickly removed from the list and, I don't think any more shiploads of children were sent to Canada.

At home our back garden was dug up and an Anderson Shelter was erected. They tested the Air Raid sirens to let us know what they sounded like. A wavering up and down note warning us of approaching bombers and the steady note as the All Clear signal. During the next few years the terrible sound of the sirens always struck fear into us.

All the time a raid was in progress you could hear bits of metal falling on the roofs of the houses as the bombs and shells exploded and a new hobby started with the children – collecting shrapnel. Next morning we would be out early looking for bits to add to our collection. Some of the children had really impressive collections and I remember one boy coming to school with the tail section of an incendiary bomb. This was immediately taken off him by the teacher, much to his annoyance.

I got to school one morning to hear the exciting news that just down the road a German plane had crash-landed in a field. At dinnertime a huge gang of us went to have a look at the plane, which was being guarded by one, bored looking RAF man with a rifle. It was easy for part of our gang to distract the RAF man while the rest of us were stripping the plane for souvenirs. When we went back to school many of the kids had pockets full of live bullets, which had been scattered all over the ground near the plane. The Headteacher searched everyone's pockets and confiscated the bullets then handed them over to the police. We found out later that it wasn't a German plane after all but one of ours, which had run out of fuel and couldn't make it to Ringway.

Even during wartime Christmas was very exciting although, partly because of the war and partly because of our poverty, we didn't have many material things. Every year I received exactly the same Christmas presents but it was still exciting. I knew I would find in my stocking, one apple, one orange, one new, shiny penny and a box of cream filled chocolate soldiers. Every year I would eat the chocolate soldiers while I was still in bed and every year they made me sick, as I hated the horrible cream filling. When I came downstairs I would find my main present, which was almost always a book. I remember receiving Treasure Island one year and another year the Swiss Family Robinson. I received several books in the 'Just William' series.

As I became older I became interested in nature and would spend weekends and school holidays in the fields watching animals and birds and writing in my notebook. At birthdays or at Christmas time I would often get a book about animals or nature and I used to listen to a children's radio programme called 'Out with Romany.' Romany was supposed to be a gypsy who lived in a wooden caravan but really he was a vicar, but he did live in a gypsy caravan. In the programme he would be talking to two girls about nature and animals and one of the girls was called Violet Carson and many years later she became famous as the crabby Ena Sharples in 'Coronation Street.' When 'Romany' died he had such a following of young radio listeners that his caravan was parked in the centre of Wilmslow and became an attraction to visitors.

They built air raid shelters on our school playing fields. When the air raid siren sounded we children had to march out to the shelters but many, especially the girls, screamed and fought to avoid going inside as they were cold and dark and full of spiders, slugs and beetles. During one long raid we were getting very restless at sitting in the shelter and the teacher said, "Can anyone tell a story?"

To my surprise I stood up and walked to the front of the class. I had no idea what I was going to say and I cannot understand what made me do it. As I turned to face the class I suddenly realised that this dark, cold, dismal place, with just one flickering candle, was ideal for a ghost story so I started a story about witches, hobgoblins and ghosts. I cannot remember much about the story but the teacher had to tell me to tone it down a bit as I was scaring some of the kids too much.

From then on I was in great demand during air raids to tell stories in the shelter. We knew of children from other classes trying to sneak into our shelter to hear my stories instead of saying the times tables in their own shelter.

These were the days of corporal punishment in schools. Some teachers used this frequently but others were a bit soft hearted and rarely used it. Teachers sometimes hit us with anything to hand at the time, sometimes their hand or even with a ruler. A smack with the flat part of a ruler made a lot of noise but wasn't too bad but some used the narrow edge, which could be extremely painful. At Primary School, where I wore short trousers, some teachers would pull up the leg of our trousers and smack our upper thigh. We could cope with one or two slaps but one lady teacher used to give us about ten slaps in quick succession, which left a large red mark on our leg. We used to hope this had faded by the time we got home, as our parents would often give us another slap if they discovered we had been punished at school.

Teachers would also throw things at us in class, usually the chalk duster, and some of them were experts at long range throwing. We would be talking at the rear of the class, thinking we were safe, when the chalk duster would fly through the air and crack us on the head. When I was older and at Grammar school our French teacher had a sports shoe which he used as an instrument of punishment. He called the shoe 'Henri' and at the start of each lesson he would place Henri on his desk as a warning to us. Sometimes a boy would be leaned over the teacher's desk and take several blows to his bottom from Henri. They were really hard and the boy would return to his desk trying hard not to cry. We were frequently punished for failing to hand our homework in on time.

For really serious offences we were sent to the Headmaster for punishment and this was usually administered with a leather strap or a cane. I remember one boy, who was the school 'tough guy' being punished in front of the whole school at morning assembly. He had to bend over and receive a beating from a cane. He was in tears when the punishment was over and assembly continued with him crying in the background.

During this time my mother and I used to cycle to visit her sister, Agnes, who still lived in Wormleighton, Warwickshire – a trip of about a hundred miles each way! I had done this trip several times and it didn't strike me as unusual when my mother would say "We are going to visit Aunt Agnes."

The journey to aunty's was split into two days. On the first day we would cycle from Manchester to Uttoxeter. This was about sixty miles and it would take us about six hours, or more, with plenty of rests. We always stayed at a Youth Hostel, called Barrow Hill. This was a huge mansion, which had been donated to the Y.H.A. and I remember it had a magnificent oak staircase, which was wide enough to drive a bus up, and oak panelled walls.

On the next day we would complete the journey having an easy day of forty miles. After staying with aunt Agnes for a few days we would return home the same way.

Shortly after the war ended, my mother created a great stir in the neighbourhood when she announced that she and I were to go to Switzerland on holiday. Not only was Europe still in turmoil after the war but also taking holidays abroad astounded everyone as only the very rich were able to have holidays and going abroad was unheard of. I have no idea where the money came from but I think that mum and I were among the first British people to travel to Europe after the end of the war.

We travelled by train to London, Dover, then over the Channel to Calais where we were horrified to see all the war damage as even the houses were full of bullet holes. Again it was by train to the border with Switzerland at Basel. As we travelled across Switzerland I was spellbound, as I had never seen such beauty before. Everything seemed so clean and green after dismal war torn England and France. We stayed at the resort of Lugano, which was on the border with Italy. The Swiss people, who were so glad to see the British tourists starting to return again after the war, welcomed us. I was amazed to see chocolate, sugar and other luxuries on sale in the shops and we could buy as much as we liked, it was heaven on earth.

Mrs M Dance lived in Poole

Dummies

I was just five years old when war broke out; I was living near the gas works in Poole. I remember the barrage balloons, I was terrified of them as I thought if a German plane hit one we would all be gassed. One day we were all in the garden, a plane went over and my uncle said, "It's alright its one of ours," then suddenly, it dropped the bombs. We all rushed indoors in the cupboard under the stairs, those of us that couldn't get in went under the table.

Afterwards my two uncles went to see where they had landed, which was a direct hit on the Fifty-Shilling Tailors. They were horrified to see what they thought were dead bodies, which fortunately were tailors' dummies. I also remember the night when the flares were dropped all round us, but we were saved by setting Brownsea Island on fire, and we all went down on the quay to watch it.

Derek Hyamson lived in Liverpool

Flying Helmets and a Famous Comic

The only teachers I can remember at my Junior school were Miss Thaxter who was a strict woman, who used to give you a stout whack with her hand on the back of your leg, if you upset her. And a woman of mixed race, which was unusual in those days, called Miss Price. I remember on Empire Days, pupils were allowed to come in uniform i.e. Scouts, Lifeboy etc. Another thing I remember were the fights held after school behind the shops close to the Granada cinema. These were performed in a fair manner, using bare fists only. If anyone kicked they would be ridiculed and skitted at. Quiet a crowd of pupils would gather to watch. The proceedings would often be broken up by an adult.

Some of the clothes worn at that time were flying helmets (smaller versions of RAF pilot's headgear), balaclavas and clogs. Clogs were a common form of footwear, because of the shortage of leather boots and shoes. Cord shorts and windcheaters were also worn by many. Some parents, my own included, bought clothing coupons from other parents who couldn't afford the clothes anyway.

At this time the blitz was on, and in the mornings we would go collecting shrapnel and looking at bomb damage. In the evenings we would hang around the street in the blackout. There were no lights visible at all, and you could hardly see a couple of feet. The kerbstones, trees, and lampposts had white bands painted on them to help you see them. We would then go home and prepare for the air raids, a terrifying experience for me. During the May blitz in 1941 we would go straight into the Anderson shelter in the garden, in which my father had made some make shift bunks out of doors. He had made a steel door out of some sheets of metal, for the opening. We had a small paraffin lamp, for light and heat. The sound of the sirens would start (a terrifying sound) and we would wait for the sound of anti-aircraft fire, and then the drone of the German planes, followed by the sound of exploding bombs. I would be praying to myself for them to go away. After a while it would go quiet, and I would think they had gone. Only to return, wave after wave. Then the relieving sound of the All Clear would bring yet another night to an end. Although on one occasion, I remember the All Clear didn't sound at all. It was the night an ammunition ship (I think) caught fire and explosions continued through the morning. I felt the blast of one while standing at the door. On another occasion a raid had started before we got to the shelter and when I was nearing the entrance I heard a 'swish' pass me, followed by a bang. The following morning we found a long jagged piece of shrapnel embedded in a bin alongside the shelter. I had a lucky escape.

In about 1942, the houses in what was then the new Woolfall Heath Estate were used for Italian POWs. These prisoners were later allowed to leave the compound. They were dressed in British battle dress, dyed purple, with a large yellow diamond patch sewn on the back. Some of them used to go to the Granada cinema on Saturday nights. I think they were given this privilege after Italy surrendered. There didn't seem to be any animosity shown to them and when the National Anthem was played at the end of the film, they always stood up.

Ken Dodd is about five years older than me, but I remember him at school, I saw him in the school concert. He was already telling jokes, with his ventriloquist's dummy at that age. His father and older brother had a coal wagon and used to deliver our coal. After the war, Ken started delivering 'Aunt Sally'(a liquid floor cleaner) and chandelries in a small ex-army van. He later used an old removal van. He used to have a little old man who lived with his family, who was a well-known character in Liverpool. He had very small legs, and had bow yanks tied around his trouser legs to raise them up, and he always wore a bowler hat. He used to sit on the tram step and never pay. I'm sure Ken got the idea from him for his 'Diddy-men.'

Patricia Saxon grew up in Cambridgeshire

School Uniforms and Flying Bombs

The Forties should have been a major part of my formative years as I entered Grammar School in 1941. Whatever opportunity I was excited about through school, the war seemed to get in the way.

Before I began this school, I looked forward to wearing the school uniform, which signalled much to the locals. Everything was made to the best - but by September 1941 the war was taking effect. Brushed felt for winter hat and panama for summer were almost unobtainable so I had my sister's rather battered headwear and plain cotton blouses instead of silky Egyptian cotton. The good thing, these were not so expensive for my parents and, instead of feeling slightly embarrassed at being one of the few in the not-so-posh uniform, staff seemed to see this as being very patriotic!

Before Grammar School, in Battle of Britain times, we spent many hours in the Junior School air raid shelters. When the sirens sounded, which was frequently, a line of quiet, well-behaved, obedient children were shepherded to the shelters, each carrying over-shoulder on string, gasmask in cardboard box. On our person, we had a small tin of Horlicks tablets to sustain us over the long hours.

For a while attacks always happened on a Friday evening after dusk. One Friday afternoon I was playing in a friend's house about fifteen minutes walk away. The sirens started up and we hoped the raid would be short before the All Clear siren. This time the raid was particularly long and dusk turned to night.

My friend's parents were concerned that my parents would be worried and finally decided after some long hours, that during a lull, my friend's brother should walk me home. We were loaned the family steel helmets and sixteen-year-old lad and ten-year-old girl set off. The lull soon ended and the sky was full of flak, flashes and lights. We could hear the whiz of dropping bombs all round. We arrived at my home and hurried inside. The lad decided he had better get back home as quickly as possible. He must have hurried because we later knew he arrived home safely. We were all relieved because, minutes after he left us, the six flats opposite our house were demolished by a direct hit.

Flying Bombs began when I was in 4th year at Grammar School - again much time was spent in school shelters. One of the events I had been looking forward to was cancelled. Parents had paid for a group of us to spend two weeks at a Cambridge college to speak only French. We were just getting into the language and beginning to enjoy it but it had to be cancelled owing to the Flying Bombs.

Another event which had to be cancelled was rehearsals for the annual school house play - our house was doing a few scenes from Shaw's 'St Joan.' I can still recall my bitter disappointment at not being able to play the part of Joan, for which I had been selected.

I don't know why these particular two events have remained so vividly in my mind. They were missed opportunities.

Judith Keel went to school in Church Stretton

School in the '40s

Our boarding school was in the Stretton Hills some twenty miles away from Bishop's Castle. 'The Mount' had recently been evacuated from the Home Counties and had found a new home in a generously proportioned Victorian house in its own grounds near Church Stretton. Miss Benson, the headmistress, agreed to take us in as weekly boarders and so we joined this small school of no more than thirty pupils which included a few local children who attended daily. At first there was a problem as to how we would get there, as there were no private cars on the road. Petrol, which was on coupons, was only available to certain priviliged groups. One of these was the farmers. Luckily for us it turned out that a farmer's son who lived about seven miles away from us was starting at The Mount at the same time as us. The farmer said that if mother could get us up to his farm by eight o'clock on Monday mornings he would give us a lift and return us to be collected from the farmhouse on Friday afternoons.

Mother got hold of two old secondhand bicycles, a child's size one for me and a 'Sit-up-and-beg' bike for herself with a basket on the front and a carrier on the back for my sister to sit on. This was how we got ourselves up to the farm with our week's luggage on board. Rain or shine we got there and I well remember the ache in my legs as I pedalled or pushed that bike uphill, my suitcase on the back packed with clothes for the week, teddy bear, gas mask and ration book.

The farmer's car which we transferred to for the second stage of the journey was an old green shooting brake covered in mud and smelling of goats, chickens and the dogs which always rode in the back wherever he went. Worse still was the very strong smell of petrol fumes. We rattled and bounced our way down lanes where lines of Nissen Huts filled with stored munitions were hidden behind the hedges, until we reached the main road to Church Stretton. On our arrival that first day we were herded up the front steps then up the carpeted front stairs to our dormitories. This was probably the only time we ever used the front stairs as later they were out of bounds and we had to use the bare wood backstairs. Carrying my luggage I was shown the attic room with lino on the floor which was to be my 'dorm.'

It proved to be extremely cold in winter, there was no heating, and suffocatingly hot in summer. There were four iron bedsteads with spring bases and thin horsehair mattresses. Beds had to be made before breakfast and we were shown how to tuck the sheets in using hospital corners. It turned out that we only had a bath once a week when two would share in a bath with a red line painted around the inside allowing only six inches of water, the regulation amount in wartime. After breakfast we formed a line for our daily dose of cod liver oil and malt, then a line for the lavatory where our bowel movements were closely monitored. Joining the line for syrup of figs might follow this! If you complained of a headache or felt otherwise unwell you were given a dose of grey powder dissolved in milk, which was a remedy applied to all ailments. Heaven knows what this actually was but it really was not wise to confess to illness!

The Mount had just three teachers. The headmistress, Miss Benson, taught all subjects to the older children. Miss Whately, the daughter of the local vicar and probably no more than eighteen years old, looked after the little ones. The formidable Miss Beaumont was part time and had a reputation for getting her charges through entrance exams to other schools. She was very strict, drilled us hard in mental arithmetic and would not tolerate any slapdash work. The housekeeper Miss Tease, used our combined ration books to put meals on the long mahogany dining table. Miss Benson sat at the head to serve and we noticed that she always kept a generous portion of the best for herself.

The food was very plain but that was usual for children at that time. Nobody sat down until grace had been said and we took turns to say it. Saying thank you for the food that we received had a special meaning in wartime. 'Bread and scrape' featured at breakfast and teatime and jam was only allowed on the last slice. On Mondays we looked forward to the cold remains of the previous day's roast with mashed potatoes and baked beans. The Sunday roast produced several basins of beef dripping which had a lovely rich brown jelly at the bottom and this was passed round to spread on bread. I was often hungry and it seemed a good idea to wheedle my way into the cook's affections. I would sneak into the kitchen and look at her with round hungry eyes and she would give me the jam spoons to lick or offer me some of the rind off the large round of Cheddar cheese which was usually used to bait the mouse traps! A cake tin containing sweets bought with our combined ration books was passed round after tea for all to share. The punishment for bad behaviour was not to be allowed to have any sweets.

On some weekends, in winter when the snow was too deep for example, we could not get home and so stayed. The Sunday treat was a walk up the lane at the side of the house pursued by Miss Benson in her tweeds and brogues swishing a leather whip at our heels to keep us moving. A dubious treat! Then in the evening to go into her study where a fire was lit to listen to the six o'clock news on the radio. This was followed by a character building pep talk.

After lights out at night I would often get out of bed and look out of the window over the blacked out town of Church Stretton and beyond. On the lower slopes of the Long Mynd I could just make out the shape of a large building which before the war had been the Long Mynd Hotel and Health Hydro. At the beginning of the war it had been taken over by St Dunstan's for the rehabilitation of burned and blinded airmen. The only young men to be seen in the town were these wounded airmen which brought the war a lot closer.

The return journey on Friday afternoon was a joy as it was downhill for most of the way home. Also there was time on light summer evenings to stop and talk to the two prisoners of war who had been assigned to the farmer to work on his farm. The POWs, Monti, a handsome Italian and Hans, a blonde German would stop work to chat to us.

They badly missed their families in their own countries and liked to practice their English on we children. They obviously took pleasure in talking to our very attractive mother who baked cakes to give to them in return for eggs, which they had collected in the hedgerows.

Once home we would settle round a bright wood fire for stories or do our music practice on an old upright piano which had several notes missing. By now we had a baby brother and would play with him or help to bath him. A family again!

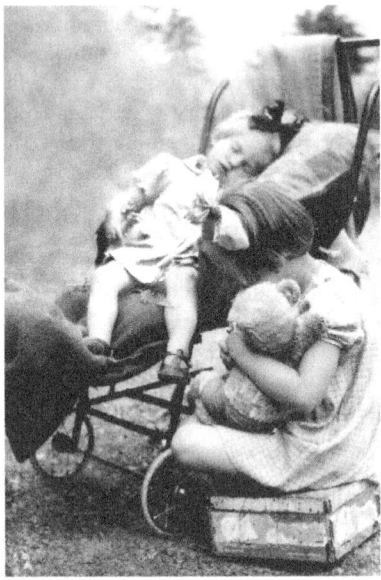

A long day!

Elizabeth Diggens moved to Surrey

The Bounded Area

My first memory of the war was being terrified by noise; this was at the start of the 1941 bombing of the docks at London. My father took me to see the burning Tate & Lyall Factory at Silvertown - we stood across the river from the factory and I clearly remember the noise and the smell of toffee. We slept at this time in an Anderson shelter in the garden. In 1941, Lockwood Road where we lived took a direct hit from a landmine and many of the people in the road were killed. We survived but when we came out of our shelter the house had disappeared. At about this time I started to stammer very badly.

My father then moved us to a house opposite the Imperial War Museum. Every night for the next year or so I was given a blanket and told to wait at the door of the museum, where all the children would be let in at 6pm to sleep in the deep cellars under the museum. I can remember crying for my mother until the warden on duty told me the Germans would hear me if I did not stop!

At the end of 1941 our new house also took a direct hit and we were again homeless. My mother wanted to leave London altogether then so we went to the Billeting Officer and were directed to go south to Surrey. We (my mother and me), my father having stayed in London, were taken in temporarily by some farm workers whilst my father went to look for some housing for us. As we had very few clothes and little else we went to an aid station and were given clothes by people in the village.

Meanwhile my father had found us an empty cottage at Abinger Common where the gardener who had occupied it had been called up. I think the cottage must have devastated my mother, as it had no running water, electricity or toilet. However, she managed and we had an outside pump and a deep well. We then found out a few weeks later that we had moved into a 'Bounded Area'. It was fenced off by barbed wire because there were two or three army regiments setting up camp and an enormous quantity of ammunition stored nearby in the woods on Leith Hill.

I started school in the village school, spoke in a broad cockney accent for which I was much teased and generally had a hard time from the other pupils for several months. We had two excellent teachers - Mrs Carpenter, who had lost her husband in the 1914 war and her son in the Battle of Britain, and Mrs Bishop who taught the younger children. Our occasional music master was Dr Ralph Vaughan-Williams who lived in the village at this time.

One day we all heard some tremendous explosions and ran to the shelter. The noises got louder and nearer and an army lorry came to the school to collect us; one boy helpfully said, "You know, they are going to shoot us all" which set everyone crying including me. In fact we were taken to a nearby school.

When we came home after about a week I was amazed to see that most of the woodlands on Leith Hill had been burnt down. A stray German bomb had landed on one of the ammunition stores, which had set off a chain reaction. The Canadian army personnel stationed on Leith Hill had to move as much of the ammunition as possible at tremendous risk to themselves.

We also eventually had a large number of Italian prisoners located near the back of our cottage. They were very hard worked by the army but always had time to speak to us children. Towards the end of the war we had V1 rockets coming over and our beautiful 14th century church at Abinger Common took a direct hit one Sunday morning as the service finished. We saw the VI coming and ran for shelter under the hedge - which would hardly have saved us! We eventually got used to the V1s and took very little notice of them unless the motor cut out right overhead - we had no air raid warnings living in the country.

Yvonne Wright moved to Shrewsbury

Prefabs

Just as war was declared we evacuated to Shrewsbury where my father got a job rescuing the parts from crashed Spitfires that were any good to put towards the making of a new Spitfire. We lived in specially erected Prefabs, which I thought were great – detached as well! We were in the country, our neighbours either side were fields of cows, which I used to talk to.

Some years later, my mother told me not to go around the corner, which I could not understand as the Prefabs were built in a circle and I always walked 'around the block'. So curiosity got the better of me and I sneaked round only to find that where there had previously been an area of grass, there were now two Nissen huts standing – and they were occupied by MEN.

A few days later, I went with friends to the area and we chatted with some of the men and we discovered that they could not speak English. Yes, it was a Prisoner of War camp on our doorstep. Most of the inmates were Italian, with a few Germans.

Pete Hepper moved from London to Kent

No Custard

We lived in a terraced house in South London - dad, mum, two sisters and me. We had a yard with an outside loo, complete with the 'ace of clubs' spyhole in the door. Dad and Uncle Jim (no relation) from next door dug a pit and half buried an Anderson shelter.

"It will not do a lot of good, but will leave the place tidy," observed dad.

One night the air raid siren went off, down to the shelter we all tramped. When the All Clear sounded, out we came to a different world. The house was flat, gone. The only thing standing was the gas stove! It still had a rice pudding in the oven.

"Sorry there is no custard," said mum, between tears.

We were now homeless but within hours we were off to Kent. Dad stayed in a bedsit in London because he drove a lorry for the Woolwich Arsenal. If we were lucky we would see him on a Sunday 'if the train was still running.'

After one big raid, dad said that he and his mate had run for cover, only to come out at the All Clear to find that they had sheltered under a lorry-load of seven tons of high explosive!

In Kent, the local school was OK. I was picked on a bit but gave as good as I got. I learned to climb tress and retrieve pidgeons eggs – you carry them down the tree in your mouth!

Don Goodwin lived in Grimsby

Railings and Red Lights

My dad had to go to London on bomb damage as he was a bricklayer. While he was away they came and cut all the railings off the walls down our street. He was as mad as hell when he came home!

When dad came home from London he always brought us some coloured matches. When struck they would burn red or green. We were listening to the radio one night as usual when mam said, "Dad's come home unexpectedly." We all heard his footsteps coming down the passage. I ran to the back door to collect my coloured matches but nobody entered the house. I was devastated. I went back into the living room and told them that nobody was there. Everyone looked puzzled. We just got settled down when there was an almighty bang in one corner of the living room on the ceiling just as if someone was in the bedroom hammering on the floorboards with a lump hammer. This was followed by two more bangs in other corners of the living room. Mam said, "Something has happened to dad."

The next day she got a telegram to say dad was in hospital but was not in danger. It transpired that he was on the scaffold when a doodlebug landed near by blowing him off the scaffold, luckily on the way down his chin hit a scaffolding pole that was stuck out, it knocked him out thus saving his life. After a few weeks in hospital he came home and I got my coloured matches.

During the war sweets were never to be found in the shops. So we went to the chemists and bought some root that tasted of aniseed or the thick black liquorice that was bitter and vile but better than nothing. One thing that sticks in my mind is the food parcel we got from my auntie in America. It contained all sorts of goodies, it even had a large tin of dried apricots that mam kept in the pantry. I would sneak in and take two then fluff up the rest to cover my tracks. I got caught and was threatened with a good hiding but mam was as soft as a brush, she never hit us. Dad was a different kettle of fish - he only had to look at us to make us tremble in our shoes.

I became friendly with a scruffy lad at school and I went round to his house. We were not well off but he was even poorer and lived in a rough area. We were playing marbles in the gutter, we did not know that we were outside a house of ill repute. Every so often a bloke would knock on the door, which was answered by a big fat woman with her hair in curlers and a fag in the corner of her mouth. The bloke would say is "Is Mary in?" upon which the woman would say "Yes love, come on in." Twenty minutes later he would come out and go on his way whistling.

I said to my scruffy friend, "I wonder what all these blokes keep coming to the house for? There has been eight gone in up to now."

My friend said, "I don't know, but I am going to find out."

"What you going to do?" I asked.

"I'm going to ask if Mary is in. Are you coming?"

Not wanting to appear a coward I followed him to the door. "Is Mary in?" he asked the fat woman.

"Come on in lads." We went upstairs to a bedroom.

"There's a couple of young gents to see you Mary." She led us into the bedroom.

There on the bed in a pink nightie was the loveliest girl I had ever set eyes on.

"What do you want boys?" she asked.

"We want what those blokes had", said my friend.

"Come over to the bed and sit down."

We did as we were told. She got hold of our heads banged them together then kicked our backsides and chucked us out into the gutter. As we sat there dazed I said to my mate, "I don't know about you, but I couldn't stand twenty minutes of that!"

Betty McCrea recalls some episodes from her early life

Glimpses of A Wartime Childhood

They fell slowly at first then gathered momentum. Not bombs, they came much later, but words. They dropped from our fretwork-fronted wireless at news time through the lips of Bruce Belfrage, Freddie Grisewood and Wilfred Pickles and from my grave faced father's lips when he read the Daily Express at breakfast. They were strange new grown up words like evacuation, invasion, rationing, propaganda, declaration and mobilization. There were foreign names too: Czechoslovakia, Poland, Goebbles, Hitler, Nazi and Mussolini. Some of the names sounded nice. I thought Czechoslovakia a pretty name. I hoped it was a pretty place. I liked Mussolini and thought it must be a girl's name, one I should have liked but I was stuck with Betty Winifred so secretly I renamed my favourite doll Mussolini instead.

There was much talk of germs and Germans. How could you tell the difference? Both were unwelcome intruders into our lives. Angry looking creatures with enormous pointed teeth, poised to pounce on any unsuspecting human not in possession of a handkerchief, glowered from hoardings threatening terrible retribution. I learned that there were German spies lurking behind every quite ordinary door, listening to our conversations, which could contain information vital to their cause. Posters declared 'Careless talk costs lives' and 'Walls have ears.' Gaumont British News at our local 'pictures' solved the problem for me. The screen showed a column of soldiers marching into Poland - the commentator referred to them as German troops (they were also called Nazis which sounded very nasty indeed). They looked like ordinary men except that they were unable to bend their knees and had to march like toy soldiers.

My mother rescued me from evacuation by grabbing me off the school coach, which was to take us children to a railway station. She took off my label, which said who I was and relieved me of my hated gas mask. She was crying and hugged me to her till it hurt. "We'll stay together", she said, "No matter what." We went home and made toast on the open fire. When my father came home he looked surprised to see me but suddenly we were all laughing and everyone was happy again.

From then on there was no school. They were shut. Instead, the children who stayed behind met in the homes of children with non-working mothers who helped supervise lessons set by a retired teacher. It was not a very successful solution. Gradually for various reasons many evacuees began to drift back and the local authority decided to re-open the schools. We attended mornings one week and afternoons the next.   All of our male teachers had been called up.   They were replaced by retired teachers of both sexes who seemed incredibly old and very, very, strict.   Even this minimal education was interrupted by air raids. When a warning was sounded by the stomach churning undulating wail of the siren, we all had to march in an orderly crocodile to the shelters, which were nothing more than reinforced corridors. There we spent interminable empty hours singing songs like 'One Man went to Mow' and 'Ten Green Bottles.'   I developed an all consuming hatred of men, meadows and green bottles which was not dispelled until I reached my teens and discovered the merits of men in meadows and white wine.

Eventually school meals were introduced and our Headmistress always ended her daily harangue at assembly about the wickedness of waste in wartime with reference to school 'dinners.'   We must eat every scrap of the awful stuff because brave sailors were risking their lives to bring us ungrateful children food.   I could never fathom how us not eating our lumpy potatoes, stringy meat and soggy greens could endanger sailors' lives. If they were bringing all this stuff through predatory U-boats etc. then, I felt, someone should tell them not to bother because all could be found here in England.

I think my enduring scepticism of advertisers' hyperbole had its roots in the war and austerity years. Our local greengrocer still displayed colourful pictures of citrus fruits and bananas although there were none to be had. Slot machines on stations did not hold the Nestles penny bars they boasted nor did biscuit tins in grocers' shops contain the scrumptious biscuits pictured on the lids.   Rich Tea or Digestive seemed to be all that was available.

The wireless was listened to avidly in our house, especially news bulletins.   The carefully modulated voices of the announcers kept everyone informed of current events. I liked to listen too although I did not always understand what was being said. The phrase 'next of kin of casualties' (have been informed) seemed like poetry to my childish ears and I would skip around chanting the words like a mantra until told to pipe down.   We listened to ITMA (It's That Man Again) and Gert and Daisy. Grandma Buggins was also one of my favourites. (She was the medium through which the Ministry of Food passed on recipes to help housewives eke out the meagre rations). But most important of all were Churchill's speeches. They lifted everyones' spirits. When we listened to words like:-

"We shall defend our island home ... and ... outlive the menace of tyranny: if necessary for years, if necessary alone ... We shall not flag or fail. We shall go on to the end. We shall fight in France, we shall fight on the seas and oceans: We shall fight in the air. We shall defend our island, whatever the cost may be. We shall fight on the beaches, we shall fight on the landing grounds: we shall fight in the fields and in the streets, we shall fight in the hills; we shall never surrender."

... then we just knew that we would win in the end.

Shelagh Crompton moved to Dunstable

Whipsnade Zoo and Percy

In September 1940 I was living with my parents in Romford. My father, a toolmaker, had given up engineering in favour of his first love, music. He was a teacher of violin at the local Academy where he was also sometimes the conductor of the orchestra. My mother had been a model in the days when they were called mannequins and had had quite an adventurous past as a 1920s 'Flapper.'

My father constructed an Anderson shelter in the back garden, which we scarcely used. On the night in question, however, my mother insisted we go into the shelter. In after years she would maintain that she had a premonition. During the air raid that night we had a land mine in the back garden.

It was said later that this was one of our land mines rescued by the Germans from Dunkirk and that the target was probably the nearby railway line. All I know is that it landed just behind the shelter causing an enormous crater and burying us beneath the fallout. The back of the house collapsed adding to the debris that covered us. It took several hours for the rescue services to find us and get us out during which time my father made holes with his bare hands to let in some fresh air for us to breathe. We were taken to a nearby communal shelter where we were given help and comfort. I had a little brown mongrel dog called Judy, who would not come in to the shelter and had been in the house during the raid. The shock of it sent her mad. She followed us to the communal shelter and was running around hysterically, foaming at the mouth. The Home Guard on duty took her outside and shot her. The pain of that moment is with me still.

There followed a period when we shared a flat with other displaced families, then my mother and I went to stay with a relative in Somerset. My parents managed to salvage what possessions they could from the house but it is a sad fact that they lost almost as much to looters as they did from the bomb.

From the early part of the war, my father had been forced to give up music and had returned to factory life. His company was relocated to Dunstable and it was possible for us to be together again. We now found ourselves in the hands of the local Billeting Officer. Looking back as an adult, I suppose I can understand the resentment the mistrust and the anger that the householders must have felt having strangers foisted on them by bureaucracy. But to say we were unwelcome would be the understatement of the year. The usual response was "We don't want dirty Londoners here."

We were billeted with a family in Dunstable near my father's work. We were assigned, grudgingly, one downstairs room, one bedroom and very limited access to the kitchen and bathroom. It was almost impossible for mother to prepare an evening meal and she was not allowed to use the kitchen on Sundays so we were forced to try and eat out most of the time. In a small town in wartime, this was very difficult indeed. There were two cafes that I remember, one of which did a nice line in fish and chips. Neither of these was open on Sundays. But Whipsnade Zoo was not far away and most Sundays we would go and have lunch in their restaurant. I don't remember much about the food but we got to know the animals really well. I loved it.

We were subjected to all sorts of petty humiliations. When my father returned from work he would be met at the front door by the lady of the house who would follow him down the hall to our room, mopping the floor behind him.

Things came to a head when I became very ill. This was, of course, in the days before antibiotics. I did pull through, albeit a thin and weedy child. One of the things the doctor prescribed for my convalescence was fresh air and exercise. Needless to say, I was not allowed in the garden of the house and so every day come rain or shine my mother and I would walk down to the far end of Dunstable so that I could go into the public gardens and play on the swings.

Eventually, my parents managed to find somewhere else to live. The Smiths were country folk through and through and some said of recent gypsy stock. They lived in a large family house with land at the rear and our accommodation was a sort of self-contained flat tacked on to the back. Mr Smith was a bit of a dealer and there was a constant procession of farm animals occupying the outhouses. It was all a bit of a culture shock for my poor mother, the sophisticated townie, but she struggled manfully even befriending a young goose who would waddle up our outside staircase to be fed titbits and who answered to his name.

Ever kind and generous, the Smiths, at Christmas, presented us with a plucked and dressed goose for our Christmas dinner. Yes, it was our Percy. Whether or not we ate it has been erased from my memory but not my mother's distress.

Babs Henderson moved with her family to Troon

Troon

My father died in November 1941 aged thirty-seven. He had been in bad health, which is why I presume he was not called up and worked as a chef in a large local hotel in Troon. The hotel in which he worked was the Marine Hotel, which sits at the first few holes of the Royal Troon Golf Course and has accommodated many of the rich and famous, even in those long ago days. As Head Chef he commanded a reasonable salary which allowed us to live in a beautifully appointed semi-detached cottage. However, when he died we were impoverished and had to move immediately to a string of undesirable furnished lets, many from which we fled, so dreadful were the circumstances. However, after hopping around for some months, we ended up in the back kitchen of a tenement block, with a small scullery and the use of a toilet in the hallway of the house, which was lit by gas light.

We kept warm in front of a large black range and while my mum and I slept in one of two set-in beds, my sister slept in the other. The gentleman and I use that loosely, not that he did us any harm, was a bit fearsome and scary to look at. He was a small man with only two teeth in his head, one on top and one on the bottom and a bunnet (flat cap) on his head at all times. He used to visit Glasgow from time to time, marching the streets with a banner, proclaiming to all who would listen that Christ was our saviour and judgement day was coming. We knew this because my mum hailed from Glasgow and had lots of relatives there who visited us at this hellhole, met the man, and recognised him. Periodically he would come through our room with a large pressure cooker and plonk it on the gas stove which took up much of the scullery and we sat terrified waiting for this monstrosity to explode!

We were in this hovel, which my mother did her utmost to keep clean, for six long years; I had no idea what electric light in a house was until I went to school!

My mother visited the local Town Hall week after week, to plead with the then Housing Convenor for a council house. She was treated to the sight of the top of his head, which he never lifted, but balefully told her, week in, week out, there was nothing he could do for her. Despite this I remember happy times there, when our relatives arrived from Glasgow bringing goodies of all kinds. Each week, mum trotted down the few yards to the shops, for the weekly shop. Standing in queues at each one with our ration books, for half a pound of butter, or a quarter of tea. Every penny had to be carefully managed and it was the procedure when she got home to go through all that she had bought over a cup of tea and tie it up with what she had left in her purse. She would not be settled until every penny was accounted for. Mum started 'charring' for little or nothing, and when I went to school, managed to get a job as a dinner lady, which she remained at until she retired at sixty-five.

Good as mum's family were, and they tried to persuade her to move back to Glasgow so that they could be of more support to her, she was determined that we should remain in Troon. In those days when we visited Glasgow and returned on the old steam trains, our noses were full of black soot and our clothes similarly discoloured with the atmosphere wraught by the many factories and huge works which once chuntered away in the city. Here in Troon, a benefactor by the name of Charles Kerr Marr had bequeathed his fortune so that a secondary school could be built for the children of Troon to have the education similar to that of many of the fee paying schools in the country. It was a wonderful chance for children in those early days, and Troon as a result grew in size, as many people removed to the coast.

We had three more moves between the time I was nine, in 1948, until I was eleven. All to furnished rooms, all a bit better than the last. Finally one old lady remembered my mother, and wrote to tell her that a house was becoming available in one of the last buildings we had been in, she was applying to move into it, and would mum like her to recommend mum for the one she was vacating. If you had given my mum a million pounds, she couldn't have been more pleased. Subsequently, I was married out of that little house, which boasted two rooms, a scullery and a toilet on the stair landing.

My love for my Mum knows no bounds and that she suffered so much to keep us in this lovely seaside town was the greatest gift she could have given us.

Maths homework!

Michael Yarrow recalls an anxious episode from his early life

I Hope He Will Come Soon

An owl screeched in the darkness outside the window, momentarily turning the young boy's stomach with fear. "I hope he will come soon", he thought, desperately stifling, as best as he could, the anxious gnawing within.

He was maybe eight and a half years old and alone in the house. His dad was out somewhere in the country roads in his car, hopefully on his way home. His mother had left home some year and a half before and a divorce was pending.

The year was 1948 and the shortest day was just around the corner. The day had been much like any other school day – the lessons were good, the school dinners pretty awful, and Vic the bully carefully avoided.

He had walked home, found the back door key in the outside privy, unlocked the door, lifted the latch and went in to the stone-floored scullery. He locked the door behind him, went into the wood-panelled living room, hung up his coat. It was too cold to stay outside, so he collected up his books and comics and moved a chair to the window where he could read until night began to fall.

He settled down to read with a biscuit from the tin in the food cupboard. Time passed until it was getting hard to read properly in the failing light from the north-facing window. The time had come to light the light.

Taking the matches from the mantle shelf above the range, he climbed onto a chair then onto the table that stood in the middle of the room. He stood on the green piled, tasselled tablecloth to reach the gas light. He hoped the gas mantle was all right. Once or twice it has been torn, making the gas roar and burn too close to the thin glass globe. He looked, it seemed to be intact. He knew how to change it, but wouldn't have wanted to do it all on his own in a room three-quarters dark.

Striking a match, he let it burn for a moment, then held it up into the hole at the bottom of the globe. Carefully he pulled the chain on the gas valve and the gas began to flow. The lamp lit with a loud pop. Then he adjusted the gas flow to minimise the roar of the flame but maximise the light in the room. The light was lit.

He was an avid reader and soon became engrossed in his encyclopaedia, imagining what it might be like to travel to Mars or Mercury. One day he would be a space man. Having read that chapter he went on to some gripping episode in one of his comics.

He could actually read for hours, rainy days would pass almost unnoticed. Reading took him through the portals of the Wizard, the Hotspur, the Adventure, and the like, into another world full of exciting people and things. The world of Amazon adventures with the Iron Teacher robot, and of gruelling races run and won by the mysterious Wilson or the fish and chips loving Alf Tupper.

However engrossed, from time to time he surfaced to see the clock on the mantle shelf had moved on only so slowly. "I hope he will be here soon!" he thought each time he came up for breath, and, coming back through that portal, into the real world, he would worry.

"What if it's got foggy out there?" He never was quite sure where 'out there' would be today. Dad travelled across several counties in a little black car, an Austin Ten, selling toys and fancy goods to village shops. He could end up two hour's drive away from home. Pea-souper fog was common in winter, fog so thick you could sometimes not see the grass verge from the passenger seat or the white line, when there was one, out of the driver's windscreen. These fogs slowed you down to ten or fifteen miles an hour and driving that slow threatened to, and even did sometimes, run the car battery flat.

"What if he's got a puncture?" Punctures were common, tyres were not replaced until the inner tube showed through. Tyres were expensive and hard to get in those early years after the war. Changing a tyre on your own in the dark with only a hand torch to see by on an unlit country road was far from easy.

"What if he's run out of petrol?" With an empty spare can, running out was always a fear on a long journey. In country areas, petrol could only be bought from a single pump at a local village garage. These often closed at five thirty when the man went home.

"What if he's forgotten to take his coupons with him?" Petrol was severely rationed and you could only buy it if you had petrol coupons. Dad, because of his job, had an additional allowance.

And if any of these or some other mishap occurred, how would he know. Like most houses, there was no telephone in the house.

The hands of the clock crept slowly round.

5.30.

5.45.

5.55.

6.10. "Please come soon!" He pressed down hard on the growing desperation. Home alone had a different meaning in 1948.

6.25. The rats were gnawing at his stomach, not just the hunger. Had dad ever been so late before?

6.35. The clock ticked inexorably and uncaringly on.

6.42. Then there was a sound out front. Yes, it was a key in the front door lock. The sound he had been longing to hear. The boy opened the living room door into the dark front room to see his dad coming in. He ran to him, his fears draining away.

Dad tasted of petrol as he kissed him. Three times the car had broken down in the dark. Three times he had taken the carburettor apart, by the light of a torch balanced on top of the engine, and blown the dirt from each jet in turn. Dirty petrol was common just after the war. How many times he had been out with his dad in the daytime and seen him blow the jets, even helped him do it. But now, at last, dad was home, cold and hungry.

The boy hurried to the scullery and lit the gas light there. He took the kettle from the top of the grate to the gas stove in the scullery, and lit the gas to bring it to the boil. A cup of tea would wash away the taste of poor quality, stinking Russian petrol.

He was all right now. Dad was home, safe and well, and he was safe too. All was well with the world – until tomorrow night!

Margaret Weeks grew up in Devon

Solland Farm

I think our first tractor arrived at Solland farm when I was quite young. It was a Standard Fordson and cost £120. Father had a variety of tractors during the war as the War Ag, as it was called, provided implements to contractors to plough up everything available to feed the nation. I can remember the first combine harvester arriving. I think it was American, and I can remember riding on the platform where they bagged the corn. It was not self propelled and had to be pulled by a tractor. The biggest tractor father had was a Minneapolis Moline. It was a very big yellow American tractor with a winch, and was used to pull the thresher. As there were no specialist mechanics at the time, blacksmiths carried out most repairs.

During the war Land Girls were employed by the farmers to cover for men who had to join up. Doris Jennings arrived in or around 1941. She had been lodging in Okehampton with a lot of other girls, but stayed with us until she got married to Frank, who worked for father, in April 1945. I was bridesmaid. Doris spent a lot of her time on the thresher, and doing most of the jobs that the men would do.

Indoors, mother always had help from somebody who lived in. We had three girls during the time that I lived at Solland. The one that I can remember most was Betty Parker. She also married someone who worked for Father.

I had bronchitis several times while I young. I had a bed in mum and dad's bedroom because there was a fireplace there, and a kettle was put on the fire, with a piece of rubber hose pointing at me, so that I could inhale the steam. This was one of the only ways that the cough could be helped. A long way before antibiotics! One of my bouts of bronchitis was bordering on pneumonia, and I was supposed to take M&B tablets. I hated them - mother tried everything to try and get me to take them. I had my tonsils out when I was five years old, and I didn't get much illness after that.

Being a big draughty old house Solland was very cold sometimes in the winter. We had a very big high-backed settee in front of the fire, in the dining room, where we sat mostly, and a big screen behind it. If you sat right in the grate, your front was warm and your back was cold, so you had to keep as close to the fire as possible. The front room fire was only lit on high days and holidays. Probably when the preacher came to dinner. Two or three times a year, the person who had preached in Exbourne Methodist Church came to dinner and tea, as he would have to preach again in the evening. All the best china and cutlery was brought out and there always seemed to be trifle for afters. It was one of the only times the dining room was used for meals. Most of the meal would be prepared the day before, so mother could go to Chapel and bring the preacher home. Whoever was at home would do the cooking, and father always had to be indoors by the time they arrived home, so that he could talk to the preacher. He was always made to go to chapel in the evening. This was usually the only time mother could get him to go! If it was a cold winter's day he wouldn't take off his working shirt, but put his best one over the top!

Ann Bush moved from Southampton to Bridport

Auntie Daisy

In June 1940, I was sent to Bridport to stay with my auntie Daisy who was in service with a Miss Sara Edmunds. The large house was called 'Providence Cottage' and it had three gardens - the Kitchen garden, which was across the road and the Field garden where flowers and other plants were grown, especially Sweet Peas. Then there was the main garden with greenhouses and a large lawn where one could play croquet.

Symes, the gardener, looked after all this. The Summerhouse was a lovely place for a small girl to play in.

The water for everything hot had to be pumped up from under the ground. Symes used to turn this large wheel every day so that the house had a good supply.

I missed my mum and dad and brother Arthur but I was lucky to have my auntie with me. She used to take me on her half-day up to North Allington to clean for her father. He lived in a garrett up some stairs on his own. Sometimes he played his mandolin for me. Grandad seemed very old to me and the place had a funny smell of stale tea. Auntie and I walked both ways, it seemed a long way to my short legs. Sometimes for a treat auntie would buy me a packet of Smith's crisps (with the little blue screw of salt inside) on the way home.

Every afternoon I was allowed in to the Sitting room to listen to Children's Hour on the wireless and have what Miss Edmunds called 'a little refreshment.' This was kept in the sideboard cupboard and was usually a peppermint cream covered in chocolate, a great treat. There was a horsehair sofa which I did not like sitting on because it used to scratch the back of my legs. The Breakfast room had a big bookcase in it and there were lots of back numbers of 'London Illustrated News.'

The house where I was staying had lots of rooms and was three stories high. At the very top were the rooms the maids used to sleep in, also the Nursery. I think there were five or six children in the family. A lot of their toys had been kept and I was allowed to play with them but had to be very careful not to break anything. Another room which fascinated me was the Box room. In it was wrapping paper, real silk ribbons all the colours of the rainbow and of course, lots of boxes of all shapes and sizes for packing things in.

In December 1942 I came home for Christmas and became very homesick. After a lot of discussion my mum and dad agreed that I could stay home with them. My auntie missed me a lot and I shall never forget her kindness. When Miss Edmunds passed away in the early 1950s she left me £5 and a little gold brooch.

Ann and her sister Leonnie

The 1940s - Month by Month

1943
January
- The German forces at Stalingrad were forced to surrender
- The first daytime bombing raid on Berlin took place

February
- Britain's largest charitable trust was set up by Lord Nuffield

March
- Mass bombing raids caused severe damage to Germany's industrial heartland

April
- The remaining Jews in the Warsaw ghetto fought back against their Nazi oppressors but were hopelessly outnumbered

May
- The RAF carried out the famous "Dambuster" raids, breaching the Mohne and Eder dams
- Part-time war work became compulsory for all 18-45 year old women who were not in full time employment

June
- King George VI visited the Allied troops in North Africa

July
- Allied forces landed in Sicily, the start of the invasion of the European mainland
- Fascist dictator Mussolini was deposed after twenty-one years in power

August
- Lord Louis Mountbatten was appointed Supreme Commander in South East Asia
- Sicily fell to the Allies

September
- Italy unconditionally surrendered to the Allies

October
- Italy declared war on former allies Germany

November
- Allied leaders Winston Churchill, Franklin D Roosevelt and Joseph Stalin met in Tehran, their first meeting to decide the map of Europe at the end of the war

December
- The 'Bevin Boys' were founded. 1 in 10 of all male conscripts between the ages of 18-25 were chosen at random to work in the coal mines instead of joining the armed forces
- The German battleship 'Scharnhorst' was sunk by the Royal Navy

===============

The Blitz

Frank Stonard remembers the blitz in The City of London

St Lawrence Jewry

December 28th 1940. My brother and I were on leave and were due back to our squadron the following day. We had decided to travel back together and met on the afternoon for tea at his wife's place, which was in the old BFC House in Gresham Street in the City of London, where there was a large underground shelter.

At about 6pm, the air raid siren went and very shortly we heard the sound of gunfire and the drone of the bombers; showers of incendiary bombs began to fall. After clearing them from the roof of the building, it became obvious that this was to be a heavy raid and we retired to the shelter.

When it came to about 9pm and there was a lull, we decided to make a break for it and emerged from the shelter to find the entire city seemingly ablaze. The Guildhall, close by, was alight and the air was filled with smoke and burning debris. The glare from the fires, as we made our way down Cheapside to the Bank Underground station was so much I believe one could have read the small print in a newspaper.

By some miracle, there were some trains running short distances and we picked our way over the packed platform of people to get in to a train. At Charing Cross we alighted, along with many other Servicemen who were bound for Waterloo station, across the river. As no trains were allowed under the Thames during a raid, we had to walk down to the river and cross Hungerford Bridge.

The sight was almost indescribable. There were hundreds of Servicemen trying to cross the bridge; the sky was lit up all around with blazing fires. It was like a second Great Fire of London. At Waterloo station, a great throng of Service men and women had gathered, hoping to get a train back to base, but all trains had been cancelled.

My brother and I decided it was hopeless to try to return to base so we went back to the shelter in Gresham St. Huge fires were raging.

The scene at the Guildhall was disastrous. The building was on fire and sparks blowing in the wind had caught the wooden spire of St Lawrence Jewry Church, across the Guildhall Yard. The spire eventually crashed on to the church and another of Wren's beautiful churches was destroyed. I remember a solitary fire appliance arriving and the hose being directed through a priceless stained glass window into the burning interior, but there was no time to consider that. Mercifully, the raid died down and we returned to the shelter for the rest of the night.

When we emerged next morning the scene of destruction was unbelievable. The Guildhall was still smouldering, the church was just a shell and in Cheapside it seemed the whole of the buildings had collapsed into the street. Grimy, weary Firemen and ARP personnel continued their tasks of dampening down and rescue.

Later that day, we arrived back at the Airfield, tired, dirty and somewhat dishevelled. We presented ourselves to the Guard Room. The SP on duty looked us up and down.

"I hear there was some activity up in the Smoke," he said.

Jillian Elms lived in Coventry

Jillian's mother, who lived in Coventry, wrote to her son, while he was serving abroad in the Royal Corps of Signals.

Hullo Son!

How are you darling? You should have arrived at your destination by now. Do you think you'll be able to let us know where you are – after you've got there?

Anyhow, having no idea where you are, we've sent your Christmas cake along, there is a little card which I think is very nice indeed. You'll never be without a friend if you put your trust in God. We, as a family, have been most blessed. We certainly have been protected and abundantly cared for. November 14th 1940, with its night of horror I can never forget. Nor shall I, <u>nor do I,</u> forget how I felt no fear whatsoever after the first few hours. How I prayed 'Lord! Have mercy upon us!' Our prayers now are for you and your safe return Son. Have a happy Christmas and <u>will you</u> go to communion at least on that day? All our love Son,

Ever your own Mum xxxx

On the night of November 14th 1940, Coventry endured its worst bombing raid of the war. Some facts, provided by Jillian:

The air raid on Coventry was the single most concentrated attack on a British city during the war. Codenamed, Moonlight Sonanta, the raid lasted eleven hours and involved nearly 500 Luftwaffe bombers. The smell and heat of the burning city reached into the cockpits of the German bombers, 6000 ft above. More than 43,000 homes and more than half the city's housing stock was damaged or destroyed in the raid. Coventry Cathedral was destroyed. 1,236 people died during the blitz. 111 buses were destroyed or damaged and the tram system was totally destroyed.

Auxiliary Fire Service in Coventry

Jean Williams also lived in Coventry

Coventry

In November 1940, Coventry suffered terribly from the German bombing raids. Every night, as soon as it became dark, the sirens sounded, and we had learnt by now that it really did mean that German bombers were coming.

The Council had begun to build air raid shelters in the streets for people (like us) who could not have one in their garden. These looked rather like a garage, which isn't attached to a house. There was only a small entrance and a brick wall was built about 45cms away from the entrance. There were wooden benches down the sides and I suppose they would hold a dozen or so people.

Two or three families would use the same one. Unfortunately, our's was never finished.

Every evening about six o'clock the sirens would sound. My dad, who was head porter at one of the two big hospitals in the city would get back on his bike, although he hadn't been home long, and go back to work. He didn't have to, but his hospital was next to a very large factory, which used to make Morris cars. My father knew that this factory was a very likely target for the bombers so he knew that if any bombs fell in the area, everyone possible would be needed to help to move the patients to safety. This left my mother and me at home. We used to go into the 'bogey hole.' This was an enclosed space under the stairs where the electricity and gas meters were. It was very dark and had just about enough room to lie down. On the night of 14th November 1940, more bombs than ever seemed to be dropping. We could hear the whistling sound as they came down. Suddenly there was a loud knock at the front door. An air raid warden said that an incendiary bomb had hit the factory a little way further down the street. The factory made elastic, which meant that a lot of the material used would burn very easily. He said that we must leave our house and go into one of the street shelters that had been finished. We all sat in the shelter listening to the bombs dropping. The All Clear siren sounded about 7am.

When we came out of the shelter that morning, the street was covered in broken glass and roof tiles. We, like many of our neighbours, had no roof left and all the windows had been blown out. The council sent men to fix tarpaulins over the roof and to nail a sort of waterproof canvas over the windows until, many weeks later, someone could come to repair them properly.

When we got inside the house there was no water, gas or electricity, and it was about three months before they were all restored. Tankers came round with water and we had to fill buckets and all water had to be boiled. We had to manage with candles for light. Some of the people in the street had had modern fireplaces put into their houses instead of the old range. We were lucky, we still had our range and could at least cook hot meals.

Later in the morning we found out that three or four families had asked permission from the factory to be able to use the air raid shelter under the factory which was for the workers in the daytime but was not used at night. They thought it would be safer than those in the street. They were in the factory shelter that night, and all died, including children I had been playing with the day before.

Inside our house there was dirt and glass all over the floor. A quite heavy china cabinet which had been fixed to the wall had fallen down and lots of china ornaments which my mother treasured were all broken. In the bedroom a piece of shrapnel had gone through the wardrobe door and burnt a hole in a new dress which my mother had bought with her clothing coupons to wear at my brother's wedding on the following Saturday. We didn't get to the wedding, in Birmingham, because all the roads out of Coventry had large craters in them so no buses were running. In fact, my brother got married not knowing whether we were still alive; telephones were not working either. Hardly anyone had them in the house, but there were public ones.

The raids continued for a long time, but not every night.

We children didn't understand what it was all about. We hated the Germans, although I doubt if any of us had any idea where Germany was, or France, for that matter. None of us had ever been abroad and we didn't learn any Geography in junior schools in those days.

Years later, when I was a teacher and was asked to take a choir to Germany I learned how very kind and friendly the German people are and I still go to visit many friends there.

Dennis Darney also suffered from the bombing

Black and White

In October 1940 we had five or six friends in a room above our shop playing snooker. About 8.20pm there was a huge 'yushing' noise and explosion, we were lifted off our feet, the lights went off and the ceiling came down. My mother called up to ask if we were OK. I managed to open a door and we walked down stairs. My mother laughed at us, we were covered in white from the ceiling. I told my mother to look in the mirror, she was black from soot down the chimney! Father had people in the shop so got me, plus the eldest of my friends, to go and investigate. After only a few yards we found the edge of a crater - a bomb had completely filled the road. We could see about five or six houses up the road with no roofs or fronts but the back walls were standing. The young chap and I decided to go to the rear of the premises where we found all the people safe; they had all been in the back rooms. The only casualty was a young chap on a small motorbike who had been dispatched by the ARP to find where the bomb fell. He found it, going straight into the hole at a slow speed!

Alan Ottoway recalls the bombing in Manchester

Christmas Eve

On Christmas Eve 1940, the sirens sounded to warn of German 'planes approaching, aiming for the Trafford Park Industrial Estate in Manchester where numerous munitions factories were sited.

We all moved in to our Anderson corrugated shelter in the garden and climbed in to bunk beds to get some sleep and to forget about the impending danger approaching. As I was only eight years old, I did manage to drop off to sleep, the rest of the family evidently could not sleep. How could they, with Trafford Park only one mile away?

When I awoke it was daylight and we all ventured out of the shelter to find that our house was still standing but six houses to our right were demolished as well as eight houses across the road. Since our house was blitzed we couldn't live in it so we gathered up some bedding and mother insisted on taking some pots of homemade jam. We put these in my old pram and in our pyjamas and dressing gowns, set off walking to my grandparents, approximately two miles away.

On arrival at about 7.30am, can you imagine five people all in their night attire with all their possessions in an old pram asking to be let in. Well, we were turned away by my grandad! (make what you will of this man who was an ex regimental sergeant major.) So we set off again for another two to three miles to my mother's mother's house, who welcomed us and gave us her front room. We were re-housed in Urmston about ten days later.

The sad end to this story is that we found out from the police that across the road where the eight houses were felled, a land mine had exploded in a back garden. It didn't occur to me at the time but the explosion was in the garden of my pal from primary school and all the family were wiped out. It was told that the youngest girl of the family was approached by a fireman and as she lay dying, her last words were "Has Father Christmas been yet?"

The Anderson Shelter

Roy Bartlett recalls the bombing in Wednesbury

Bartlett Hardware

It was about one-o'clock in the morning that the 'Big One' fell. I was sound asleep until it struck with fearsome force. My first conscious awareness was that my head hurt, presumably having struck the wall at the side of my bed. Also, why was I now lying on the cold stone floor? In fact, all sixteen people in the shelter that night had been heaved out of bunks or chairs and deposited to one end of the cellar in a milling heap of confused bodies. With a brick wall at my feet, I was left alone in that section. Upstairs in the kitchen, Dad, Ivy and Arthur, who were not on duty that particular night, were awake and very aware of enemy aircraft droning overhead. They had no time to be frightened as the descending whooshing whistle was overtaken and obliterated by the exploding crescendo of noise and glare like Dante's inferno as the bomb struck somewhere very close. Choking masonry dust rolled in through every shattered window as my family recovered from being hurled into a terrified yelling jumble on the floor. Coughing and spluttering in the dark confusion they shouted at each other to counteract the ringing, singing, deafness in their ears. Fortunately, the window sticky tape and the heavy blanket blackout curtains, although shredded to destruction, had contained the flying glass and none were cut or injured in any way apart from bruises.

Downstairs in the cellar we were fully aware that this one was very close. We must have looked quite a sight. One end of the cellar was partitioned off as a coal store and all the coal dust wafting around added to the dirt and dust filtering down through every crack and crevice, our ears were popping and painful from the explosive vacuum.

A frantic exchange of shouts with those upstairs verified that everyone was OK. I can remember tea and water being passed around to slake throats and nostrils tinged by that peculiar dry sulphuric taste of high explosive. Flannels and hankies soon followed, to wipe away some of the grime from grubby faces.

So, the big question, where had it struck?

A couple of soldiers had missed the last train and stayed in our shelter, they joined our regular copper and together with dad, Ivy and Arthur, the group ventured outside.

With trembling apprehension they emerged from the shelter entrance into a 'Pea-soup' fog of choking dust to be immediately misled by a red glow from the road opposite.

However, this proved to be a single terraced house set ablaze by an incendiary bomb, presumably dropped by the same aircraft. The two soldiers stayed there to see if they could do anything and to ensure that people were not trapped inside. It was subsequently discovered that the lady of the house was in fact, in our cellar, together with her son home on leave from the Navy. He had persuaded her to take shelter. By now, everyone was saying "Where's the bloody fire brigade?" It was unknown then, but the auxiliary fire lads, some of whom were injured, were fighting desperately to extricate themselves from the wrecked school, then, having done so, finding the two vans and pumps little more than mangled heaps of scrap iron.

As visibility improved it became evident that the seven nearby shops had been reduced to a huge expanse of rubble and wreckage that straddled the road and beyond. The people beneath that grotesque pile of masonry were close friends and fellow shopkeepers.

The rescue services were now arriving to commence a search for any survivors. By next morning the toll was grim. Ultimately, bodies were recovered from the wreckage, twelve people were injured and three members of one family were never found. We knew them all. The cold light of day brought an awful reality to the scene. Every window in our house was shattered and frames loosened. Everything and everywhere was covered in a thick layer of dust contaminated with lumps of rubble and slivers of glass. What a nightmare for my house-proud mother. One of our customers returned a paraffin oil stove found in her front garden some one hundred yards away. Incredibly, a cardboard label, entitled BARTLETT HARDWARE was still attached by string and the stove was only slightly damaged.

To add to my mother's anguish, I was in trouble, being unable to walk. Evidently, when those in the shelter had been flung to one end, my right foot had slammed against the wall at the end of my bed. Relaxed by sleep, my ankle had suffered impact damage to the cartilage between the bones. Dad took me to the local hospital, already overstretched by more urgent casualties. Eventually I was fixed up with heavy strapping that remained in place for many weeks until some mobility was restored. Opinion was that the ankle should have been put in plaster, but there was none available due to heavy demand. This ankle was to remain a problem throughout my life, with an inherent weakness.

Reverting to that morning, a young soldier arrived to stand guard outside the shop with rifle and fixed bayonet to deter any would be looter. Anyone caught stealing from bomb damaged premises could be shot! Mum's pride and joy, the back garden greenhouse was not a pretty sight. All the young vegetable plants being nurtured through the winter months were either mashed by glass and debris, or had been blown away.

I was not much help, but everyone set about the big clear up. Despite a chaotic jumble of stock and debris in the shop, dad decided to open for business - we were open already, like no door! Mum stomped around muttering "The man is mad!" Customers were rare and their requirements a challenge. I watched with disbelief as he scrabbled around in an effort to satisfy.

Really, my parents were the epitome of the spirit that prevailed in those dark days, a determination to carry on regardless, whatever the circumstances and all this compounded by a severe lack of sleep. The word 'stress' was not familiar to the English language in those days!

Meals were now a problem. Minute particles of glass had infiltrated every possible nook and cranny. Mum was so apprehensive that despite a most stringent examination of food, a piece may be missed. Due to the severe rationing, provisions could not be thrown away. We ate so very carefully for many days, to the constant accompaniment of mum's entreaties "Eat slowly, chew it up."

Dad had a sale of 'Blitz Damaged' goods, which included the flying oil stove. This was successful and suggestions were made to the Bank and Off-Licence that they should follow suit! That reminds me that all the smashed stock from the Off-Licence left the area smelling like a gigantic cocktail!

It was raining when I came home from school one lunchtime and I could see that water was pouring over the top gutters. Mentioning this to dad, he said, "I know, I've asked old George to have a look at it."

He duly arrived the following day and clambered up the ladder with a scoop and bucket. As usual, I was being nosy and watching from below, when he suddenly descended with abnormal haste. As he reached the bottom rungs I could see that something was wrong. His face was white and one hand was clasped to his mouth. Racing to the kerb he was then violently sick. My first reaction was that he had a few too many down the pub, but I was hastily ushered out of the way, despite protests and mounting curiosity. From whispered snippets of conversation I gradually worked out the grim grisly story.

The poor man had found the gutter to be blocked at the junction with the down pipe with a jelly like substance. Trying to scoop this out it was not only clinging together, but attached was a flowing mane of obviously human hair.

One could never be certain of course, but the awful conclusion had to relate to the family that were never found after the bomb fell on the adjacent shops. No wonder my parents were anxious to keep all this from me!

Denis Sheehan recalls an incident at Bethnal Green

Bethnal Green Tube Station

The date was the 3rd April 1943; the tragedy at Bethnal Green tube station. That evening I had visited the hospital at Cambridge Heath Road, about a hundred or so yards from the station. Within minutes of leaving the hospital, loud gunfire started, ack-ack, there had been an anti-aircraft battery recently installed at the adjacent Victoria Park. It was more deafening than any gunfire heard previously and it sparked a panic in the crowd of people trying to get down to the tube station platform.

I was unaware of this taking place, I had to pass the station on my way home, with all the noise of gunfire and aircraft and was frightened and decided to try getting shelter in the station. At the head of the stairs was, I think, an air raid warden and he motioned to me as if to say, "just don't try it."

That night, one hundred and seventy three people died in the tragedy, most from suffocation – many were women and children. An inquiry was held in secret and published at the end of the war. The report was headed by the right honourable Herbert Morrison.

I joined the Navy in July of that year and thankfully survived to tell this tale, but I was never more frightened than on that night.

Mr J Shepherd lived in South East London

A Low Ceiling

We never knew whose house/home it once belonged to for it only belonged to us temporarily, and it was ours only for a very short time before 'Jerry' blew it to pieces. It stood on the top of a hill overlooking Tunnel Avenue leading to the Blackwall Tunnel, the Thames and a large Industrial area. As such it was on the German's prime bombing run! We watched German tourists at Greenwich photographing this whole area before the war. Now they came night after night, dropping Incendiary bombs to create fires to light their way along the pathway and we were right in the middle of the bombing run!

One night they dropped a 'Big One.' It landed in our front garden, collapsing the front of the house, bringing down the ceiling onto the piano in the back room. That piano saved us from being buried alive. My brother Cyril usually slept under the stairs, in what was considered a safe spot, whilst my pal Arty and myself slept in the bedroom that wasn't so safe. That night as per usual the deep pulsating throb of the German bomber's engines lulled us into a deep sleep. Odd that it should have such a lullaby effect. Our own coughing and spluttering woke us. Sitting up, I bumped my head, it was the ceiling! Sitting down on the bed quickly, I yelped in pain, it was full of broken glass. Arty was shouting about we can't go out naked so we scrambled around for some clothing to put on.

Dressed, he joined me in shouting out for my brother, "Cyril, are you alright? What's happened?"

His muffled answer led us to him under the stairs, but we could no longer see through the darkness and choking dust.

"I'm buried and can't move - get help quickly." Cyril was almost at screaming point.

We stumbled amongst the wood, bricks and rubble, trying our best to help but couldn't see. Eventually, by crawling around, we found the back doorway then lurched through it, into a dark figure with a torch who bumped right into us.

"Any more of you? Steady lads, this way, follow me", he encouraged us.

We followed him to the front, trying to talk properly about Cyril being buried. He then disappeared. Others led us to an ambulance, and we stood watching as they stretchered Cyril out. Fortunately he only had minor injuries, just cuts, bruises and of course, shock.

Whilst waiting outside we looked down the hill and up into the coal-black sky studded with stars. Fires were burning everywhere, bombs were still going off, whilst searchlights scanned the sky for the German Bombers, lighting them up as targets for the Ack-Ack gunners. Red-hot shrapnel fell all around us like rain, 'Pinging' on the road and pavements. It was dangerous just to stand around.

As Cyril disappeared into the ambulance, the ARP man standing beside us suddenly raised a fisted arm, shaking it violently at the sky as he screamed out, "You murdering bastards, you'll pay for this, we'll get you, just you watch."

Brian Moran lived in London

The Dark Days

When most of the children were evacuated, only seven of us young lads were left at home out of the whole school. There were no teachers as they went with the evacuated children so we had no school to attend and roamed the streets for the next three years playing in the streets or on the waste ground that was close by.

The school board inspector who came around the streets would ask us why we were not at school and when we said that we were from Farmer Rd he would say, "Oh" and walk on.

In the evenings lots of radios would be tuned in to the station of Lord Haw Haw. On one occasion he stated that Walthamstow town hall clock was three minutes slow. A number of people who lived near by went to look and found it was true. He also stated that the beautiful town hall would not be standing for very much longer. On the 15th September 1940, a bomb hit it. A few minutes before the end of Lord Haw Haw's broadcasts the sirens would wail and off to the shelter we would go. Mum carrying the saucepan filled with cocoa and me with a pack of cards and some books to read. The lady next door to us was a widow called Florence Page with three teenaged children. Flo would come in our shelter until it was time for us all to go to bed. Cocoa was drunk and Flo would supply the bread pudding, this was being kept warm on a very low heat in the oven while the raid was in progress. It would be fetched during a quiet interval in the raid.

One night Flo went to fetch the bread pudding during one of these quiet periods and while she was indoors the planes came over and very heavy gunfire broke out overhead. In a fit of panic she grabbed the pudding in one hand and a saucepan in the other putting it on her head as a tin helmet, thinking it would give her some protection on the way to the shelter. When she went to take it off it was stuck fast and the next morning she was taken to hospital where it was removed!

On Monday mornings my mother and aunt Pixie would go to my nan's to do their washing. On this particular day my mother and I arrived in Pearl Rd to discover that a bomb had fallen the night before. All the local people were out in the road sweeping and clearing up the glass and plaster and banging carpets to get the dust out from the fallen ceilings and broken walls,

Two parachute land mines had exploded very close together. One had landed on the Express dairy and Co-op building, the basement of which was being used as a community air raid shelter. All the twenty-two people in the basement lost their lives in that night's incident alone. As I walked down Pearl Rd to see the damage, I was confronted with pieces of human bodies laying every where that had been flung from the Co-op shelter. It was not a sight for an adult to see let alone a young lad.

I walked back to the house where my mother and I started to help with clearing up the glass and plaster on the carpets. Time was passing and there was no sign of my aunt Pixie. Nan began to worry and asked mum if she would go to Pixie's house to see if all was well.

Mum had a long distance to travel from Walthamstow to East London. It was a long time later that I saw my mother walking very slowly and unsteadily down the road holding on to the fences. As she came down the hill she looked ill and white. Some time later I was informed that my aunt Pixie and uncle Bill had both been killed that same night, with a bomb on their home. Pixie was only thirty-two years old.

One night we were asleep in our shelter and in the early hours of the morning we were awakened by a very loud swishing noise and the most almighty bang that shook the shelter so hard that it lifted it up a few inches in the air and then came down again. We thought it was going to be lifted right out the ground, all the earth that had been covering the top of the shelter was now flung down the garden path leaving the top of the shelter bare.

In the morning as we emerged we found that the house was still standing, but a little battered. The bomb had gone over the top of the house and the shelter and exploded on a Doctor's surgery nearby. We found the garden littered with surgical instruments. People along the road were picking them out of the flowerbeds. What we found we returned.

Derek Allen also lived in London

Big Boys Don't Cry

I was really excited when the invitation to my cousin's wedding arrived because it meant that I could have a rare day off work. We overheard our parents whisper that my uncle had spent £200 on the reception; a fortune to a sixteen-year-old in 1940.

After the church service we went back to my uncle's large house situated near the top of a hill. It was a perfect autumn day and photographs were being taken in the garden, when suddenly we heard the eerie note of the Air Raid siren.

My grandfather called us in, with the prophetic warning "You will see plenty of this soon enough." Reluctantly, some of the children went indoors, but to show how brave we were the older boys stayed outside and enjoyed the spectacle.

Not for one minute did we consider that women and children may be getting killed. Surely they would be safe in shelters and the bombs were only falling on the docks and old warehouses, weren't they? To our mind it was only the horrid Germans who were being killed, those that we had been brainwashed into hating.

Around midnight the All Clear sounded. My father drove his parents to their home in his ramshackle old Ford 8, which often had to be pushed to get it started. He then returned to take my family home, but I was enjoying the company of my cousins, boys and girls, so was allowed to stay the night.

Unexpectedly, there was a second attack during the night and this time the explosions sounded a little nearer.

Before breakfast next morning, the All Clear having sounded for the second time, I walked the two miles home. Everything seemed normal, the milkman doing his rounds and a schoolboy delivering the Sunday papers; normal that is until the shock of seeing a pile of rubble, where yesterday a house or two had stood. Arriving home I was surprised to find that my parents were already up and dressed. By the atmosphere I could sense that there was something seriously wrong.

"What's the matter?" I asked.

It was my father who answered, "My best two mates have been killed." he replied.

As he had just been discharged from the army on medical grounds, I assumed that he meant two of his soldier friends, but it was worse. My grandparents, having been taken home by their only son, had been killed outright when their house received a direct hit.

In those days we were taught 'Big boys don't cry,' so I managed to keep a stiff upper lip until I soon found that I needed the toilet. Once out of sight, I locked the door and sobbed uncontrollably.

Leslie Oppitz grew up in Croydon

Surviving the Blitz

I lived with my parents and sister in Sanderstead, near Croydon. By mid 1940 the daytime bombers came and inflicted damage but many never reached London because our fighters did a good job. I still vividly recall standing on Farleigh Common watching German Stuka bombers dive-bomb Croydon aerodrome while a few of our Lysanders hovered helplessly around them. Thankfully Churchill had foreseen the war (while others in power hadn't) and we were prepared to some extent. Spitfires and Hurricanes massacred the daytime German bombers.

My father and I were regularly on duty as 'fire fighters' against the incendiary bombs. I recall as a schoolboy collecting these bombs (about fifteen inches long with an explosive cap one end and a fin the other). I learnt how to defuse them but I was very foolish because the Germans later added explosive charges, which were set off if you undid them. But I was spared that and I used to quietly sell incendiary bombs at school for 2/6d each! Of course I'd removed the detonator. But one chap didn't believe me and reckoned they were harmless. He bought a bomb and then thought he'd be clever, he put the detonator back and dropped it from his landing window. His mother was furious because it burnt down their back door.

On another occasion walking to get a bus to school I noticed everywhere – road, pavements, gardens – there were thin strips of metal foil lying about. We learned that this was dropped by the Germans to confuse our radar systems.

As time passed, war debris was everywhere. Crashed planes in woods or fields with dazed pilots spared death and walking for sanctuary. I remember walking a normal local road and seeing a large round hole in the middle of the road. I peered down to see the large fin of what was probably a 500kg unexploded bomb. I didn't hang around. But many such bombs never did explode since workers on the continent forced into armament manufacture made bombs that wouldn't go off.

Mr A Gilleland grew up in Battersea and Brixton

Childhood Memories of the London Blitz

My brother and I where looking out of our Battersea bedroom window at about eight o'clock at night and we were watching the bombing of the docks, the whole sky was lit up, an orangey red. Suddenly the air raid siren sounded off, and we all went rushing off to the brick shelter in the road. As we got inside my mother said, "I've forgotten Johnny."

He was my baby brother, so I went rushing back to get him, picked him up from the cot, ran down the stairs and then I heard the screaming of the bomb as it was coming down. Just as I got to the shelter door the bomb landed, and I felt the ground heave up and the noise was terrifying.

The next morning we went out onto our balcony, overlooking the back gardens and the houses opposite. The house about a hundred yards away to our right, the bomb had landed in the garden. Sadly, the family was in the brick shelter, they never stood a chance. As my mother said, "If they had dropped it a few seconds earlier, it could have been us!"

We then moved to Brixton, just up from the school. Lovely area, we backed on to the allotments. It was whilst living there that we had our second near miss. I think it was a pretty heavy raid that night, but cannot remember the year, I think it was 1943. The warning had gone off and we crawled into our Morrison shelter, a strong metal frame with wire mesh around it, to stop any rubble coming in, if the house collapsed. Then we heard the drone of the bombers and then the bombs started coming down. I heard my mother say, "I think this is our lot." Then we heard the terrible explosions. We stayed there all night. My brother, as always, slept through the lot. The next morning we got ready for school, only to be told it was closed because of the bombs dropping just down the road from it. So off we went again to look. I'll never forget that sight, they reckoned about three bombs landed. The most awful site was an Anderson shelter, full of holes.

In June 1944, we were playing out in the garden on a sunny Sunday afternoon, my brother and a friend, when we heard this droning sound, looked up and saw what looked like an aeroplane on fire. It was low in the sky, suddenly the flame went out, and it started to come down and at the same time banked towards us. We all dived very quickly into the Anderson shelter. After the explosion we left the shelter to see smoke coming from up the road, so off we went. It had landed just the other side of Brixton Prison, at the rear of some houses. As we got near them we saw what I think was the remains of the flying bomb, lying in the road. It was very quiet, I think we were the first there. A front door was open. I don't know why but we went in, and there was a body of a woman lying in the hallway - we ran!

Elsie Warren worked in Edmonton

The Jewish Girls

During the war I worked at Dunlop in Edmonton sewing buttons on uniforms. When I went to work on the 14th February 1944, it seemed strange that all the machines were not working. I knew that after a week of heavy bombing something was very wrong. Then my boss told me that during the all night raid on London, Aldgate Tube Station had taken a direct hit and was flooded. Eight of our Jewish girls were taking shelter there and we lost all of them. I have known many sad events during the war but this was the worst ever.

Mrs M Rudge lived in Birmingham

The House Next Door

In the late summer of 1940, aged eighteen, I was working at an ARP depot on the outskirts of Birmingham. I took several phone calls for help and then came one for the house next door to home.

As the Rescue Squad left, I asked them to tell me, when they returned, if my parents were safe. When they returned I was told that my parents were OK and my father had even helped them, but the next door neighbours and another neighbour and her son had all been killed. There had also been a bomb on the drive of a house two doors below. At that time, the bombs were light, so although my parents were in the main shelter, in direct line to the one bombed, they were unharmed.

I went home at 6am feeling very tired and said to my mother, "If there's an unexploded bomb, please don't wake me up."

Luckily, there wasn't!

Mary O'Boyle worked in Norwich

The Blitz in Norwich

At the height of the Battle of Britain, I was a very young fire woman in Norwich. Fire sub-stations were set up around the city and I was stationed in what had been a glass-roofed milk depot. During April 1942 there was very heavy nightly bombing of towns and cities and Norwich was no exception. In late April, I was on duty manning a telephone area to take the calls of fire incidents. This night the bombs were falling fast and the city was ablaze. The glass roof around me crashed in and fire bombs exploded around. I sat under a very thin desk in my tin hat and tried to log the calls. Unable to get a response from the duty fire officers, I left the office to find out what was happening. There were no firemen or fire engines to be found. They had not waited for my information, but had all set off to fight the nearest fires. It was an impossible task of course, the city was unable to cope, and houses just burned. Firemen rescued what people they could and helped move possessions if possible. The water, which should have been available to use, was dried up. It was a fairly typical example of how impossibly prepared we were to fight this war. Of course, things improved later. I might add that Norwich lost many citizens that night and much property.

In the second half of the 1940s there was still much food rationing and shortages of everything. In the latter half, some cars and electrical goods were beginning to appear. I now had a job as a demonstrator of the first post war washing machine to come on sale. There was enormous interest in this and people queued for miles to place an order, even though there was no firm delivery date.

Ted Watson worked in Bournemouth

The Model

In the 1940s I was a police constable in Bournemouth. One Sunday, there was a daylight raid by fighter-bombers on the town. Several department stores, a cinema, and numerous houses were destroyed. A department store known as 'Bobbys' in the Square was damaged - all the shop windows were gone and several female models had been stripped of their clothing by the blast and lay around on the floor.

When the red alert siren sounded every police officer had to report in person to the police station.

A hotel on Richmond Hill just off The Square had a direct hit. There was rubble on the street, everywhere. The rescue parties were hard at work.

We had a PC named Randall and because he was the father of twins became known as 'Randy' Randall. There was a Police Box in the Square with a white light on the top, which flashed on and off when they needed a policeman to attend an incident. During the dark hours of the night I heard one of the policemen say to Randall, "The light flashed on the Box so I answered it and HQ wants to have a word with you."

Randall walked to the Police Box, opened the door with his key and a nude female figure fell into his arms. It was a trick that caused a chuckle after all the sombre incidents we had witnessed. Of course, it was a model taken from 'Bobbys' store.

The days went on and by the third night bodies had been moved from the hotel on Richmond Hill but the civil defence still carried on their onerous duties and had reached ground level. There was no hope of finding a living person. All of a sudden there was a shout of "Quiet. Quiet please." The silence was immense. There had been no rain and everything was covered with dust. We waited. Suddenly a plume of dust rose into the search lighted air, a gasp broke the silence. There in the dust stood a Scotty dog shaking the dust from his coat. He walked across that dusty floor and someone picked him up. There was a great cheer from everyone there. He was taken to the WVS canteen that was on hand and I think he drank water and had about a couple of month's ration of meat. What drama!

Colin Holloway recalls the bombing of Coventry

Joey and Mrs J

Due to my father's tram depot being sited on the opposite side of the city, about six miles away, my parents moved to a house within a quarter of a mile of the depot. This turned out to be a mistake as the area was surrounded by factories, which the Germans bombed repeatedly – and we were in the middle of it.

There had been various small raids on the city before the big raid of November 1940. My dad had just got in from work at 7pm when the sirens went off. 'Planes were already overhead as we rushed to the air raid shelter, about two hundred yards away. My mother took our canary in his cage with us but the warden said that pets weren't allowed in the shelter. So Joey (the canary) spent the whole of the night, throughout some of the worst bombing of the war, under a privet hedge by the entrance to the shelter. The following morning, when the All Clear was sounded at 7am we emerged from the shelter to hear Joey singing his heart out. If we had left him at home he would surely have been cut to pieces as all of our windows were blown in during the night.

There were some happy times in the shelters and sad moments too, like when very young babies cried. Even now, when I hear a baby cry I think back to the air raid shelter. On a lighter note, I remember one night during a light raid when most of the occupants of the shelter had nodded off to sleep. Mrs Jerome, a lovely elderly lady went to the toilet (which was just a bucket behind a curtain). Someone shouted 'It's the All Clear.' It was actually Mrs Jerome noisily performing her own All Clear behind the curtain. As Mrs J continued her weeing, the sound of laughter echoed around the shelter bringing a much-needed break in the tension. Yes, babies crying and liquid running in to buckets always reminds me of the war!

Doris Parr recalls the Blitz

The Land Mine

One January night in 1941, it was our turn for a bit of enemy action. I can still remember it vividly. We all sat in our front room as the air raid siren had gone, and we could hear gunfire. Yvonne and me had been on our way to bed, when we were called downstairs to join the family, including the young mother and her baby, who had been snatched from his cot upstairs. At about eight thirty, or soon after, a land mine was dropped in the garden of the detached house next door to ours. It was so sudden. One minute we sat, chatting I suppose, curtains drawn against the black-out, when there was a whoosh, lots of rumbling as the lights went out, and the air was filled with dust from upstairs ceilings. My father ushered us all outside and I remember we all walked over our front door, which lay in the hall, its glass panel in splinters. Yvonne and me were bare foot, and in our pyjamas, as we went out into the snow. My mother carried David, and our evacuee had somehow lost her skirt. The women from the house adjoining ours lay across the road, in the snow filled ditch. This set Yvonne and me off giggling, though I imagine we were a bit hysterical too. No one seemed hurt, and we were invited into a neighbour's house just down the road. It was very cold, and we were glad to be by a fire again. The daughter of the neighbour had a boyfriend who was home on leave and he and our dad returned to the house to search for our coats and shoes, and goodness knows what else. We eventually spent the night with my mother's brother, his wife and our small cousin Shirley. Ten of us slept in one room, on couches, armchairs and in the case of the children, on the floor. The next day, our evacuee returned to London with her baby, and Yvonne and me became kind of evacuees ourselves, as we walked on our own, carrying our few belongings in a suitcase, to the home of yet another uncle or aunt. We had to stay there a few weeks until the local council found us a new home. Our former home was too badly damaged to return to, as incendiary bombs had been dropped through the roof. It was quite lucky that none of us had been upstairs in bed, as chunks of ceiling and bits of glass, lay on our pillows and eiderdowns. My mother stood in tears as she watched the workmen sweep the rubble down her stairs, as the stair carpet was fairly new, and had not been easy to come by. A line of washing left out to dry, was riddled with shrapnel, including Yvonne's skating dress, a blue wool knitted treasure, hand knitted by an aunt. She was upset about this.

The big house next door had to be pulled down; it was so badly damaged. The elderly occupants and owners had had a lucky escape. They had been sitting by their fireside and the chimneybreast saved them. Their chickens were all killed by the land mine.

Mary Beech was born in Coventry

Low Flying

I was born in Coleman Street in Coventry on November 14th 1940, the night that the city was flattened. The nurse put my mum and me under the bed!

My dad, Billy Cackett, always told me how, one Sunday afternoon in 1941 when he was in his garden, a German bomber came over flying so low that dad actually saw the pilot. The 'plane went on to drop two bombs in the canal which should have hit the Boulton and Paul factory. The 'plane was shot down on its way back, I don't know if the pilot survived.

Michael Barrett recalls an incident in Tottenham

The Cat Bath

This incident occurred in Tottenham, North London at the height of the Blitz. I was approaching eighteen at the time and waiting to go into the RAF. My father was an ARP Warden and I very often accompanied him when he went out on patrol. On this particular night a very heavy raid was taking place and my father suggested that I went home to check if my mother was OK. As I opened the front door a terrified cat shot past me into the house and met head on with our little terrier who was coming up the hall to greet me. The cat, having escaped the maelstrom outside, now sensed that one of its nine lives was again in danger and fled up the stairs with the dog in hot pursuit. Suddenly there was a loud splash, then a crash followed by silence, except of course for the intermittent racket outside. I ran up the stairs and when I reached the landing the dog was disconsolately sniffing round bewildered by the sudden disappearance of the cat. I entered the bathroom and beheld a very wet and bedraggled cat perched on a narrow glass shelf above the bath. The shelf had up to that moment contained glasses, toothbrushes, etc. The bath was full in order to provide water in case of fire - a wartime directive to all households. My mother dried the cat and gave it some food, a precious tin of sardines and we released it next morning apparently none the worse for its previous night's dunking!

The 1940s - Month by Month

1944
January
- Allied forces landed at Anzio, in Italy
- Russian forces smashed through the German lines laying siege to Leningrad
- Helicopters were used in warfare for the first time

February
- Plans for a National Health Service after the war were unveiled

March
- Welsh miners went on strike, protesting against a new national wage deal
- Allied aircraft bombed Nuremberg

April
- The build-up to D-Day continued with military exercises taking place throughout the south of England
- The first prefab home was built
- PAYE income tax was introduced

May
- The preparations for the invasion of Europe reached a peak with a massive build up of troops and ships on the south coast

June
- The invasion of Europe began on the 6th of June - D-Day
- US forces entered Rome
- US aircraft bombed the Japanese mainland

July
- Hitler escaped an assassination attempt
- German V1 rockets fell on London causing extensive damage

August
- Paris was reclaimed by Allied forces
- Officers implicated in the plot to kill Hitler were executed

September
- Street lighting returned to most British cities
- Allied forces reached German soil
- British paratroopers landed at Arnhem, meeting heavy German resistance

October
- German Field Marshall Rommel committed suicide when it became clear that he was implicated in the plot to assassinate Hitler

November
- Winston Churchill was given the freedom of Paris as he celebrated his 70th birthday
- 90 people died when an RAF bomb dump exploded at Fauld, in the Midlands
- The German warship 'Tirpitz' was sunk, the last major ship in the German fleet
- The Home Guard was disbanded
- Neon lights in Piccadilly Circus were switched on for the first time since the war broke out in 1939

December
- The German army tried a last counterattack in the Ardennes
- Glen Miller died when his 'plane disappeared over the English Channel

===================================

Evacuees

Joyce Ambrose was evacuated from London

My Billets

I have many memories of my evacuation from London to Dunstable, in Bedfordshire during the war and the life we had to contend with. I'll always remember arriving by train from London as, after refreshments, we were all taken to a street where the police waited to organise people who came along to choose a child or children. I must say it was very frightening.

Myself, I had several billets from the age of seven years. One incident I vividly recall was a billet where the lady of the house would go through my coat pockets at night and remove any money she found (I earned this shovelling up horse manure and running errands). To remedy this, I went to an old church nearby, found a loose brick and before going home put any money I had safely away behind a brick. I did this each day until I was moved on to another billet. I used the money to visit the transport cafe every morning when not at school to get a mug of tea and a bun. Our schooling was only part time, as we had to share the school with local children, one week they went in the morning, we went afternoons, alternating each week.

Olive Hoyles also left London

Evacuation to Devon

The war years as an evacuee from London were incredible, to the point that throughout my life they have been with me in memories and friendship, to this day.

Eventually I was taken to a family known as Mrs Daniels and her daughter Megan, who had been constantly worrying her parents for an evacuee. Many years later I learned that an organiser, Mrs Bowden, had picked me quite early for the Daniels family.

Their home was a Public House with large gardens, orchards and hen houses on separate land. I was so excited after all the worry. The family was so kind in offering supper and seemed pleased of their friend's choice.

The following days and weeks were so busy with new schooling, being introduced to the rest of their family in the village, helping in the orchard collecting fallen apples, and the collecting of eggs from the hens. I cannot express the difference my life was from my so far upbringing in London near to Epping Forest, Essex.

There were treats to Exeter, shopping with Mrs Daniels and Megan and a coffee at the coffeehouse near the Cathedral. At that time an orchestra played in the coffeehouse - such exciting days.

I received a weekly letter from home with pocket money and a comic. The local cinema in Collumpton quite often had some of the pocket money!

I returned to London when the war had finished. I went back to Devon many times to visit and the friendship with Megan is still going strong today.

Betty Goble was evacuated from Croydon

Not Wanted

When war broke out my mother wanted me to go to Canada for safety, but fortunately for me, she changed her mind, as that ship was lost at sea. My two sisters were to be evacuated with their secondary school and an exception was made to enable me to accompany them. We were well looked after in various addresses in the Brighton area, then a few months later, when all seemed quiet on the 'home front', I was returned home to Croydon.

However, before long the blitz started and I was sent off with countless other little children, by train, to Woking. Two ladies lined us all up in pairs and then we walked and walked in 'crocodile' formation, for what seemed hours. I became very tired and the string of my gasmask box was cutting into my neck. The system was that one of the ladies would walk up to a front door, say a few words to the occupant, then hand in one or two children - then the door would be shut and the crocodile of children would proceed further along the road. I was near the back so many of the children had been billeted by the time my turn came.

Struggling with my little case, and rather tearful, I eventually reached the front of the line. A lady took me to a front door, knocked, and a small, shrivelled, little woman answered. At first she appeared surprised, but this quickly turned to dismay and annoyance. I was thrust forward and, in no time, the front door was shut behind me and all was quiet. I peered up as the woman, in a wrap-around apron of the times, looked crossly down at me. I found myself in a dark and gloomy hallway, not knowing where I was or indeed, why I was there.

It transpired that there was a daughter, a girl of about my own age. She had vivid ginger hair as I had never seen before, and a very pale complexion. Perhaps unfortunately, her name, too, was Betty - but we never came to know each other so I felt very lonely.

My recollections of living in that house were not happy. The mother would put my food upon the bare wooden kitchen table and then they would both stand behind me, smirking. I could see them in a mirror. They seemed rather amused or scornful of my manners; and I recall swinging my legs furiously under the chair - doubtless I was quite a curious sight.

At home, I was well used to washing in a family bathroom. However, I never saw such a facility in that house. Hence, my only washing was achieved by reaching up as best I could to get my hands under the tap at the stone sink in the kitchen. I have strong recollections of watching rivulets of water running up my arms, leaving little clean wriggly lines through the grime. I remember sitting in school, looking in wonderment at these lines along my arms.

Then, one day, very unexpectedly, I was taken by a strange lady to what I later recognised as a small room in a clinic. I was told to strip off all my clothes. In my ignorance, I fiercely resisted and screamed loudly as my garments were pulled off me. I soon stood naked with my dignity badly assaulted. There I was in this little room, looking round me and wondering whatever was happening. I learned many years later that I had caught scabies. I was hand painted, all over, with a yellow, strong smelling lotion, as was the treatment then. When the lotion was dry I dressed and I was then returned to my Irish hostess. The whole episode was repeated a while later. I lived in this house for some months before I was moved elsewhere.

Miss P Strickland was evacuated to Cornwall

Cornwall and Cows

One morning soon after the war began we all assembled at school, with gas masks and our bags. We were transported to a main railway station in London, then journeyed to Cornwall. My sister and I arrived there in the late afternoon and slept on camp beds in a school. The next morning we were served with watery cocoa and bread and margarine. In the afternoon two old ladies came and took us to their cottage for tea – strawberries and Cornish cream. It was the first time that I had ever seen a cow – they came right up to the cottage fence.

We were eventually taken to live with a lovely family in Lewannick, a tiny village with no gas, electricity or water laid on. The beds were heavenly, mattresses and quilts filled with chicken feathers from the plucked chickens.

Their cooking was delicious. They made their own bread, saffron cakes, pasties and biscuits.

The village school was so tiny, one half of the children were sent out to play whilst the other half had lessons – no paper, just slates and soft pencils. The headmaster's wife ran a knitting circle and even at the ages of eight and nine, we all knitted scarves, balaclavas, gloves and socks for the forces.

Mrs B Norfolk journeyed to Barnsley

Mushy Peas

As a child, I was sent to Barnsley from London to get away from the bombing. My sister said that she was going for some sweets - I never saw her again until 1945 when my mum came for me. Happy times with a miner's family. When I arrived, the mother and her two children were in the kitchen, where they ate. I had to stand to eat my meals even though there were chairs in the house.

On Saturdays, the Mushy Pea man came. Hot peas in a bowl for 1d or 2d, I can't remember exactly. We would go into this wooden trailer, which contained a table. We would sit down on the left and move around the table, eating. When you got right round the table and back to the door you would leave, as by now you had finished your dish of mushy peas.

I can remember going up to a big house to get clothes and shoes to wear. I'm not sure if they were new. We wore clogs and we clattered down the street.

Overall, these were happy days with the miner's family.

Anne King was sent to Devon

My 1940s Decade

My early life in West London came to an abrupt halt when I was evacuated. We lived on the upper floors of a house whose ground floor was occupied by the owners, brother and sister, Mr and Miss Sills, who were both Jehovah's Witnesses. Mr Sills suffered from Parkinson's disease. Although my mother was not of their faith, she always accepted a copy of the Watchtower from Miss Sills when it was offered, and so Miss Sills told mum about the school to which I was eventually sent. The school was being set up for children of Jehovah's Witnesses, and particularly those who as conscientious objectors might be sent to prison or directed to work on the land during the war. On Miss Sills' recommendation I was accepted.

I knew nothing of this background negotiation, my mother simply took me to Paddington station one day bearing a small suitcase, a gasmask (with some sandwiches on top of the mask in the cardboard case) and a label attached to a coat button, identifying me and my destination.

I found out later that my mother had been drafted into civilian work at the Chiswick factory of London Transport, which had stopped making buses and started making three-ton army lorries for the war effort. She had been allowed time off to take me to Paddington but not to travel with me. So she walked along the train looking for an elderly kind-looking lady to look after me on the journey, and hopefully to be travelling at least as far as I was. Eventually, we found such a lady, who was delighted to look after me. So I sat down opposite this kindly temporary guardian, and after a brief hug, was left alone with her. My mother's heart was breaking, she told me later, but she had to be back at work, the strict injunction helping her to cope with initial separation.

I must have been a little more phlegmatic, or confused. A young couple joined us in the compartment and the young man put my case on the rack, together with my gas mask, after I had extracted the sandwiches. Some four hours later the train drew into Newton Abbot. There I parted from my temporary guardian and met my new one, a much younger lady I later found to be called Audrey. I was whisked away in a taxi, possibly the first time that I had ever ridden in a saloon car. I still remember the smell of leather.

I was soon introduced to the large three-storey house called Craigard, that would be my home for the next five and a half years. There were about fifteen of us, more girls than boys. The largest ground floor room had been adapted as a dual dining room and classroom. Along one wall there were several large boxes later found to contain an assortment of toys donated by local sympathisers. One box was crammed with Meccano which I was not expected to be interested in as a girl. I was. Two upstairs rooms had been turned into boys' and girls' dormitories.

The school permanent staff comprised two elderly ladies we were allowed to call auntie Watson and auntie Donald, and a cook called Mrs (Annie) Eckhart. There were also several girls and the occasional man, all in their early twenties, as far as I remember. Each disappeared at some time or another to face their tribunal for refusing military service. Some came back, their work at the school being accepted as sufficient reason for not joining up. Others were either sent to prison for a while or directed to take up work on farms.

At holiday times, most of the children were collected by their parents in August and presumably taken to safe destinations for family holidays, perhaps in north Devon or the mid-Wales west coast. My mother and father came down once, staying in Newton Abbot and taking me out for days; next year only my mother came. My father was in the RAF by then, and as I also learned later, had divorced my mother since their first visit. I have sometimes wondered if a 'friend' accompanied my mother on the later visits. I shall never know.

For the rest of the holidays, three or four of us had the run of the toy boxes on wet days, including the Meccano, and also were taken out for weekly trips to the beach at Paignton or Dawlish, the journeys being by train.

On Sundays throughout the year we were walked to Kingdom Hall in the town for a service, and were encouraged to read the Bible or participate in short playlets from Bible stories. Once or twice a service was cancelled, again I heard later that local youths had smashed the front plate-glass window of the hall, that had once been a shop. Jehovah's Witnesses were not popular locally because of their conscientious objection to military service. I also saw the only example of actual mudslinging at this time, mud covering much of the white gate at the entrance to our school quite often, although there was no more extensive damage. Inevitably we had no contact with other local children, because of our affiliations. Local farmers were more sympathetic, and we sometimes found boxes of windfalls from an orchard, or vegetables and eggs left on our back doorstep. An old chap called in the morning sometimes with mushrooms gathered from local fields and another, Gaffer Gumble called selling bunches of watercress for a few coppers.

Once we had an allocation of oranges, which were immediately turned into marmalade that all could share.

During the build-up to D-Day, endless convoys of American military vehicles streamed through the town on their way to Denbury Barracks. One sprayed us with handfuls of sweets which we eagerly snapped up, only to have them taken from us. A senior girl then heroically ate one to make sure that they hadn't been poisoned by fifth columnists. When she didn't collapse and die, the sweets were given out again and eagerly consumed.

Needless to say we had no idea of why the Americans were around, they were just a momentary source of sweets, long rationed and mostly unavailable in England.

In late 1945, this pleasant life came to an end. I have often wondered if I was really happy or just suppressed my home-sickness. As one gets older, more early memories seem to return; I still cannot remember being unhappy, except for about five minutes after my mother left at the end of each holiday. I was easily cheered up by a combination of the usual formula of milk and biscuits, a hug of the house dog Chum, and the lure of the toy boxes.

As my mother was divorced and living with her mother, she could not have me to live with her when I returned to London. My gran (who was a widow) refused to have a boisterous child in the house all the time. So when mum met me at Paddington, she had to explain hastily the new arrangements she had made. Once again I was farmed out, to a family in Richmond.

The household included three sisters, one called Mary, the others, Dorothy and Jean, who were in the Wrens at the time. Mary worked with my mother and offered to ask her mother if I could live with them for a while. I went but was able to see my mother every weekend. At the age of nine, I was travelling between Richmond and Fulham (two buses, or one train and one bus) on my own, unthinkable today, I suppose.

During this time I attended the local primary school and in due course took the equivalent of the 11 plus. I was not very popular when I earned a place at the local grammar school while the son of the house (same age) only qualified for the County Secondary School.

I had some difficulties at the grammar school. The school expected pupils to return to pre-war standards as soon as possible. For example, we were expected to wear a school blazer, and a badge sewn on to the pocket of an old or wrong-coloured blazer was not acceptable. It was embarrassing to be reminded of this in front of a class. How could I tell them that my parents were divorced, my mother only had a small income and that my father allowed her 12/6d a week for my keep, with no extras for clothes etc. For most of the girls, coming from middle-class families meant that money was not an issue …

Another problem was that my 'landlady' was prone to headaches, which she tried to relieve with vinegar and brown paper, which I had only previously heard of in a nursery rhyme! Anyway, on such days, Mrs Brown would tell me I would have to stay off school to do her shopping. This was fine until a man, who identified himself as the School Board man (in the butcher's shop) insisted on seeing me to my home, where he informed the ailing Mrs Brown that I must go to school immediately or face the possibility of expulsion. Off I went, to be humiliated again by our Latin teacher in front of the class; she informed me that many others would like to take my school place if I didn't want it. But that was nothing to the rows at home that evening; somehow it was my fault that Mrs Brown, poorly as she was, was harangued by a Truant Officer.

It took nearly a year for my mother to convince gran that I was not a riotous tearaway, but quiet, understanding child. Finally, gran relented and I moved to Fulham, with my mother at last.

The next complication was that my mum started looking for a second husband. A series of gentlemen called to see her and perhaps take her out dancing. I used to wonder why they were all so nice to me, not dreaming in my innocence that they were working on mum through me. Anyway I had a few little gifts or half-crowns given to me. After gran died, the man who would eventually become my step-father moved in. Someone else to dislike, I supposed, although he was very good to my mum.

My paternal grandparents lived in Hammersmith, and I used to visit them occasionally. This gran was very different from my mum's mum. She was a Conservative, a member of the Primrose League, and in her earlier days had been quite an orator and a great campaigner for the party around election time. My mother's younger brother was a rampant Socialist who enjoyed nothing better than heckling my gran at local halls when she was canvassing.

Grandad was a darling; he had been a Hansom cab driver in his early days and later became a builder's labourer. Although my gran was perhaps a cut above him socially, she married him on three conditions. He was to stop drinking (she was strictly TT), he was to wear a stiff shirtfront ('dickie') every day and always wear a bowler hat when he was out. He kept all the conditions throughout their sixty-two years of married life. He was a delightful little man, and I loved him dearly.

Mr Duquemin was also an evacuee, from Guernsey

Evacuation and Reparations

Ever since 1563, when it was founded by Queen Elizabeth 1st, Elizabeth College had occupied the site of a former monastry, to the west of St Peter Port, on Guernsey. In June 1940, the local authorities decided to evacuate all men who wanted to join the armed forces in the United Kingdom, as well as all the children and women who wanted to leave.

On the 20th June, after waiting, seated on a single suitcase for two days, the staff and the boys of Elizabeth College walked down to the harbour and embarked on the SS Batavia IV. They joined the other three secondary schools, the Ladies College and the girls and boys of the Intermediate schools. There were about one thousand souls in all. The ship was Dutch and had previously been used for transporting cattle. We were sent down to the lowest deck, a low-ceilinged hold still containing hay from its previous voyage.

With hindsight, it was folly to pack the majority of the island children into the same boat. Had the boat been sunk during its journey across the Channel, Guernsey would have lost an entire generation of future schoolteachers, clergy, lawyers and civil servants.

The sea was calm and the crossing was uneventful until early the following morning. As the ship steamed into Weymouth Bay there was a flurry of activity, sirens were sounded, naval ships sent signals by Aldis lamp and the ship turned sharply to the west and proceeded under escort to Weymouth quay. It was rumoured that the captain of the Batavia was unaware of the minefield laid to protect the naval base at Portland!

By noon the children and staff had disembarked and were served an al-fresco lunch in the station waiting rooms. There followed a long delay, but as night approached the evacuees were loaded on board a train that headed north. We ended up in Oldham, where we were bedded down on the floor of the Co-operative hall.

For the next fortnight the people of Oldham entertained the boys. The municipal swimming baths, including the individual bathrooms, the cinemas, the local buses and a park containing a boating lake were placed at our disposal. The school staff attempted to keep the examination candidates revising under difficult conditions. Their task was made easier when the school was transported to the village of Great Hucklow, in the Peak District.

There, the junior school was accommodated in the Unitarian holiday homes and in corrugated-iron huts on the edge of the village. The senior school was housed in the Clubhouse and hangar of the Lancashire and Derbyshire Gliding Club.

The German army now occupied the Channel Islands and the Battle of Britain was being fought over Southeast England. News of old boys, who had only left school a year earlier, being killed in action, started to arrive. A steady stream of names that was to continue for the next five years.

On a personal level, my older sister Thelma ended up in Rochdale. My mother and two younger sisters were housed in a former nursing home in Cheadle Hulme. The accommodation was shared with two other Island families. The remainder of our family remained in Guernsey. We had lived in a house at the east end of the main runway of the island airport. The Germans began extending the runway soon after their arrival. Within a year the house, outbuildings, greenhouses and vegetable garden had disappeared. My elderly grandmother tried to salvage the contents, but with only a neighbour's horse and cart for short periods at a time, most of the contents disappeared.

My father was a Sergeant in the local police force. In 1942 some members of the police force were caught pilfering, from both the German army and civilian food stores. There followed a brutal interrogation of the miscreants and the others involved were soon revealed. My father was sentenced to two and a half years hard labour by a German tribunal. Later, he was confident that he would be reinstated and have his pension rights restored, as he claimed he had only been following advice from Colonel Brittain, who had regularly broadcast to occupied Europe. But the local authorities refused, several of whom he had regularly chauffeured to and from German HQs to attend receptions and celebrations and who had received packets of sugar, coffee and the like, that he had conveniently left on the back seat of the police car, in which he drove them back and forth. He died nine years later, a taciturn and bitter man. Ironically, my widowed mother received £2,300 in compensation in 1964 – from the Germans!

Maurice Rudge was evacuated from Bristol

Table Tennis Tables and Postal Orders

When the war started the Bristol area was deemed to be safe so no form of evacuation of the children was seen to be necessary. The authorities had hundreds of children from the London area billeted in the surrounding villages. This was soon to change. Mother was sent a note from school saying that I was on the list for evacuation but my two brothers, not being in the same age group, would not be required to go.

My turn came in early May 1941. Off to school I went with a pillowcase with few belongings, my gas mask and a bag with cucumber sandwiches supposed to be for our dinner. On arrival at school we were issued with a big label to tie around our necks for identification purposes. We were now truly evacuees. There seemed to be hundreds there and quite a lot of mums with young children. Double decker buses were lined up along the street, one of which I eventually boarded. None of us had a clue where we would land up. I was transported to Stapleton Road Station, Bristol to start my mystery journey by train.

Evacuees

We all had visions of travelling to Wales or up North somewhere but we soon had some idea as we travelled south through Bristol, making our first stop at Bridgewater, where a couple of carriages emptied. Our turn was to come when we got to Williton Station, about six miles from Minehead.

There were charabancs outside the station waiting to transport us to the various villages. Ours was to take us to Watchet where we were duly set down at the local school awaiting allocation to various houses. By now I had palled up with Barry Redwood. It did not appear that any child was given a specific person to go with as the local residents just came in and selected whoever they took a fancy to. Anyway, Barry Redwood and I were the last two left - nobody seemed to want us so by then we were really down in the dumps.

Eventually a lady came in with two little children in a pram and Barry was whisked away with her. Nobody left for me, so out of the goodness of his heart, Mr Young, the headmaster of the school, decided he would take me until other arrangements could be made. Mr Young, his wife and two children lived in a big house on the main road out of the town.

The first thing that happened at Mr Young's was that I was given a room of my own. This was unheard of at home, as I had always slept in with brother Roy. Being the headmaster's house, it was quite posh. You even had to wash your hands before meals and Mr Young would say grace at the main meal of the evening. It was all very strange to me and one thing I was never going to get used to was going to bed at 7pm as, back at home I was lucky to get to bed at all if there was a raid on. There was also church three times on a Sunday with the family.

My friend Barry landed up quite the opposite. The lady he was billeted with was on her own with the kids, we presumed that her husband was away in the army but we never did find out. He could do just what he pleased and quite a few times he baby-sat while his good lady went out.

Our schooling was most haphazard. Our school was the Conservative clubroom on the esplanade and our classroom was made up of card tables and a large table tennis table. Can you imagine what it was like with about a dozen of us sat around this table tennis table and four to a card table. I think there were about twenty-five of us, ranging from about seven years old to nearly fourteen so Mr and Mrs Hayward, the teachers, had their work cut out trying to drum some sense into us.

After about two weeks I moved to another billet and I cannot say that I wasn't sorry as, although they treated me very kindly, their middle class background was not the same as I was used to. After saying goodbye to the headmaster and his family, I was taken to stay with Mr and Mrs Stacey, the village postman and his wife. They had no children and lived on a small council estate. This was more what I was used to. I had much more freedom and no more church on Sunday. I could even go to the pictures. I could go around to my pal's billet on an evening and get back at about 10pm. Barry was usually baby-sitting. I used to often wonder why the postman would give me a couple of shillings to go out. Never mind it was very acceptable!

There were no visits from mum or dad but plenty of letters and the occasional parcel with some goodies in and perhaps a postal order for 5/-. I used to be a loner mostly going out on my own over to the dock area. There seemed to be no security and I often thought that the Germans could land there easily. I used to talk to the sailors, quite a few of whom were over from Cardiff with a cargo of coal. I used to think, "Shall I stow away?" At least Cardiff was near Bristol.

I was getting homesick by now. This country life was not for me. So every time I wrote home I would say, "Come and get me." Eventually, after a few months mother relented and back home I went. Thus ended my spell of evacuation. Quite a few kids stayed until the end of the war and got jobs and stayed on.

Dianne Scapens lived in Liverpool

The Silence

My mum and dad grew up in Liverpool and were married at nineteen, in 1943. Mum went to work in the munitions factory working twelve-hour shifts, six days a week. She did this from aged 15 - 21 and often speaks of friends who were there one minute and gone the next, all young women. They still seemed to retain a zest for life though. Mum said they used to rush home via a long tumbling tram journey and several miles walk in order to have tea, get washed and get out to the local dance hall before the sirens sounded. "It was better being locked in the dance hall over night when the bombs were dropping, than squeezing into the air raid shelter with everyone else!"

The most poignant tale mum tells is when she was coming home one evening after her day shift, 6am - 6pm. There was a stillness, an emptiness, a desolation never ever experienced before. As she was walking from the tramcar she felt the overpowering sadness in the city - all the children had been evacuated!

She recalls the empty streets, no after-school release of energy. No kids playing football, sitting in the gutters playing marbles, charging around on a steering cart, half a dozen skipping ropes being turned at the end of various streets, one end being tied to a lamp post. Just the quietness, women standing either alone or in small groups bereft of their families, their men off fighting and now their children taken from them. There were women silently sobbing, some inconsolable, others in total shock, numb with pain. Mum's younger sister, two brothers and several cousins had boarded the train in Lime Street with hundreds of other youngsters from the city.

This is an experience for which I thank God that neither myself nor my generation and fortunately not my children's generation has had to bear.

The 1940s - Month by Month

1945

January
- The Russians liberated Warsaw and entered Germany
- President Roosevelt was inaugurated for a record fourth term as President of the USA

February
- The city of Dresden was flattened by Allied bombing, causing much controversy
- Churchill, Stalin and Roosevelt met at Yalta, to agree the shape of post war Europe

March
- Beaches on the south coast re-opened as the war drew to a close. Unexploded mines were a local hazard
- Allied forces crossed the Rhine and drove on towards Berlin
- Lloyd George died, aged 82

April
- US troops landed on Japanese soil, in Okinawa
- The million strong German army in Italy surrendered
- Mussolini was executed by Italian partisans
- Soviet troops entered Berlin
- Hitler committed suicide on April 30th
- President Roosevelt died of a cerebral haemorrhage

May
- The war in Europe ended with the German surrender on May 8th

June
- The post-war map of Europe was unveiled, showing that Germany would be split between East and West

July
- The Labour Party swept to victory in the post-war election
- The first atomic bomb tests took place in New Mexico

August
- Atomic bombs were dropped on the Japanese cities of Hiroshima and Nagasaki
- Japan surrendered on August 14th, five days after the second bomb was dropped

September
- British troops regained control of Hong Kong and Singapore

October
- The first Far East prisoners of war returned to the UK
- The United Nations was established

November
- The German war crimes trial at Nuremberg began
- Charles de Gaulle was elected President of France

December
- The International Monetary Fund was created
- Controversial US General George Patton died following a car crash

=================

Doing My Bit

Alistair Duncan did his bit in Leith

Stop or I Fire!

At the outbreak of War I was seventeen and just left school. I took up work in the office of McVitie & Price Ltd and joined the LDV-later the Home Guard.

We were on duty two nights each week and every so often did a third night. My nights were Tuesday and Thursday and my extra night was Sunday. The routine was one-hour training, one-hour guard duty and two hours patrol, either 10pm to Midnight or 4am to 6am. We reported for duty at 8pm and finished at 6am.

During the first six months when we were on patrol, watching out for German spies trying to land or other enemy activity - we carried rifles but no one knew we had no ammunition!

One night in late 1940 or early 1941 I was on guard duty outside our post, which was directly opposite Newhaven Harbour (Leith, Edinburgh) when a motor boat engine started up. This was between 1-2am in almost pitch darkness. I ran across the road to the steps leading to the harbour and called "Who goes there"? Needless to say there was no reply. I then called "Stop or I fire", still no reply but I could see the image of the small boat approaching the exit. I then fired but missed the moving target.

As you can imagine, all hell broke loose and there were all sorts of enquiries about the rifle being fired. I often wonder if I was the only member of the Home Guard to fire at the enemy!

At breakfast that morning, I was relating the story to my dad who was repairs manager in Henry Robb Ltd, Shipbuilders in Leith. He immediately called the dock police who instigated a search of the docks and the culprit was found still beside the little motor boat on a lower pier at sea level. It turned out he was a German spy obviously hoping to escape into the community when darkness came again.

So all was well in the end and I suppose I was partly responsible for capturing an enemy spy. I still await my reward! I then survived five years in the army and am still here to tell the tale!

John Barfoot recalls the Home Guard in Berkshire

Memories of the Home Guard

Before joining the Navy in 1943, I was a member of the Home Guard, in Hurst platoon. Our commanding officer was Captain Reggie Palmer and the second in command was Lieutenant Tomkinson, both veterans of WWI. The members roughly belonged to four categories. Those that had served in the first war, people in reserved occupations, youngsters like myself, killing time until old enough to join up and a few who were over call up age.

We were all issued with American 300 rifles, which we kept at home together with the necessary equipment to keep them clean. These were regularly inspected at every parade. Our regular parades were on Thursday evenings, in the village hall and Sunday mornings. On Thursdays we practiced arms drill, which came easily to me having been a member of the Army Cadets at Maidenhead School; weapons training, which consisted of stripping down and re-assembling Bren and other automatic weapons; first aid; map reading and other associated military subjects.

On Sundays our training was more active. It consisted of platoon drill, battle drill and occasionally live practice with a Stoke's mortar, the grenade throwing rifle and hand throwing of Mills bombs.

A weekend school used to be held at Binfield. Those attending slept in some converted pigsties. A Captain Parmentier, assisted by an army sergeant ran the school. The subjects, as far as I can recall, were unarmed combat, street fighting and learning to drink beer army fashion at a nearby pub!

Another Sunday activity was going to the firing range at Kiln Green. Here we had the opportunity to fire our own rifles and register their peculiarities. In fact, I believe I fired more small arms ammunition in the Home Guard than in my time in the Navy.

From time to time we had to mount guard overnight on various stragetic sites in the village such as the Post Office and Telephone Exchange. On these occasions the guard met just before 10pm. We then did a two hour stint at our allotted post before or after which we tried to get some rest in the Scout hut which was equipped with camp beds before dispersing at 6am the following morning. Rest was not easy. Being near his shop, one of our members, Mr Pibworth the butcher used to bring in his typewriter and accounts and spend the night busily typing his correspondence on a table in the corner, much to the annoyance of the rest of us.

On some weekends we held exercises in conjunction with neighbouring platoons. On one of these occasions, whilst exercising with Twyford, an incident occurred that could have come straight out of the script of 'Dad's Army.'

My section had instructions to go along the banks of the Loddon to the railway bridge and see if it was guarded. If so, we were to drive the guard off, put on our own guard and the rest proceed to Twyford Mill. For this we were armed with replicas of Mills bombs made of clay, which dispersed with a small bang and a cloud of dust, and also crackers at the end of the rifles operated by string on the trigger guard.

We decided to change the plan and approach along the Hurst Road as we would be expected along the bank. As we neared the allotments we could see a guard of about four men, nonchalently smoking under the bridge. We decided to cut across the allotments to surprise them. As soon as we started we were confronted by several angry allotment holders telling us that 'Digging for Victory' was more important than playing at soldiers. Deciding that discretion was the better part of valour, we put plan two into operation. This involved going on to the railway embankment at the station and surprising the guard from above. As we tried to enter the station we were blocked by a ticket collector demanding we obtained platform tickets before setting foot on the platform. Putting on our best 'Don't you know there's a war on?' attitude, we pushed past and carried on down the platform. The collector dashed over the steps to the stationmaster's office. This produced an enraged Mr Huggins, shouting at us to get off his railway. By now committed, we doubled down the platform and onto the embankment. Not to be outdone, Mr Huggins followed us, wildly gesticulating. Reaching the bridge we looked over the parapet and saw the guard still smoking and blissfully unaware of the drama unfolding above. Quickly dropping some bombs and firing crackers, we surprised them and they rapidly disappeared towards the mill. By this time Mr Huggins was getting near so we scrambled down the embankment and without placing our own guard, followed our Twyford colleagues as quickly as we could along the river bank to the mill. Stationmaster 1, Home Guard 0!

How effective would the Home Guard have been if put to the test? Undoubtedly we were good for morale. We felt we were well trained and knew our locality well. However, how we would have fared against heavily armed and fully trained airborne troops is open to question. I, for one, am glad we never had to find out.

Richard Wright recalls his father's exploits in Cheshire

Home Guard

My father, Clifford Wright, was the second person to enlist in the Bollington (Cheshire) LDV ('Look, Dash and Vanish!'). 'Exercises' were frequently held and one Sunday, American GIs who were camped locally were given the task of defending Bollington and the Home Guard had to attack and capture the US HQ, situated at the local council offices.

They started their attack from Poynton, a village five miles away. The Americans had set up a series of road blocks and my father thought of a way to enter Bollington. When the local bus arrived, our valiant Home Guard boarded and my father had them lie down on the floor (after he had paid their fares!). Being a local service bus, the GIs waved it through their check points and when it arrived at Bollington Council Offices the platoon debussed and promptly 'captured' the US HQ.

But an 'umpire' disqualified them for cheating. My father appealed and said, "We did what the Germans would have probably done."

The appeal was quashed because, "We Brits don't play underhand tricks like the one you employed!"

Dr Tony Husain remembers the Home Guard in Croydon

The Pikemen of England

Since my father was Professor of Mathematics of Osmania University of Hyderabad, and my mother's family came from Colchester we, as a family of five boys, travelled frequently between India and England and were finally sent back in the Spring of 1939. We were accepted into Whitgift School in South Croydon, and at the tender age of fifteen, I became a prefect. When bombing began I was allowed to look out of our dugout around our parade ground during an air raid and saw the swirling around and the distant machine gun fire in the first dog fight over Biggen Hill. It reminded me of the old silent film called Hell's Angels, which I had seen in the 1930s in India.

My OTC Sergeantship got me into the Home Guard, where I had to drill the 'Old Contemptibles' to form three ranks instead of four.

As Home Guards, we had to defend the approaches to London. As a Platoon Commander I had some six old men, one with a Lea Enfield rifle, the standard issue for the army, two double barrel shot guns, a Mauser pistol, which I kept for myself, and the others had lead piping with a bayonet stuck on the end. Someone took a sepia picture of us, 'The Pikemen of England.'

Our main struggle every evening was to lift two angled railway lines into slots in the road to prevent the German tanks passing under a railway bridge over the road. They never came.

Later on I qualified as a doctor but even in the army, I never fired a shot in anger.

Alistair Duncan's father, Alexander also recalls the 1940s in Leith

Alexander was the manager of ship repairers Henry Robb Ltd in Leith, Edinburgh

In the early years of the war, we had a coalition government and Mr Bevin was the Minister of Labour. He introduced the 'Essential Works Order'; he was also responsible for bringing Shop Stewards into being, who have been the means of all the labour troubles ever since. One of the clauses in the 'Essential Works Order' stated that no firm during the war could sack a Shop Steward. Most of the Shop Stewards were communists. The Shop Steward of the electricians in the yard was a red-hot communist and he disappeared one day for a week and when he returned I asked him where he had been and he said he had gone to London to a Shop Stewards' meeting.

I said, "Well, I am going to give you a warning, if you leave to go to Shop Stewards' meetings in London or in any other place without the firm's permission, you will be sacked!"

A few months later he went to Manchester for about a week and when he came back I sent for him and sacked him.

The following day, the entire Yard went on strike in support and before three days had elapsed, all the firms in the Port went out as well. Sir Gilbert Archer and Lord Rosebery were known as the 'Uncrowned Kings of England'. They both visited us with a labour leader and instructed us to reinstate the Shop Steward, which we refused to do. Sir Gilbert Archer then said "If you do not reinstate this man, we will stop the King and Queen visiting your Yard in the summer." We said to Sir Gilbert, "There is a principle involved here and we are not reinstating this man."

A public enquiry was then held with Lord Wark, a Judge of the Court of Session appointed. After all the evidence had been heard, and I had explained to Lord Wark that the Shop Steward involved had been given two chances, Lord Wark decided against the man and ordered all the men in Leith back to work.

In 1944 we had HMS Wallace, which was a destroyer, in for a refit. When a naval vessel is drydocked, there is a drydocking form which must be completed. The form must be signed by the First Lieutenant. It is a duty of the Foreman Shipwright to organise this, but on this occasion he was not available and he sent one of his Chargemen, Jock Wood.

He went on board and asked for the First Lieutenant to sign the docking form. The First Lieutenant took Jock Wood down to his cabin and said "This is all in order Jock" (he did not know that his name was Jock, but naval people call all Scotsmen 'Jock'). He signed the form and handed it back to Jock. Jock examined it and found he had simply signed the form 'Philip', so he said, "Excuse me, Sir, but have you nae second name?"

Prince Philip laughed and said, "Well, Jock, between you and I and the gatepost, I am Prince Philip of Greece, and that is how I sign my name - just 'Philip', but do not tell anybody."

He then asked Jock into the Wardroom for a drink but Jock told him he was just a Chargehand and was not allowed into the Wardroom and that in any case he was a teetotaller. Prince Philip then said "Well, come into my cabin and I will give you a cup of coffee."

After Jock had drunk a cup of coffee the First Lieutenant shook hands with him and said he hoped to meet him again, and told him not to tell anyone he was Prince Philip of Greece.

Later in the day when I was going through the Docks I happened to pass Jock Wood and he put up his hand to stop my car. I asked him what the trouble was.

"Oh!" said Jock, "There is nae trouble, but I just wondered if you would like to shake hands with me."

"Why would I shake hands with you Jock?"

He held out his hand. "This is the hand which shook hands with Prince Philip of Greece." Jock was very proud about it all. Later I told Prince Philip the story and he laughed his head off. He said, "Jock did not keep his word because I told him not to tell anybody!"

The King and Queen visited our Yard in 1943 when all the Directors were presented to their Majesties. They did not arrive until about four o'clock in the afternoon instead of 2.30 pm as arranged. The King was a very tired man that day and they had been visiting some of the Clydeside Shipyards before coming to us. The King did not want to climb the stairs to the Boardroom so it was arranged that we should line up in front of the office for the presentation to their Majesties. After that was over, they walked through the shipyard and the Queen was always about twenty yards behind the King; she spoke to whom she chose and not to those who had been chosen for her.

After they finished going through the Yard, we had one of our latest frigates lying at the West Pier ready and the King and Queen went aboard her and were presented to the Captain and all the officers. The Captain was Peter Scott, better known as the 'Birdman.' This frigate was his first big command.

During 1946/47 the King and Queen again visited Edinburgh and were in residence at Holyrood Palace. They visited Trinity House in the Kirkgate. The Lord Provost at that time was Sir Andrew Murray and he being the Vice-President of the Master Mariners Club, which was immediately under Trinity House in the same building, managed to persuade their Majesties to visit the Master Mariners Club. Being an Honorary Member I was invited to meet the King and Queen. Very short notice was given of the visit so there were only about twenty persons present when their Majesties arrived at the Club.

The King was very tired and he just stood at the entrance with Sir Andrew Murray but the Queen walked round and spoke to each Member. The Queen has the art of putting anyone entirely at their ease when being formally presented. On this occasion she merely spoke to each Member without any introduction and was at ease making conversation with anyone she had never met before.

I was standing practically at the end of the line with my back to the mantlepiece. Princess Margaret was with the King and Queen and she was standing behind me at the mantlepiece with Group Captain Peter Townsend, who at that time was the King's Aide. He was very popular with the King and the Royal Family. Princess Margaret at that time was only about sixteen years of age.

Just before the Queen arrived where I was standing, I felt a tap on my shoulder and on turning round Princess Margaret asked, "What is that?"

I looked and saw it was a model of the first steam engine ever built and if one turned the flywheel with one's finger, the pistons worked. I touched the flywheel to make the pistons move and the Princess said, "I would like to do that." Which she did, moving it so hard that the flywheel having no key fell on to the floor, which made rather a noise.

"Damn it!" she said.

I then said to the Princess, "It is a good job your Mother did not hear you say that" - and she just laughed!

Just then the Queen arrived and said to me "You will be a Ship Master, I presume?"

"No, Madam, I am not a Ship Master, although my complexion might lead you to think so." and she laughed. "I am not a Ship Master but I build and repair ships which is the next best thing."

The Queen said to me "Your face seems familiar to me."

"That is very kind of you to say so", I replied, "I did have the honour of being presented to you before when you visited our Shipyard in 1943."

I said to the Queen, "Perhaps I shall recall a little incident which happened on that day."

"What was that?"

"Well, when you went aboard the frigate of which Peter Scott was the Captain, the King did not notice that the First Lieutenant was a George Cross man, but you did."

The Queen said, "Oh, I remember that so well, and the King was not at all pleased at being brought back!"

On that occasion the King had been presented to all the Officers and he was touring the ship with the Directors, including myself. After the King had walked about thirty feet along the deck, the Queen sent Captain Peter Townsend to bring the King back as he had not noticed that the First Lieutenant was a George Cross man. It was the King who brought that honour into being. One could hardly help but notice the George Cross because it is a gold cross on a plush background.

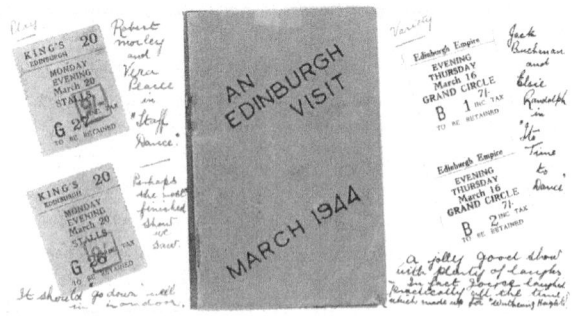

Judith Keel enjoyed the theatres in Edinburgh

Barbara Algar toured the country

The Winstanly Babes

During the war, I was with a dance troupe called 'The Winstanly Babes.' We were doing a tour of England with a pantomime, Cinderella. All the cities that we performed in were systematically bombed and we really believed we were being targeted. We began the tour in Morecambe, which was the only place that wasn't bombed (at least not while we were there) then we went to Liverpool. The night we arrived was one of the worst blitz in Liverpool – eight miles of docks were bombed and the next morning there were water carts and women dolling out food. The theatre was hit and we didn't perform for three nights. We went from there to Swansea where we were boarded at a B&B facing an internment camp for Germans and Italians. After that we went to Coventry, Portsmouth and Plymouth, all of which took a terrible bombing and finally back to Manchester into the horrific bombing again. Many of my friends were either killed or missing in the ensuing years on tour, it was an episode I will never forget.

Eric Wilson in the Wirral recalls a tragic incident

Sleeping on the Job

During the early years of the war I was too young to join up so I joined the Home Guard. I was employed on war work in the area - often, this consisted of boarding up broken windows for which we used shed roofing felt. We left one small space for a small pane of glass to be refitted, which allowed some light in to the rooms.

One day, I had to go to a village called Greasby, about three miles away. I loaded up a handcart with roof-felt, battens, nails and tools and myself and the foreman put our bikes on top of the handcart as well. It was a very hot May day and after about a mile along the country road my mate, who was about 70 years old, suggested that we have a five minute rest on one of the wayside seats. So, we sat down and rested. There were no passing cars or vans (because there was no petrol) but there were a few passers-by on bikes, a couple of Land Girls, another man on a bike and somebody on a large horse and cart. I noticed that people were staring at us as they passed. After a while I said to my mate that I thought we had better get going to board up the windows. He didn't answer and I turned to him and noticed that he had fallen asleep. But when I gave him a gentle nudge I realised that he had died, peacefully, whilst sitting next to me. No wonder the passers-by were staring at us. I suppose the War Office had got him to stay on after his retirement because of the shortage of younger men who were away fighting in the war.

Marguerite Lloyd lived outside of Liverpool

The All Clear

My father was a police constable in the heart of Liverpool but we lived four miles away in the suburb of Stoneycroft. My mother, as the wife of a police officer was not allowed to work. As she was also a state registered nurse, the local warden asked her if she would be the key holder of the public shelter nearby. She was given a huge key, which hung on the kitchen wall together with a certificate of which she was very proud.

One night she heard the sound of the siren, took down the key, wished she had a tin hat, eyed the dustbin lid but decided her fortnightly 'shampoo and set' deserved better and bravely ventured over the road to the public shelter. She opened the wooden door and went back home. She then put on kettle and lit a Craven A cigarette and waited ...

Half an hour later, she went down the garden path and leaned on the gate, the stars were bright and all was quiet. Along the route strolled an Air Raid Warden wearing tin hat with ARP in white letters on the front.

"Goodnight madam" he said, touching his hat in the form of a salute.

"Isn't it quiet," said my mother.

"Yes" said the warden; "the All Clear went half an hour ago!"

During the height of the blitz on Liverpool my father never talked about things he saw, except once when he told of a tall building blazing away. One whole side of the house had fallen down exposing open floors and at the top an old lady in bed, terrified and screaming for help. Fire fighters had failed to persuade her down their ladder and asked my father to try. He ascended to the top floor and called across to her, "Please madam get out of bed and come towards me."

But she pulled the covers higher under her chin and replied, "All right officer, but turn your head away whilst I get out of bed."

Even in those circumstances, modesty and good manners prevailed!

Shirley Lingwood recalls her family 'Doing Their Bit'

The Chickens

My father, being in a reserved occupation, did not have to join any of the armed forces, but became Air Raid Warden in charge of our local headquarters, situated in a chapel building almost opposite our house. He was in possession of a device called a Ripley Alarm, which indicated an advance warning of an approaching air raid, maybe fifteen to twenty minutes before the siren sounded. This device was something like an over-sized shoebox with a bell or buzzer and lots of wires inside, and it had to be plugged in to a power point. It lay on the floor beside my parents' bed and at the first buzz mum and dad were up and dressed within minutes. Dad had to go the Wardens' Post and muster his 'troops,' whilst mum and I would go down to our own air-raid shelter in the cellar.

As part of our war effort Dad decided to start keeping poultry in the back garden. A special allowance of corn could be claimed, pro rata to the number of friends and neighbours who had been persuaded to 'register' with us for their eggs. Of course this corn was not sufficient to satisfy the hens completely and had to be supplemented with adding all our potato and vegetable peelings along with any other scraps, which were boiled up daily and mixed into a mash. This was mum's job and became almost as important as making the main meal for her family each day.

An outer door from our cellar led to the back garden, basically an area of grass with a path leading to a small stone building, in past times the outside toilet, but after a little effort from dad, became a 'Des Res' for our family of chickens. It was complete with a long wooden perch and nesting boxes along one wall, each containing a deep cushion of straw and a ceramic egg, which I was told, made all the difference. Our feathered friends had the freedom of the entire garden, which had been fenced off to keep out any unwelcome intruders.

To say these birds were mere egg producers would be far from the truth. Be they White Leghorn, White Wyandotte or Rhode Island Red – each one quickly and firmly established itself as a family pet, recognised by name. Books on poultry keeping were avidly studied and the finding of the first tiny eggs alongside the larger pottery ones, when the pullets attained that certain age, was a real thrill. Charts were meticulously kept to record the production of Daisy, Maisie, Dolly, Mary and Betty (and numerous others whose names escape me) and any variance from what the textbooks said was the 'norm', had to be investigated. Maybe an addition to the diet was required and I recall permanganate of potash being put into their drinking water, though for the life of me, I can't remember what that was for.

However, it was soon to be discovered that the hens would have their problems, as well as we humans. Dad had to find solutions for soft-shelled eggs, in fighting, and the reason for the pecking of combs and wattles until the blood ran down. When one of the birds looked decidedly off colour, though showing no obvious reason for its malaise, Dad consulted our near neighbour, Mr Ellam. He'd been raised in the country and seemed to know instinctively about things rural – no need for textbooks. He gladly came to cast an eye over Flossie and declared she was crop bound. Sure enough, feeling through the cushion of feathers at the base of the neck was a hard packed crop about the size of a small tennis ball.

"No problem" said Mr Ellam, "Let's take her indoors and I'll deal with it."

He sat on a stool in the cellar with the bird firmly supported between his knees, and with a deft hand, smartly plucked out a few feathers over the crop. A razor blade made a small, neat incision through the outer skin and the wall of the crop, and before you could say 'Winston Churchill,' his finger had cleared out the offending mass. This was followed, equally quickly, by a neat stitching job, using a darning needle and linen thread from Mum's workbox, and in no time at all Flossie was back, running about the pen with her pals.

In due course, inevitably, our family of chickens became old hens and had to face the beckoning stew pot – but can you imagine how we all felt about the prospect? What may have been imagined as a very welcome addition to the meagre, weekly meat ration, became a possibility too awful to contemplate. Dad firmly declared there was no way he could bring himself to pull the neck of any of his charges, so once more had to call on the services of Mr Ellam. As for the prospect of a roast chicken dinner or chicken pies, our so-called registered customers had the benefit of those, as mum couldn't bear the thought of cooking and consuming members of her extended family.

Needless to say, the war was far from over and dad was committed to supplying eggs for some time to come, so had to decide how to augment the declining numbers of hens. Initially he had bought young pullets on the point of lay, but this time opted to buy day-old chicks, which needed to be kept in an incubator. This he had built himself and had experimented for some considerable time to ensure that the series of light bulbs under the dome, switched on in various combinations, could produce just the right temperature for the well being of the new chicks. The incubator was housed in our large attic and, as you may imagine, became the focal point for all the children in the district to visit after school. Out of a clutch of probably two dozen day-old chicks there were several weaklings which had to be weeded out and mercifully put out of their misery. Over ensuing years we did manage to become a little more detached and look on the poultry keeping more as a business. Dad got around to being able to kill, pluck and draw the birds when necessary, but I do not recall ever eating any of their flesh.

The whole experience could not have been a greater contrast from his job in engineering, where his company manufactured catering equipment – ovens and heated cabinets for the hotel and catering industry.

After the war it was good to see the back garden restored and to be able to buy our eggs at the local Co-op just down our street.

Charles Butland Horlock moved to Bournemouth

Diary of a Wartime Fireman

When war broke out we lived in London. The beloved father in law died suddenly. The mother in law was unable to cope with the shock/grief. "Could we come to Bournemouth" to help look after her and her little lad. We went and settled in.

So I had to do something. Obviously being young, fit and active I would be 'called up' soon enough – but I was not inclined to rush into uniform and get my head shot off. So I started by collecting rents for the family and painting/decorating – digging a bunker in the garden against air raid bombing – started an allotment to help with food rationing and got a job helping to build brick walls in front of windows to protect against 'bomb blast'.

In the evening I joined the Auxiliary Fire Service – went up to the fire station two or three nights a week 7pm to 7am. Here I received basic firefighting training and spent the remainder of the night in a car with big trailer pump behind at strategic points of our territory. The town was beginning to get the odd few bombs – but more important our baby was born.

Then came the official papers. Report to Southampton for a medical examination prior to call up. Thus a few days later in Southampton I found myself in a large building in what looked like a 'naturist convention'. Gangs of naked young men drifting around from one cubicle to another and soon I was one of them. Various doctors prodded and poked me and finally declared me fit A1. Dressed I was and then shunted to a room to meet a fat little chap, very ancient and dressed to kill in an army officer's uniform. He glanced at my record card and started asking a mass of personal questions. That done I told him I wanted to join "the Air Sea Rescue" boats.

"Can't do that " he said, they are recruited from the navy.

"So I will join the navy and get a transfer later," I offered.

"Navy is full up," he said.

So I opted for the Air Force and would hope to be a navigator.

"Air Force is full up," said he.

I began to dislike him.

Said he, "You will go in the army."

"Well," said I, "having worked in the big stores keeping stock of goods and being able to drive what about the Service Corps?"

"You will be sent to the first regiment that needs replacements," and so saying he bent to make a note. Disgusted I got off my seat and went out slamming the door.

Returning on the train my thoughts were black. I did not mind the prospect of fighting – I had as much chance as anyone. It was the idea of trailing across foreign lands, carrying a mass of heavy gear, shod like a horse in heavy great army boots. An idea struck - "Full time fireman." It would be a 'reserved occupation.' I would apply first chance, which I did and was accepted. Fatso was sunk without trace.

I was based in a fire station near Bournemouth. When Germany decided to bomb the western ports we became frontline troups overnight.

On a night in January 1941 I was awakened by the 'fire-bell' going full blast. Half asleep, I slipped on clothes and took my place in the 'Regional Car Unit,' which was kept in readiness for out of town work. Within minutes we were out of the station and heading east. Portsmouth had sent out a request for all help. Still a bit drowsy, I settled in the back of the car, with my colleague as our driver, heading east with all speed. The familiar bumping of our heavy trailer pump behind in our ears.

As we neared Portsmouth, the faint crump-crump of bomb explosions was eerily ominous. We were there and suddenly it came to reality. As we approached the fire area we were forced to reduce speed to bypass the craters in the road, the houses down and partly across the road. Finally, amidst a tangled web of hoses in the town center we located 'Control Headquarters.' Orders and directions received we left and arrived at our vicinity. Almost immediately we heard the high up whistling scream of a bomb shower coming down. Strange how one got the illusion they were directed straight for one's head. We immediately dived for cover. Straight under the pump I went and realized sickenly that my bottom half would not pass the narrow aperture. What a start for a tour of duty - a wounded posterior. However the bombs struck somewhere near and after the explosions and houses crashing down, somewhere round about, we were up and starting bearing our hoses on the immediate fires around us. It should be explained that with a five man crew, one was on the pump controlling the water pressure – two on the hoses, and the other two on a search and find for survivors in the burning and immediate houses. My first search was almost a disaster. The houses were well alight with incendiary bombs through the roof and a quick glance showed the stairs and bedroom impassable. So the ground floor rooms were searched starting from the back. Above could be heard the crashing of burnt supports etc. Coming to the last room, I looked in and stepping inside to make sure, down came the ceiling with plaster and burning timber alike. In a headlong dive my landing was under the table for shelter, but obviously this could only be temporary. Thus when the falling bits were finished - a quick lunge took me into the hall, which was full of smoke and darting flames from the burning stairway. This meant dropping flat and wriggling towards the door. Suddenly above my head came the swishing of a hose jet. Keeping my head down I finally scrambled clear of the house. Emerging thus, the fireman on the hose greeted me cheerily, "Didn't expect to see you again Charlie." Well I was accustomed to this rough humour and no doubt made some similar reply.

At some periods we exchanged roles and I did a fair amount of work on the hose, dousing immediately available fires. Normally many fires would persist until the houses were left as shells and our gains were marginal as the incendiary bombs were a fierce potential and in overwhelming numbers. Official figures estimated that nearly forty thousand bombs were dropped during our three-night stay. As the fires were spread further inland we moved with them.

One horrible fire we tackled gave off the most foul smells and I stood shoulder to shoulder with a colleague as we doused it with twin hoses. The fire colours were rainbow hued and the smoke very thick. It became increasingly difficult to see what was happening through the smoke. We conjectured it was a chemist shop and the drugs etc were producing the colours. We were interrupted by an agitated civilian behind us. "Come quick," he said "My house is on fire."

We told him that we had to dispose of the smelly nuisance in front of us first.

He replied "My pub will be lost if you are too late." (or words like that)

"Pub," we said "that's different." Two hoses rose in the fire lit night sky in twin parabolic arcs with a parallel symmetry, which would have brought joy to a drillmaster's heart. We concentrated our jets on his fire and soon it was out. We returned to our original fire. Later he dumped a crate half full of beer behind us as an expression of his gratitude.

Esme Hurn lived in Norfolk

The Bread Round

I left school in 1936 aged fourteen. My mother took me to apply for a situation as housemaid to an elderly couple who lived in a market town seven miles away. The lady of the house was severely disabled and I remember doing all the housework and cooking. Luckily, I had been to cookery classes while at school, plus my mother was a good cook, so her advice helped a lot. I had one half-day off a week, on which I cycled seven miles home to see my parents. My wage was five shillings per week. I later took a job as a shop assistant and again cycled daily seven miles there and home every night. At seventeen, I was admitted to hospital for an operation for varicose veins and was told on discharge "no more standing." My father told me to apply for a van driver's job locally, delivering bread to customers and also the baker took on a contract to supply the local army units with bread. My driving instructor put me through my paces and at the end of the first week I was asked if I could take five hundred loaves of bread to the Grand Hotel at Cromer, where troops were stationed. I did this, with a little anxiety and had no more driving lessons, I was on my own. I taught two other ladies to drive and did this work for four years. This entailed local bread delivery rounds to all surrounding villages and to the troops. My daily rounds consisted of carrying two large baskets; a deep one for an assortment of loaves and a flat one for cakes and flour. Owing to the weight of these baskets and the fact that, at seventeen, my bones had not fully developed, I now suffer from scoliosis of the spine and arthritis. However, I do not regret a single day of my wartime effort, it was hard work, washing the vans weekly inside and out and down to the chains on wheels in deep snow.

I was blessed with a love of music and played the accordion in our Village Hall for the weekly dances, where I met my husband to be, as he was stationed a few miles away. We were married in 1944 after which he was sent abroad - he was in the Household Cavalry - and was wounded and spent the rest of his army days in Windsor where I eventually joined him and I took a job in Timothy Whites in Windsor High Street. It turned out that my father and my husband's father were cousins, but that's another story!

Winnie Ponting lived in Chippenham

Tea and Sugar

During the war, the army used the area near where we lived for practice. One day a Bren gun carrier was tipped over and all the soldiers came into our kitchen. None were killed or injured but the diesel had spilt on them. We helped them to clean themselves up. As you know, we were on rations and the soldiers were very kind and gave us some of their tea and sugar mixed together as a thank-you for helping them.

Fred Bishop was attending Grammar School at Swanage

Trenches and Tea Duty

All of us that were available were rounded up to dig air raid shelters. This consisted of zigzag trenches across the end of the park adjacent to the school. The rain and the yellow clay soon made this a very sticky mess. The plan was simple. If the air raid warning sounded, all of the pupils would rush off in a more or less organised manner and disappear in to the trenches. Stretcher parties were organised and they went with their stretchers. I often thought that some two hundred and fifty children out in the open running to the trenches would have made a wonderful target for a wandering enemy aircraft. This system was soon abandoned when the enemy 'planes failed to materialise. Those cold wet trenches would certainly have killed more children than the enemy could have managed, I'm quite sure.

Some of us also joined the ARP – Air Raid Precautions. They needed boys on bicycles as messengers in case the telephones were knocked out. We worked in pairs and were issued with a siren which worked off the front wheel of the bicycle – 'only to be used in a responsible manner'- and a lamp glass showing an illuminated A.R.P. We felt quite important. During the height of the blitz we were kept busy although most of the time the enemy aircraft were overflying us on the south coast towards more interesting targets inland. On a typical night we were in bed by 8pm, wakened by the sirens at 10.30pm and off to the ARP post. Then Lofty (my partner) and myself set off together to wake the old and deaf people and put their kettles on for them, then went round again to make their tea. Then we reported back to the ARP post before going out on patrol again. When the All Clear was sounded at about 4.30am we went back home to bed, then up again in time for school. This went on, day in day out and the only break we had was when the weather was bad enough to keep the enemy aircraft on the ground.

Sheelagh Aranha recalls her mother in Essex

Ice Cream

In 1940, dad was sent off to war leaving mum to be a 'one parent' to us three children for six years. I will always be proud of my mum. In our village she was always known as 'Chappie' (Mrs Chapman). We lived on the coner of Barror Hill Road, where the bus turned round – some children still had a mile or more to walk home. Mum used to cycle five miles to Garon's fishmongers in Southend and buy a large block of clean ice. She brought it home on the child seat of her bike. Then, with custard powder, mashed potato and cream in an old butter churn, she would make delicious ice cream for all the kids that got off the bus.

On cold days the deep fryer was on the stove and every child had a newspaper cornet of hot chips to keep their hands warm.

These simple things meant a lot to those children.

Jeremy Woods grew up in Uganda

The War Effort

In 1941 I was eight-years-old and living in Uganda, where I was born. HMS Hood was my favourite battleship and I was devastated when she was sunk. I heard the news when the family was staying with friends on the shores of Lake Victoria – there was no electricity, a car battery powered the radio.

I had to do something for the war effort. I had two Ugandan shillings saved in my post office Lock Box so I persuaded my father to finance the cost of a postal order for 2/-, which I sent to Winston Churchill under a covering letter, helped by my mother.

I received the following reply to the parting of my worldly wealth:

23rd February 1942

Dear Jeremy Woods,

I am writing on behalf of the Prime Minister to thank you most warmly for the 2s. which you have sent him to help buy a new battle ship. The money is being passed on to the Chancellor of the Exchequer.

Yours truly,

(signed E M Watson)

The reply was enclosed in a '10 Downing Street' envelope. It is astounding that Number 10 had the time or inclination to write at that time!'

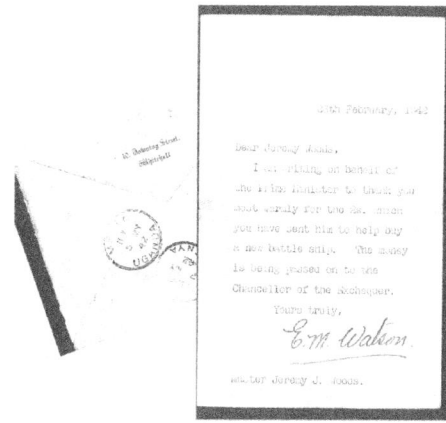

Jeremy Wood's letter

John Scrivens recalls life in Devon

The 'Arethusa'

As a fourteen-year-old in 1942, I saw the film 'In which we serve.' I left the cinema feeling that I would like to make the Royal Navy my future. Boy service then started at fifteen and half years old. In the meantime, how could I get in to the navy before then? 'Arethusa' was one way, though there were several other training ships in being at that time.

So I wrote off to the London head office of the Shaftesbury Homes and subsequently found myself in a sailor's uniform bound for Salcombe, in Devon with eight other boys. There were one hundred boys in training with an adult staff of six. The discipline was hard but fair, the food was … we always felt hungry!

The daily routine was run like a naval ship. Boys were able to go ashore on Saturday and Sunday afternoons. In the eighteen months that I spent there I had lots of good times and some not so good. The overriding memory was the build up of the US forces prior to D-Day. Landing craft and men arrived each day, all destined for Omaha beach where they suffered heavy losses. Most of all was the sight of the invasion fleet seen from the top of 'Bolt Head,' ready to go the next day. Hundreds of ships as far as the eye could see – battleships, cruisers, landing craft, destroyers, etc. I remember thinking to myself, "I wonder how many will return and how many will not survive?"

Joyce Watson was stationed in Portsmouth

The King's Visit

In June 1944 I was an 18-year-old Wren stationed near Portsmouth as a radio operator at the combined ops communications headquarters.

Shortly after D-Day King George V1 was coming to visit and a few hours before he was due, the officer of the day (male) did an inspection, we all had to stand up and raise our skirts to show we were wearing issue knickers.

At the time we did not think anything of this, the phrase sexual harassment was not in our vocabulary 60 years ago.

(Is it too late to sue?)

Kathleen Dicker remembers 'Doing Her Bit'

The Women's Land Army

I joined the Women's Land Army as a volunteer as soon as I was old enough, at eighteen. Women's calling up age was actually twenty but most of us were keen to do something and some of us even thought that the war might end before we had got into the thing, so we wasted no time. Training was non-existent, you picked it up as you went along. Looking back, I realise this could be quite dangerous as there were sharp tools and large animals to deal with. In fact, I did cut myself, fall around, etc. I was doing milking and general farm work and the men were showing me how to go about it (very patiently).

A lot of people imagine that we lived in hostels and went off to work in gangs. Most of us worked alone on our farms. The farmer was responsible for finding our lodging, the cost to us was one pound two and sixpence per week and this was full board. My first lodging was in a farm worker's cottage and it was basic. No bath, an outside loo. I was used to that, but the real problem was that my landlady was the world's worst housewife. Food was rationed, but if you were clever with it you could do satisfying meals. My landlady was able to cook well, but she did it all at the weekend and the rest of the week we starved. I lost a stone in weight and never felt good that first winter. I don't think anyone in that house washed unless they were going out! After eight months, I got transferred to another job and this time I lodged in the farm manager's house - super! The poultry farm where my sister worked had closed and she joined me at this new job where we were milking and doing general farm work again. But it was different. My first farm was run by a struggling farmer who economised in lots of ways. For example, I had to try to get my little calves on to artificial food too early, so they did less well. The whole herd had a bad attack of bovine ringworm and all the men got it too - I was the only milker to escape! My new farm was on an estate. There wasn't a shortage of money to do things as they should be done. We ate extra well because my new landlady traded things like onions with the soldier cooks and we got tins of pineapple and other delicacies in return. Her husband was also serving on the war agricultural committee - a body of experienced farmers appointed to go around the farms in their area to make sure that every tiny scrap of land was being utilised to the best advantage. They were not all that popular and I imagine sometimes they were passed the odd pheasant and piece of venison to look the other way when someone didn't want to plant any more potatoes. The biggest food joke was Woolton pies. Lord Woolton, the food minister, decided that, as land workers had no opportunity to eat in works canteens they must be given something extra apart from cheese. The result was pies issued weekly - dry pastry with gristly meat and veg in them. Warmed up with gravy they were edible if you were starving. I imagine the pigs had most to them. But it was a kind thought!

I think that forty-eight hours was probably a working week in the 1940s but farm work could be dawn to dusk in the summer. As a land girl, I had a half-day weekly, but this was put together to make one day off each fortnight, so that I could go off home. Saturday afternoon and Sunday were not working days on the land but since most of us were milkers or had animals to feed and look after, such time off meant very little. For me, Sundays had six hours solid work anyway and Saturday afternoons meant just a longer dinner hour when I could cycle in to town and do any shopping and change library books.

An interesting time thing was 'double summer time.' This was official and we all adjusted to it but some of the farmers made a fuss and said that the changes upset the cattle and they would work 'to the old time.' This was OK, so long as you bore in mind that things like buses and trains would be on the official time whatever you did individually. Otherwise it didn't matter, the sun was the important thing!

In about 1943, the Land Army girls had a rally in Windsor Great Park. We would have stalls and displays and wear our uniform. We practised our curtsies, only to be told that this was not suitable wearing trousers - we should stand still and call her "Ma'am" if she spoke to us. Beryl and I were given the job of serving HM because we had the longest service. When she arrived she had the princesses with her (wearing pink and looking rather bored). The Queen sailed up to our fancy goods store in hyacinth blue and with a lovely smile. She looked for something to buy and picked up the dressing table mats that I had made.

"Did you make these?"

I opened my mouth but no sound came. Meanwhile she asked a price.

"Three Guineas" said our lady organiser.

I was appalled! It was more than two week's wages!

The material was a four and sixpence remnant. The silks for the embroidering were still available and cost a few pence. But her Majesty had taken out a little purse, extracted some money and said very softly to her lady in waiting, "is this enough?"

"Didn't she understand money?" I thought, shocked.

I was well off during the war. Once I'd paid my lodging charge, all I needed was cash for railway fares on my days off, cinema tickets and little things like toilet things and cycle puncture repairs. These last were mostly used for patching gumboots, which I wore all the time when working. Only dairy working girls got them as part of their uniform and only the one pair when we joined. You could then buy second-hand ones from the Land Army stores, but after patching they always leaked and my feet were always damp, however many socks I wore. There was nothing to spend money on and I had £100 in my post office savings at the end of the war.

Land Army Girls

Mrs Marjorie Harvey also recalls the Land Army, in Kent

Nine Lives and the Land Army

I was on my way to school when the air raid siren went. I decided to return home in order to be with my mother. We had been evacuated from Medway to Faversham, in Kent - much nearer the coast! I got back home and sat in the lounge to do my homework with the cat sitting on my lap. We could hear the bombers droning overhead. Suddenly the cat got off my lap and lay down in the hall. For some reason, I followed him. I heard the first bomb come down - a noise like an express train followed by a crump. The next one could have my name on it but instead it landed opposite and the heavy ceiling under which I had been sitting crashed down. It was so heavy I surely would have been killed but my cat had saved my life!

My friend Phyl and I gave up any ideas we had of becoming air hostesses, pilots, top line models or going to university and decided to give any local farmers the benefit of our talents! Why the Land Army? Mainly because in my case I am a fresh air fiend and would rather be outdoors than in at any time. Perhaps that is the reason the garden is in better shape than the house.

Anyway, Phyllis and I took the plunge and signed on. That part is rather hazy as I am not sure what form this took but obviously the most important statistic was height. Being of stock size and weight I did quite well uniform wise but my friend, although being the same weight, was tall and thin therefore the breeches hung in folds giving the appearance of a saggy elephant. It is surprising however what can be achieved with a sewing machine and she soon had them licked into shape. Needless to say like most of our contemporaries, when working in the fields, up trees, on threshing machines etc, our most popular forms of apparel were the cool airtex blouses, green sweaters and dungarees. In the summer, our breeches were hacked off well above the knees to become not the most elegant of shorts. Our stout shoes weighed a ton but were most comfortable when 'broken in' and our feet had become adjusted to them after court shoes and we rarely suffered from aching feet although we were on them most of the day.

Our outward appearance changed considerably as we were out in all weathers. Our hair became straw coloured and like it in texture and our skin mahogany. Incidentally our blood became quite black and we saw quite a lot of it as we frequently hacked ourselves with billhooks or stuck forks through our feet. We certainly became very healthy but also very tired. It took us about two months to stay awake after 7pm and our social life was about nil. Phyl and I were assigned to a small farm, owned by an army major, where there were only two permanent labourers to whom we were a constant source of amusement. We were either told things that would horrify us or not told anything which would have been to our advantage. Wherever we went we had to suffer the usual comments with variations e.g. "That pig is climbing on the other pig's back to look over the wall."

One day we had to be involved in building a huge bonfire on to which the men took great delight in throwing anything that came to hand such as rats, hedgehogs and nests with baby birds in them no matter whether they were dead or alive. On another occasion we were wheeling barrow loads of rubbish from 'a to b' singing to keep our spirits up and in our path was a deep ditch which, being covered with weeds, we couldn't see. Our labouring associates of course knew of its whereabouts. Somehow Phyl managed to negotiate it but realised it had gone quiet at the back. She eventually found me in the ditch with my head in a bunch of stinging nettles. We could hear our co-workers laughing behind a hedge.

We went home one weekend having made up our minds never to return. I rang up another farmer near our major to ask if he needed any land girls. He obviously thought he was speaking to our representative.

"I do want some girls Miss Foster" he answered, "but not the two who worked for Major 'B', they're far too lazy."

I hung up saying I would look into the matter.

Meanwhile, as we lived in Kent, which had a large farming community, a local farmer who knew we had joined the Land Army had called on my mother to see if we were looking for a job. We were and started the following week, he having decided we looked reasonably fit. Luckily he didn't ask for references.

Once again we had to start with all the mundane jobs such as hoeing, muck spreading etc, but as there were about six other land girls on this farm the days went quickly. There are few better things than walking through the dewy grass in a cherry orchard midst the sheep and lambs in the early morning sun. However, there can also be few worse jobs when the weather is freezing than chopping the tops off wurzles or cutting brussel sprouts off their stalks. Frequently our hands stuck to the knives with the cold and tears poured down our cheeks with the pain. Another particular 'fun' job was trying to light a bonfire with a heap of wet sticks and a few matches. Occasionally one or other of the farm labourers would take pity on us and light it with <u>one</u> match.

My friend eventually found the life too hard for her and transferred to working in a munitions factory and gradually all the other girls left for various reasons. I was living at home with all the attendant comforts so it was easier for me. I was given the opportunity to drive, first of all the tractor, none of which in those days was equipped with a self starter or a cabin. There's nothing quite equal to starting a tractor with a starting handle about 6.30 on a winter's morning (remembering to keep your thumb the right side as they certainly had a kick) to warm you up.

I had quite a few exciting moments. One day I was digging between the pear trees in an orchard with a caterpillar tractor, looking behind to make sure I was not touching the trees (there would be trouble if I tore any bark) and I felt a pressure on my chest. A hefty branch was pushing me down, forcing my hands and feet off the controls but the tractor continued to go foward (it seemed like a horror film as I thought no one was near and my neck would be broken). I screamed and amazingly, from behind one of the trees came one of the workmen who had been pruning. He threw the tractor out of gear and I was never so pleased to see anyone in my life. On another occasion I was knocked off a Fordson tractor in the same sort of circumstances and broke an arm this time. I also got smothered with tar oil spray when carting this commodity to the men who were spraying the trees. No protection was ever provided for any of us. I felt alight for several days and looked Chinese, my skin was so yellow. My poor mum became resigned to the fact that I would frequently be brought home in all sorts of conditions. One of the pleasures for me was that, as my boss was lame and the hunter he was riding learnt a trick of getting close to a tree and knocking him off, he used to allow me to exercise this high flyer while he drove the tractor. Also like most farmers in those days he hated all paper work so he built an office on the farm where I could attend to it all, which was particularly pleasant in the winter. As I was the only land girl there then, there was no jealousy.

I was also taught to drive a car and a lorry. Certainly it was easier in those days as the traffic on the road was minimal. It was a pleasure to drive then and one only needed a provisional licence, in fact on the second day I got into the lorry I was told to pick up fifteen sailors from a nearby camp to come and work on the farm. With shaking hands and feet I did this, telling the navy this was only the second time out. "Blimey miss, we're walking back," they said. I also had to collect German and Italian prisoners of war (at different times) from various camps. There was never any thought that I should have somebody else with me. Out of all the work forces we had and there were many, the Germans worked the hardest and if I ever had any trouble with car, lorry or tractor they would fix it for me.

Rona Reardon Smith shares some of her sister's memories from Birmingham

Extracts from a letter written by Rona's sister, who was a probationer nurse at the Queen Elizabeth Hospital in Birmingham in the days following the evacuation from Dunkirk in May 1940

It will no doubt be some days before I finish this letter so I shouldn't take over much notice of the date at the top.

We will begin in the evening of the evacuation, the actual date of which I don't remember.

Everything had gone on as normal throughout the day – I had had a morning off so was on duty in the evening. About 6pm the RSO plus registrars did a round with Sister and said that we may have to evacuate some patients to make room for some casualties.

At 7pm I went to supper with one other nurse. In this we proved lucky as no one else had any supper that night.

At 7.10 a phone message came that the whole hospital was to be evacuated and to be prepared for five hundred wounded soldiers from Dunkirk. All those already decided on and all others that the Houseman thought could go were therefore bundled onto stretchers and wheeled off to Casualty. Our ward had thirty-two beds. We had at the time I think two or three empty beds - three admissions that afternoon. They were given their clothes and sent home. All patients who got up had to send for friends, clothes etc, and pack up and go. Those to be operated on the following day were given their clothes and told to get up. There were others sent home, one woman I remember who had had radical amputation of breast and had had her stitches out that day, had to walk out. A private patient having deep X-ray treatment for inoperable carcinoma of the abdomen was packed off. Having eliminated the possible evacuees we were left with about ten patients, who had to be packed off to other wards.

We had been given forty-eight hours notice of the arrival of the soldiers. It seemed longer than that. The following morning there was a move round of some of the nurses. All the foreign nurses were put on civilian wards. That day we cleaned and trotted from ward to ward trying to find our patients and doing their dressings. It was chaos! All the patients were under different doctors and the Sisters had no idea what was the matter with them half the time. Somehow the time passed until the night and the forty-eight hours were up.

They started arriving just after 2am. Each patient was examined rapidly and labelled. Red, dangerously ill etc. Officers, yellow, according to wards they were to go to. At 2.30am every nurse in the home was knocked up and either told to get up or go back to bed again. Damn silly as no one is at their best at two in the morning having worked till 10.30pm the night before. At 6am, when we were called again, I looked out of my window and there was an ambulance train creeping along in the semi-darkness and the bus loads unloading at the casualty entrance. You got a cold mesmeric feeling.

Well at 7am we went on duty as usual. On West 1, the whole of the big ward was full and I think about two outside. We walked down the centre of the ward and on every bed were lain men in various clothes from womens' knickers, soaking dungarees, to full uniforms. Some were fit enough to 'cooee,' but most were in such a state that they just lay. Sister set us to bed-bath. We had three nail brushes between us which had to be passed round. First of course you asked them where they were hurt and then proceeded as best you could to undress them. We usually had two to undress two patients then we separated and washed a patient each, then joined again for the backs and beds. Their clothes for the most part had to be cut off. Their pockets were full of sand, their feet blistered and sore. After a bit of breakfast was given out they just drank and drank. They would wake up and ask for a drink and by the time you had got it they were asleep again. And Bottles! Many of them used two bottles at first. On being asked when they had last had their bowels open the answer was "somewhere in France." After breakfast Mr Ward came to do a round with dozens of students, Housemen, and others. For this, every field dressing had to be removed. This was Hell. Two nurses and two students each with a trolley went round taking dressings then two nurses followed up doing the treatment ordered. Every dressing was stuck. Field dressings are thick pads, which you place on and bandage. They have some antiseptic quality. As each patient had at least three wounds it took some time - some of course you couldn't move.

One sailor had his arm sticking out and to touch that made him scream, so he was taken straight to theatre. Then two Frenchmen were black from the waist up with burns from swimming hours in burning oil. One boy aged nineteen had two legs black with gangrene - and a hundred other dreadful things. One youth - very handsome - aged twenty-seven, married with a child had a hole in his shoulder so big you could get both fists in, and when the dressing was removed we found it crawling with maggots. He said he could feel them crawling about. The smell was so awful you had to burn cones in the room. His wife never left him. Another had his buttock blown away so that the sciatic nerve could be seen. Well you could go on forever as we had three hundred and fifty of them in finally, I think. The last lot we were expecting to make up the five hundred were sunk coming over.

The whole of that day we worked non-stop with no off duty until 9pm taking endless patients to X-ray and theatre. Then, a day after the first convoy, the second arrived at about dinnertime - so we started all over again. I know during the whole week we hardly had any off duty.

On Sunday in the evening the church bells rang for evensong while I was taking the temperatures. It was marvellous. One of them looked up and said "I say Thirwell, it's a long time since we heard them things." It was the last Sunday that they rang, so it will be a long time before they hear them again.

Well for a few of the cases: There was a boy with shell shock. He lay in bed for three days before he came round, it may have been longer. If you went to him he didn't see you, just looked glassily through you and murmured all the time "guns." He was young and when he was better and was given his uniform to go out he was absolutely TERRIFIED. Another I took to theatre had a fractured left humerus and fractured femur. By the time they had excised the arm you could see right through it. Mr Allen packed it with vaseline gauze and put it in plaster and left it to stew in its own juice. The leg was put on extension. He had two haemorrhages from the arm, was a dreadful patient to nurse because not only was he all pinned up, but also he used to swear and curse as though you did it for fun. The youth with the shoulder died. He went to theatre to have it cleared up and had intravenous blood etc and covered the theatre with maggots. He suffered terribly and was super conscious. He had enormous doses of morphine and had to have a male attendant in the end he was so restless with the pain. The boy with the legs had a double amputation. For three days he had a drip in the arm, and for a week at least his stumps were irrigated with Eusol without the knowledge of his having his legs off. He raved for days and then took on suicidal tendencies when he knew he had no legs. He used to ask us to move his legs and swear at us for not doing it, and for pretending to when he knew they had not been moved. After amputation you can feel your limbs.

One boy - about twenty-five - had a bomb explode in his face; he was unrecognisable. He was peppered with bits and absolutely unable to open one eye at all and the other only after seven days he could just open. He had two enormous gashes in his head, one so big it had to be stitched with two enormous sutures, all septic. He suffered agonies. He was a darling because he always looked - this was not in the normal method, 'looking' to him was listening - to see which nurse was coming to do his dressing, and when it was me he felt relieved because I was so gentle! He got better in about nine months and went out looking most respectable and with his sight. It was a week before he could see the colour of his blanket and a fortnight before he really saw the ward.

Well to get back to what happened on that first day. Every patient had an intramuscular injection of anti-Tetanus serum. Tetanus is a bacteria, which causes certain muscular contraction, and nervous trouble like lockjaw - this is Tetanus. Also an intermuscular injection of anti-Gas Gangrene. Every person having a dirty wound is given these two injections. Every patient was then given four tablets of M and B 693, a preparation of Sulphanilamide, the new drug - and then on two tabs every four hours. This drug must have saved 90% of the lives.

Well, after the first few weeks things began to settle a bit and they began to wake up. There was of course the round of dressing when great holes had to be packed and they just gripped the bed and bore the pain. Then the plaster cases (all fractures, etc) were put in one ward. The smell was dreadful; when they sat up there was a squelch of the puss in the plaster. When they got really too high, about once a fortnight their plasters were changed. Several of them died unfortunately. One man had a crushed foot I think it was, and he got a clot of blood in one of his vessels. One morning he was laughing as usual, and then when asked to lift up in the middle it moved the clot into his heart and he crumpled up and died.

Then of course they started to get naughty. You would give them a thermometer and when you turned round you would find they had put it in their pipe and were smoking it! They had unending tricks and always called you darling, etc.

There isn't really much more to tell. Of course they all had their souvenirs. One man had a doll for his little girl wrapped up in a bloody bit of paper, another had some coins, a piece of paper etc. They were all brave and nearly all swore worse than miners. But often if one swore at a nurse another would tick him off after she had gone. They were the grandest men from all over England, Scotland, Ireland and Wales. As conceited as you like, as noisy and impossible as you can imagine, but we all miss them. Fred Turner - a sailor - wrote to me the other day and told me how very happy he had been. Those that were in for six to nine months began to get very depressed and difficult but you cannot blame them …

Audrey Mason also recalls her nursing days in Sheffield

Maggots and Lost Buttons

At the time of D-Day I was nursing in the Sheffield General Hospital. All the military hospitals in England were full and they asked General Hospitals to allocate beds for the wounded. We allocated a whole block of sixty beds. On the nights we were informed that the convoys were coming in, the nurses had to work from 2am and all through the following day. Our first priorities were to get the casualties cleaned and fed and then seen by medical staff. Then to put on fresh dressings on wounds as those they had on were put on in field hospitals and probably had been on for days.

When plasters on fractured arms and legs were removed, they were often full of maggots but the wounds were clean, as the maggots had eaten all the pus. Then the trek to theatre started with many having deep embedded shrapnel removed.

At one stage all the POW hospitals were full as well so we had Germans down one side of the wards and British on the other, with a German SS officer in a side ward. There was never any trouble between them as the Germans were young just like our boys and didn't ever want a war. They showed us photos of their families and one had even been in the Luftwaffe and bombed London, under orders.

There was a continual movement of forces and as soon as beds became available in the military hospitals, they were moved on and we admitted other convoys.

As they usually stayed only a few weeks in our hospital, their uniform and kit was kept on a huge landing on the first floor. When it was time for the SS officer to be moved all of his buttons and medals had been cut off of his uniform. Nobody admitted to the theft and as many of them were walking wounded, it could just have easily been one of the German boys as they hated the SS men.

Jeannette Howell moved to Cheltenham

Nursing and Nurseries

In 1944 when I was eighteen, I joined the Civil Nursing Reserve. We were Nursing Auxiliaries and our blue uniform dresses had NA in red on the front. Being an Army family, I felt I wanted to do some war service. We were from all walks of life and I remember a store buyer and a ballet dancer. We had two weeks initial training in Devizes Hospital seeing operations and learning basics. Particularly memorable was a hilarious bed-bath which I gave to a wounded Italian prisoner of war who knew no English and I had no Italian.

I was sent to Sunnyside in Cheltenham, two big houses converted into a maternity hospital, not to nurse the wounded soldiers as I had envisaged! My two years there were the hardest work I have ever done - endless stairs as wards were up and nurseries down and we washed the nappies in the basement. Mums had two weeks in hospital then and didn't get up until their eighth day. Discipline was strict and some sisters terrifying. Matron was a stern, upright Plymouth Brethren lady who did her share of nursing. We had patients evacuated from the London bombing, local ladies and single girls with American boyfriends and babies. Before the birth Matron employed some as domestics and I remember trays being balanced on 'bumps.' They and we lived in nearby large houses and on night duty nurses had to go round with a torch and check that the 'girls' were in. After the births many went to homes for unmarried mothers since there was no other financial support for them.

Night duty was hectic. One night we delivered eight babies with two midwives and two auxiliaries on duty. There were Caesarian operations and forceps deliveries. Premature babies survived despite basic incubators. The smallest I remember was two and a half pounds. Despite the almost slave labour there was great camaraderie amongst the night staff. When we had time, we told stories of our lives and of our men folk away fighting. Because of the common purpose in wartime there was for so many people a sense of working together. I have a special memory too of a Christmas Eve with nurses in cloaks with candles going round the wards singing carols.

After only about a month at Sunnyside an infection caused it to close to new patients. I was sent, alone, to a remote old manor house five miles away where patients convalesced or awaited delivery, but now we had to take deliveries there. A sweet little Sister had coped alone and after I'd been there a week another midwife was sent, but meanwhile Sister and I were alone. I did night duty and called her when delivery was imminent. New patients from London were received into the huge, stone-flagged hall with a vast fireplace.

My nights there were awesome. Apart from receiving new patients I had regularly to go from my base in the Aga-warmed kitchen to check on mums and babies. Wards were small, pretty rooms and the nursery had mostly only drawers for babies to sleep in. As I remember, there was some problem between Sister there and Matron so that we had no cots or nappies, just drawers and rolls of lint!

No one had told me that the owner still lived in a top floor flat of the requisitioned Hall. On one of my solitary rounds I saw her in the panelled corridor with two greyhounds on leads. She didn't speak and I, fed on stories of the resident ghost, felt I had seen one! There were even wallabies in large enclosures in front of the Hall!

Bert Triggs in Portsmouth chose to join the army

Stains and the 'King's Shilling'

I joined up on the 2nd of September 1944. About thirty of us assembled at the recruiting office in Portsmouth for despatch to Chatham, the Royal Engineers depot, via Winchester. Railway tickets were issued and we were soon on our way to join His Majesty's Forces. At Winchester barracks we were 'sworn in', taking allegiance to the crown and received the 'King's Shilling' to seal the oath. They gave us dinner before we left – I can still remember the pudding; prunes and custard – and escorted us back to the railway station to continue our journey to Chatham. Eventually we arrived at our destination to find that we had to walk a further four miles to the barracks. It was a tired and thirsty party of new recruits that walked through the gates, filled with a mix of excitement and trepidation as we considered what lay before us.

Next day we were kitted out with our uniforms. Our 'civvie' clothes were parcelled up to be posted home; the end of our boyhood days.

We were required to attain a high standard of Drill, or 'square bashing.' Unfortunately, I was kicked in the knee by an army boot within the first few days and spent the next four weeks recovering in hospital. On returning to the barracks I found that all of my 'entry' had passed out and had begun their trade training. By this time my reputation has somehow caught up with me and I was drafted to the 'football section'. All of the best footballers were included in the same section to ensure that we had a reasonable chance of performing well in competition. I played in the team for three years, the highlight of which was finishing Runners Up in the Army Cup.

One of our 'chores' was changing the sheets on our beds; a task performed every two weeks. In the morning we bundled the dirty sheets up and left them in a pile before going off to our workshops. On our return, fresh sheets were waiting. We collected our sheets and proceeded to make up our beds. They were of a flax type material and not particularly soft. I opened my sheets to find that they appeared not to have been washed and were badly stained. I reported this to the NCO in charge. He quietly took me aside and informed me that all the sheets were the same. They had been washed but the stains were the evidence of the 'wet dreams' of previous users. I was horrified but had to accept the situation as normal! My sheltered upbringing had not exposed me to anything like this before. Some time later, cotton sheets were issued and the stain problem disappeared with proper laundering.

Roy Cox spent some time in Leeds

The Glasshouse

Being posted to a holding company around the winter of 1944, we were just hanging around Leeds waiting for a posting somewhere, possibly to Burma. One morning, five privates and myself were told to report to a regimental police corporal who would allocate us to do jobs. One private and I were given red armbands with R.P. on in black, told to parade the streets nearby and pull up any soldier who was improperly dressed. We had been pulled up ourselves many times so now it was our turn. We saw three sergeants coming towards us, hats under their epaulets. This was it, our revenge time. We walked over to them our armbands thrust forward, we were in charge.

"Put your hats on sergeants", we said, with what we thought was great authority. They looked at us with disbelief. They shouted something which roughly translated meant "Please go away you silly young fools." My mate and I looked at each other, then did as they requested and went and hid in a café for a cup of tea.

Next day we were assigned to the 'Glasshouse' for a day's duty. We knocked on the huge wooden gate which was opened by a police sergeant who made us double (run) everywhere. We were feeling quite annoyed, we hadn't done anything wrong but were made to feel we were being punished. Eventually, we were ordered into the prisoners' area. Here we were lined up, one to each cell. Each cell door was opened in turn and the other four guys got a prisoner handcuffed to them. I thought to myself, "I hope mine is OK." To my horror, the man I got was around fifteen stone and about six feet two inches tall. I was only five feet nine and under nine stone. I was supposed to take <u>him</u> for a walk round the exercise yard where in fact, <u>he</u> took me!

I and the other RPs were so relieved when we were told to 'double' to the big door and get back to the outside world.

Lionel Barnett recalls an incident at Henley-on-Thames

Painful!

In 1940 I was a Gunner, serving in the 35th Searchlight Regiment. We were based just outside Henley-on-Thames. I remember being on the Henley site for many reasons. One astounding thing was that we had a London taxi cab, complete with civilian driver stationed with us. We used the taxi for moving sandbags around the site and other chores. The main reason he was there though was to take us soldiers to any spot locally where enemy paratroopers were reported to have landed. At that time we feared invasion and everyone was on the alert. The wireless was constantly keeping us on our toes twenty-four hours a day. This unfortunately resulted in many false alarms; people were reporting paratroopers landing everywhere. Fear does a lot to your imagination. That was the atmosphere that we were operating in. Although I was in uniform in a strange area to me, more than once a civilian deliberately sent me in the wrong direction or refused to help.

Us young soldiers had to standby around the searchlights and sound locators from dusk to dawn beside other daytime duties and on two-hour guards; we were always tired. We were supposed to have twenty-four hour's leave every week but it seldom happened. However, I did get ten days leave in June and returned to the camp on July 1st 1940. I reported to the sergeant and he told me to get some sleep, as I would be on standby that evening. I went to my hut to find another soldier asleep in my bed. There were no other beds available so I ended up sleeping just inside the door of another hut on a trestle table. I next remember being woken by another soldier saying I would have to go and round up some enemy parachutists that had been reported. We lined up quickly and ran towards our transport, the London taxi. I remember an order being shouted about loading our rifles, next thing I know I felt a terrible burning pain in my left buttock and the forced pressure of hurtling to the ground made worse by my running towards the taxi. The cause of all this was a double mistake by a fellow soldier who unfortunately pulled the trigger and failed to point the muzzle to the sky. The bullet, after passing through me struck the twin tyres on the generator vehicle, puncturing both. I learned this later. At the time I was laid on my back and my left buttock felt that it was on fire. I was only eighteen at the time and quite able to stick it, luckily I didn't suffer from shock. I recollect the sergeant putting a field dressing on the wound – we all carried one in a pocket on our battledress. I didn't lose much blood because I was only a few feet away and the blast from the barrel of the rifle burned at the same time as the bullet hit me, I must have been lucky. A military ambulance was not available and after some time I was told that a civilian ambulance was on its way. I was eventually lifted on to a stretcher and somehow got to the ambulance, which took me to the Henley-on-Thames Memorial Hospital. I had to have an operation to stick up the wound. I was told later that it was a new operating theatre opened that day and I was the first patient. Whether that's a fact or not I don't know.

So I have a painful reason to remember July 1st every year!

John Chambers lived in Derby

Railway Experiences

One evening I was sitting in the cinema in Derby when the screen showed a message 'All troops report to barracks now.' The cinema manager slapped us on the back and said, "Get home safely" and gave us a free ticket. We had no wireless so did not know what was happening but knew it must be serious to call us so urgently. I thought, "If I'm going to France tomorrow I am going to have some chips tonight - they might be the last chips I will have."

We were not going to France but soldiers were returning from Dunkirk. We had to erect tents for the returners, carry blankets and prepared a meal. What a dreadful sight! The soldiers had not washed for a week; they were covered in oil and could hardly walk. They slept for twelve hours, were given new uniforms and sent home on leave. Imagine the surprise of the cinema manager when we turned up to claim our free seats!

The Germans caught us half asleep one breakfast time. A lone raider plane came overhead (it was the first time this had happened). He was looking for the Rolls Royce factory but the roof had been painted to look like a forest so he let the bomb drop any old where. If he had had a magnet he could not have been more successful - it dropped on our quartermaster's stores and killed the occupants. About this time we went on a route march outside Derby, sleeping in the open with our blankets. We saw the bombs falling on Derby and later heard of the civilian casualties. The soldiers had escaped. One time we were not so lucky. We heard the sirens and got into our hand dug trenches. I thought, "I am not standing in four inches of rain water" so I crawled back into bed. I woke up next morning surrounded by shrapnel that had come through the tent. Several sergeants in the next field were killed, others were injured. Men were coughing and sneezing - but not me.

We moved to Melbourne near Derby. I had sentry duty at the home of the former Prime Minister. The Methodist ladies darned our socks.

Another soldier -Williamson - joined us from the same school as me. I said "Stick with me and I will show you what to do."

We were taking a trainload of empty coal wagons ten miles to Ashby-de-la-Zouch colliery and returning with eighteen loads of coal which was the maximum allowed on a falling gradient. The Sergeant Major said he was a man short and so Williamson would have to take the train himself. Williamson explained that he had only arrived that day and could not do it as he did not know the line. He was taken to the Officer for disobeying an order but the Officer agreed with Williamson.

"No man can take a train where he has never been - case dismissed."

It made the Sergeant Major look foolish. Not long afterwards there was a notice of soldiers going to France and Williamson's name was there.

Next we went to Horbury near Wakefield. Horbury was famous for a vicar, the Reverend Baring Gould, who wrote the hymn 'Onward Christian Soldiers.' We had a chaplain who said, "You can have any hymn you like except that one. I am fed up of hearing it."

We moved to Stranraer in the Scottish borders - from a good town to the worst. We were half way up a mountainside, in rusty Nissen huts with peeling paint. We arrived with ballast, sleepers and rails and in eighteen months had to construct ten miles of main line and one hundred miles of sidings. Westinghouse built two proper signal boxes. The Sergeant Major said, "You, you, and you go and learn signalling."

We were three miles from the town and only had transport on Saturdays and Sundays. Each day we would sit in the NAAFI after work and learn the rules of signalling. No wonder we all passed. So in Stranraer I took charge of my first signal box - the career I was to follow for the rest of my working life. From Stranraer I went to Bicester, Westbury, Sandwich and Southampton. After Southampton I went to Arromanches then Caen. Here the cathedral only had broken windows whilst everywhere else was flattened. At Calais the RAF bombed us thinking they were over Dunkirk.

I went to Lille in France and Nimegan in Holland. By this time the war was over but discharge did not occur immediately. We were employed taking trainloads of potatoes from Brunswick to Spandau-Berlin. We did not control the trains but had to guard the potatoes to stop thefts.

On my last day in Germany I remember a party of schoolgirls in a park singing Brahms' Cradlesong. It was a beautiful memory of normal home life after the horror of separation and war.

I returned home to get to know a five-year-old daughter and an eighteen-month-old son and renew acquaintance with my wife after six years away serving my country.

The 1940s - Month by Month

1946
January
- The Bank of England was nationalised
- The first aircraft took off from Heathrow airport
- The United Nations held its first session in London

February
- The first electronic calculator was introduced by IBM, the forerunner of the computer

March
- Winston Churchill warned of 'an Iron Curtain' descending across Europe
- Details of the new National Health Service were announced

April
- The Grand National was run for the first time since the war and was won by 'Lovely Cottage'

May
- A joint Anglo US report recommended the partition of Palestine to create a Jewish homeland and refuge for victims of Nazi persecution

June
- A referendum in Italy voted in favour of a Republic, effectively ending the Italian Monarchy
- The 'Bikini' swimming costume was shown for the first time

July
- The US carried out atomic bomb tests on Bikini atoll in the Pacific Ocean

August
- Civil war broke out in China between the communists and the nationalists

September
- Football League matches were held for the first time since the war

October
- Ten Nazi war criminals were executed after being found guilty of war crimes at the Nuremberg trials
- Muffin the Mule first appeared on BBC TV

November
- The Biro went on sale

December
- MPs voted to nationalise the railways and the ports

The View From Over the Water

Joan Thompson lived in South Africa

The 'Dookling'

I grew up in South Africa and the way that we experienced the war was, of course, very different from those of people who lived in the British Isles. One of my earliest memories is of the evacuees who were sent out to the safety of Cape Town. There were always several in the class with me and I can remember our singing teacher had to ban 'The White Cliffs of Dover' as the entire class would be in floods of tears. We were so sorry for the poor little mites who, in two cases, had been blown through walls in the East End of London. Post was, of course, erratic but the evacuees had a monthly radio link with their parents in the UK. My parents were strict but those radio link nights were sacrosanct and I would not go to bed until I'd heard the complete broadcast.

Living in a large seaport we had many convoys passing through and my family was one who opened their home to the troops and sailors passing through. They'd be shown the sights of the Cape Peninsula and come to us for meals. I well remember two soldiers from northern England who had not long been evacuated from Dunkirk. On route for the beaches they had given a small Belgian girl some chocolate and she had given them a 'dookling.' The duckling arrived safely in England and grew up very happily on a farm in the north of England!

Of course, there were many people who did not think we should have anything to do with 'England's War.' When the two-minute pause was introduced at noon there would be all sorts of goings on to disrupt the silence. My father did duty as a special constable, wielding a truncheon against these agitators. I'm afraid he enjoyed it hugely!

The sailors at the naval base at Simonstown had a Great Dane called Nuisance who was a law unto himself. He travelled into Cape Town by train all by himself and would really have a go at anyone trying to disrupt the two-minute silence.

We could see all the shipping movements from our balcony on Signal Hill but it was "don't talk about ships or shipping." The exception was the Queen Mary, which was just too large to enter the harbour and had to anchor outside – everyone knew when she arrived in Cape Town!

Pat Barham recalls the WAAF

The Opera and the 'Hund'

As soon as I was eighteen, I volunteered to join the WAAF and I was called up on the 10th October 1941. I was posted to HQ Balloon Command at Stanmore which was not very exciting, but one incident sticks in my mind. I went out with another girl, much more sophisticated than I was, to the local pub, which was filled with Polish soldiers. Two of them shared our table and it was arranged (by the other girl) that they should escort us home in the blackout. As soon as we were outside, she attached herself to one of the men and instantly managed to lose the other two of us in the dark streets. Then the moon came out and my companion suggested that we walk back via Stanmore Common. Even a twelve-year-old today would have enough sense to refuse, but those were more innocent days and I was more naïve than most.

At the top of the common we sat on a tree-trunk and he told me how he had escaped to England. He had killed his German guard with his bare hands. He explained to me that if you want to strangle someone it is best not to press with the balls of your thumbs (he demonstrated), it was better to turn your thumbs in so that your nails went straight in to his neck (like so). I think it still did not occur to me that I was in any danger from this young killer and indeed, I was not. He took me home in good time and on my doorstep asked very politely if he might kiss me goodnight. Then he very gently did so. Other days, other ways! But I soon learned that he was not typical.

Members of the WAAF were not allowed to serve abroad until they were twenty-one. As soon as I came of age I volunteered to go to India. I was sent to Italy - well, they got the first letter right!

We travelled in convoy and were told not to go too near the rails of the ship because it would not stop to pick us up if we fell overboard - that would endanger the convoy.

I was stationed in Caserta, near Naples, where I worked first in the Royal Palace, amid painted ceilings and marble columns. I was later moved to a converted cowshed. We were the first English women the troops out there had seen in years and we were made very welcome. In this war torn country it was thought too dangerous for us to go out after dark without a male escort, so it became essential to find one. They had to sign for us at the Guard Room, giving number, rank and name. Then they signed again when they returned us. Fortunately, there were far more men than women stationed there so it was not too difficult.

One boyfriend was a man called Jack Jones, from Liverpool. He was a very pleasant chap; kind, very devoted and very generous - but not too sensible!

One day he took me to the opera in Naples. He wanted to buy me a box of chocolates, but as this would have cost a week's wages, I persuaded him to buy me a miniature crate of nuts and raisins instead. These were a local product and cheap.

The San Carlo, if I remember rightly, is unusual in having no circle but just tier upon tier of boxes in a semi-circle. We had one of these and as Jack didn't care for the music he put the wooden crate on the edge of our box and tried to open it with a penknife. The lid suddenly split with a crack like a pistol-shot and nuts and raisins rained down on the people in the stalls. I think we might have been thrown out if we had not worn the uniform of the occupying power.

Fortunately, Jack was soon posted to a place a long way off but he wrote to say that whenever he saw a box of nuts he thought of me!

I was posted to Kasfareet in the Suez Canal Zone in 1946. The highlight of my stay in Egypt was a stay at Luxor, where I was able to see the Valley of the Kings and the temple at Karnak. It was a male dominated society - the men rode on the donkeys, the women walked behind. I didn't actually meet a woman to speak to in my eight months in Egypt.

I did, however, meet a remarkable young girl. She was perhaps eleven years of age, had one leg and one wooden stump, like a broken off broomstick. She was the leader of a gang of young rogues in Ismailia. Sometimes she had a tray of oranges hanging around her neck and as she approached she would pick up a handful of sand, indicating by her gestures that if you didn't buy an orange you would get the sand in your face. Among her entourage were bootblack boys who would spill liquid bootblack on your clothes if you refused to have your shoes cleaned.

I have never met so many thieves, knaves and beggars but, of course, there was appalling poverty and ignorance. It was not only the very poor though, who were dishonest. I once went in to a shop in Ismailia to buy shoes and in the middle of the transaction the shopkeeper got out his prayer mat and said his prayers. Having finished he gave me my change and shoes. When I arrived home I found that the latter consisted of out-of-date currency, which was worthless.

The WAAF compound was surrounded by barbed wire, searchlights and had occasional armed patrols with dogs. The thieves still managed to get in a couple of times on pay-night and rob us as we slept!

At this time, we still had thousands of German prisoners of war on our hands, as Germany was too devastated to rehabilitate them. We had one of these prisoners working in the orderly room with us as an interpreter and we became quite friendly. One day, Erwin asked me whether I would like to go to the prison camp concert that evening and I went along. There were two armed guards at the entrance and they were not keen on letting me in. However, they couldn't find anything in King's Regulations to say that a WAAF corporal might not enter a POW camp.

I found it all very interesting. It was a tented encampment and on the roofs of some tents there were small amounts of leaves and blades of grass drying, to make a kind of 'tobacco.' The men had rigged up a little beer garden, with coloured lights where they drank the small ration they were allowed. The concert was enjoyable, with a very good male voice choir and various instrumentalists. The comedy was more than a little bawdy but to spare my escort's blushes I pretended not to understand what was going on.

Afterwards, Erwin took me back to the gates only to find them closed and the guards gone home. They were over ten feet high with a barbed wire entanglement on top. I was horrified at the idea of spending the night with about a thousand of the ex-enemy and perhaps even more appalled at the thought of what my sergeant would have to say if I failed to return to the WAAF compound by midnight and they had to send out a search party for me. However, Erwin said, "Don't vorry, ve hav a vay out!" To my surprise, I found that they had dug a trench under the wire at the back of the camp and filled it with soft sand that was easy to remove. We cleared away a little of the sand to enable me to wriggle under the barbed wire like a snake. When I was halfway through, Erwin shouted, "Achtung! Hund!" I knew there were sometimes alsation dogs patrolling the perimeter and I shot backwards so fast I caught my khaki drill shirt on a barb and tore it from end to end.

As I lay panting in the hot sand at Erwin's feet, half-naked in the moonlight, I thought it might be a setting for a scene in a romantic novel. But Erwin merely said, in a rather severe tone, "You should vear a vest. You can easily catch cold in zis climate."

Oh well! I got away at my second attempt and was home before the magic 22.59 hours, but I had some difficulty in explaining to the Quartermaster why I needed a new shirt.

I was demobbed in August 1947 and was never more pleased to see again England's green and pleasant land. The troopship docked at Southampton and the Navy went ashore first, as the senior service, followed by the WRENS. Then came the Army, the ATS, the Queen Alexandra's Nursing Service, the RAF and then - an announcement on the loudspeaker that the WAAF would stay behind and clean the ship!

Tom Dunn was shipwrecked

Abandon Ship

I was a twenty-year-old RAF Corporal and along with five others, was attached to the FAA. We sailed as passengers on the Anchor liner SS Britannia from Liverpool in March 1941 in a small convoy with an impressive looking escort.

On the thirteenth day out whilst steaming alone and unescorted in the South Atlantic we were shelled by a heavily armed German raider who fired at will causing many casualties and heavy damage. The captain ordered a smoke screen and tried to outrun the German but it was hopeless and eventually 'Abandon Ship' was sounded. I found myself in a lifeboat with three of my RAF friends and about sixty other passengers and crew.

In charge was a commander of the Royal Australian navy who was, I believe, on his way to join the Australian cruiser 'Perth.' We had a few gallons of fresh water, forty-eight tins of Nestles milk and the usual supply of hard ship's biscuits.

Most people including myself were very seasick for about two days before everyone settled down to a daily routine of looking forward to our small ration of water and milk in the morning and evening. Then, on the fifth night, we saw searchlights sweeping across the horizon followed by the lovely sight of a brightly lit ship with the Spanish flag illuminated by floodlights along the hull. It turned out to be a liner en route from South America to Cadiz. A number of survivors had been picked up in the afternoon, amongst who was a young naval rating who had had one leg bitten by a shark. Luckily the ship's doctor managed to save his leg despite the fact that gangrene had already infected the bite.

We were extremely fortunate that a Spanish/American baroness was on board and insisted that the captain searched for a few more hours as she was sure there could be more survivors in the area.

We were all treated handsomely on board, kitted out by donations of clothing so everyone of us found something to fit eventually.

All of the service personnel were put ashore at Santa Cruz in Tenerife where we stayed in two English run hotels for the next four months. Then, one day, they told us to pack up and we left on a Fyffe's banana boat bound for Gibraltar. We eventually arrived back in the UK in August, five months after leaving for the Middle East.

Of the four hundred passengers and crew who 'abandoned ship' on the 23rd March, two hundred lost their lives.

Joe North recalls his Royal Navy days

Search and Report

I joined the Royal Navy in August 1943 - I don't know why the RN because I was a landlubber being a scoutmaster at the age of fourteen also platoon sergeant in the Army Cadets for three years. However, my cousin Harry said that he was going to Portsmouth to join the RN and said would I go with him - so off I went. We arrived at the recruitment office and went in together - the recruitment CPO asked if we wanted to join the RN and we both said yes!

I knew that I was not old enough but when it came to asking the date of birth, I added one year on to my real age. About one week later my father had a letter asking for my birth certificate, which he duly sent. My mother was pleased because she said "They wont take you because you're a year too young." However, when my next birthday came around I had a letter asking me to report to HMS Royal Arthur, in Skegness. The RN had taken over Butlin's holiday camp and that's where I spent the next four months training to be a wireless telegraphist. The Morse code and semaphore signalling was a piece of cake because I had learnt these in the Scouts. However they taught me the technical side of radio and the methods of coding and decoding and I came out with flying colours and was immediately upgraded to TEL T.O.

I was then sent to Colchester with six others. On arrival we were taken to two MTBs, to be told that we were to be trained and recruited to the S.O.E. The physical training was carried out by the SAS, the more technical side with special radio equipment and map reading was done by the RN on the MTB in the evenings. We were told that we would become 'sleepers' aboard ship and to be ready when called. After this I was sent home on fourteen days leave - when recalled, I was to report to Portsmouth. I had one night in Pompey and then with about two hundred or more sailors departed by train to John Brown's shipyard in Glasgow. There, several ships in various stages of construction berthed in the yard and I was allocated to a brand new destroyer, HMS Wager.

After running in trials up and down the river Tyne and some short trips out to sea, we were despatched to Scapa Flow, the base for the Home Fleet. From there we did six sorties to Norway up the fjords bombarding oilfields and army shipping in sight, also hunting for U-boats. After about three months we joined a Russian convoy and diverted to the Faro Islands to pick up a relief weather station crew and transport them to Spitzbergen in the North Pole where we stayed for three days off-loading the crew and loads of stores. In those days they were doing three years at a time in this weather station. There was, or is, a coalmine from which they got their fuel - they needed plenty because it was a full-time job chipping the ice from the upper deck.

On return from Spitzbergen we were given seven days leave, then on to the Middle East. First stop was Gibraltar, then acting as escorts to merchant ships going to Malta to join the British fleet taking part in the invasion of Italy. From there onwards we moved to Malta, chasing subs and foreign merchant shipping en route. We stayed for about three weeks patrolling the Med and aiding in the defence of Malta - then south to Algiers before proceeding through the Suez Canal to the Indian Ocean and on to the main Middle East base at Columbia. From here we carried out many patrols in the Indian Ocean searching for Japanese subs and other shipping. We did six fleet raids on Burma during this time and this is where the S.O.E. operations became apparent. On each raid onto Burma, the Wager was despatched twenty-four hours ahead of the main fleet and I was dropped ashore to search and report, on my special crystal controlled set, locations of troops, ammunition dumps and aircraft etc. I would be picked up twenty-four hours later before any action commenced. I often thanked God that we had a first class pilot and an extremely determined and first-class seaman as our Captain because they never failed to find me. On the last raid we did on Burma we were ordered to proceed to Darwin, North Australia, going through the Straits of Sumatra and Java - which was uncharted waters and in some places we were very close to land and were actually fired on by Japanese soldiers. After Darwin we made our way to Sydney. On arrival at Sydney harbour we were welcomed like pop stars - there were hundreds of people waiting for us - how they got to know we were arriving I'll never know!

We stayed in Sydney for about a month doing exercises with some of the American Fleet - all of us telegraphists were sent to a commercial school to learn touch typing because the Yanks worked at 33wpm and we could never keep up with that speed writing long hand. The Aussies treated us very well and one particular family took me in and invited me to Christmas Dinner - on Bondi Beach, it was fantastic! I'll never forget it - December 25th 1944.

After all these exercises were over we proceeded north visiting many of the Pacific islands and joined the main American 5th Fleet in Guam - I think that with the American 5th and the British Pacific Fleet joining forces it must have been the largest fleet in history! Forty-eight hours before the landing on Okinawa began we, the Wager, were despatched to do the scouting. I was dropped - usual procedure to do my scouting and reporting. All went well until about two hours before the actual landing commenced approximately 4am. I was captured and tortured. They hung me from a tree and beat my right foot with bamboo (I still have the scars) to get me to talk. When the landing actually started there was tremendous noise, as you can imagine, the Japs forgot about me and left me hanging. However, sometime later the Yanks came and cut me down and transported me back on a tank landing craft and later on to my own ship.

At this time the battle was raging - the worst part was the Kamikazes. The Wager was hit by one of these but fortunately it only took the mast and part of the bridge and we were still operational. After the ceasefire was declared we went up the Tokyo River and anchored overnight. We tied up alongside the American battleship Missouri and watched the signing and handing over of swords - a moment in history. Sadly, one of our crew was buried in Tokyo.

Jack Shepperd recalls an incident in Boulogne

Ave Maria

Boulogne had fallen two weeks previously and my Naval W7T unit was stationed in a school opposite the Citadel. Its entrance had two very large doors opening to the playground, one always open to everyone, through which a khaki painted van with two very large loudspeakers on its roof, now appeared - bringing music to the Forces. A few matelots and civilians gathered around it, making requests.

After songs like 'Pistol Packing Momma' and such-like someone chose Deanna Durbin singing 'Ave Maria.' Within a few seconds a crowd of French people came and stood with us listening in silence. As the music died away they slowly dispersed one by one and went about their ways.

In those days music was on 78rpm records, they were very scratchy and got worse as they wore out. But nevertheless in Boulogne, war-torn to pieces, it was an eerie moment in time listening to that wonderful record echoing round the playground and out into the Citadel.

This was a real live event and has stayed with me all these years. The French were very grateful to us then. If we tried to queue up to buy those wonderful pastries etc, (bread was not allowed), with no more ado, they pushed us up to the front to be served first.

Colin Paine recalls some excerpts from the War years in Europe

Day Excursions and The Berlin Philharmonic

In late 1944 our group of D/Ops (Driver/Wireless Operators) was sent to a bell-tent canvas camp at Eastleigh, nr Southampton. In a sea of mud and floating duckboards we were confined without any outside contact until we were taken by army lorries to the docks at Southampton and embarked upon 'The Ben Ma Cree', a pre-war Isle of Man packet ship.

That night the ship moved to Dover and in the early hours we headed out across the channel. The sea, according to the crew, was the roughest that they had ever encountered. It was no better when we eventually arrived at the approach to our destination port. The sea was considered too rough for us to attempt to enter the harbour, so the ship about-turned and returned to Dover.

Next day the conditions were better so we set sail once more, but this time our arrival outside the French port was greeted with the news that the enemy had mined the harbour the night before - so back we went to Dover for another night.

The crossing, with a solid mass of troops on board, had been intended to take less than 24 hours, so by now provisions had virtually run out and the troop's emergency rations were being broached. The ship's 'heads' were too disgusting for words and the decks weren't much better.

Great embarrassment lay ahead. The following morning the Ben Ma Cree took us back to Southampton where we all disembarked to the loud applause and cheers of the population on the dockside who imagined us to be returning heroes instead of just returning from a somewhat prolonged 'day excursion!'

Next, we were martialled onto trains and taken to Newhaven where we immediately embarked on a gathering of Landing Craft and were transported within hours to Dieppe. On the quayside at Dieppe were gathered lines of German prisoners who would be transported back to Britain on the Landing Craft.

After a few days spent in an old flourmill at Corbie (on the Somme), we received our postings to active regiments and I was posted to replace a Driver/Op casualty with the 285 Battery, 90th HAA Regiment Royal Artillery at their location at Helmond, in northern Holland.

The regiment was, when I joined it, providing the defence of an airfield. This airfield, along with others, 'intelligence' had reported as being under threat from a German airborne attempt to retake for use by the Luftwaffe, as the German army retreated from their attempted Ardennes ('Battle of the Bulge') break out.

Apart from the cold and the mud at Helmond there were two incidences which I remember.

On guard duty one night I had taken a few minutes of relief in our bivouac in the hope of thawing out. I turned on the NAAFI supplied radio and heard (somewhat tinnily) soul stirring orchestral music - but then I was horrified to feel hot breath on the back of my neck and I feared that my last moment was about to come at the knife edge of a German paratrooper.

However, the voice accompanying the breath just said, "Beautiful isn't it? That is Max Bruch's violin concerto No1 ... and it's played I think by the Berlin Philharmonic Orchestra."

It was my first introduction to classical music and I later discovered that Bombardier Eric Lawson, (the voice behind me) had been a 1st violinist with either the Halle or the Liverpool Philharmonic - I cannot now remember which. I gather that he would have recognised the style of the orchestra - this still strikes me as amazing. It also struck me at that time that it was somewhat odd that we should be standing there admiring a German Orchestra playing music by a German composer whilst in the background we could hear our artillery exchanging death and destruction with the German artillery!

From one of our deployment locations we had the unhappiness of watching the trails of the V2s as they were blasted off on their way to England from the German launch sites. We had however, during our movements forward, had the satisfaction of seeing the remnants of several 'Doodlebug' launch structures that the advancing allies had destroyed.

On January 1st 1945, Hitler in desperation threw every aircraft he could muster into one last offensive fling - and a number of them swooped extremely low over our site.

They were flying too low to engage by artillery fire but small arms were brought into action and one of our bombardiers manning a Bren gun shot down a ME 109F.

The CO and another officer dashed off in their Jeep in order to claim the 'kill.' They returned with a souvenir propeller from which I obtained a small portion and then over ensuing weeks and with some help from our workshop, I fashioned into a brooch depicting the 2nd Army shield badge. My wife still has it.

The pilot of the 109 had died instantly from a bullet through the head. It was the first day of a New Year and sadly one has to realise that some mother/father/wife/ child would never see their loved one again - they would certainly not have a 'Happy New Year.'

Later the regiment moved 'onwards and upwards'. We carried out counter battery work over the rivers Maas and Ruhr. When stationed near Roermond we 'adopted' The Café de Peel as our battery headquarters, complete with two dear little old lady residents who would periodically take to the cupboard under the stairs if things got too noisy.

Morse Code

At one stage we drew lots to see which Dvr/Ops would go to an OP (observation post) at Boxmeer. I was one of those with the short straw and we arrived to be told that the nomansland deserted town was, at night, occupied variously by both German and Canadian troops. The OP party locked itself in the terraced house which was our night time base and kept very quiet whilst any footsteps were left to 'pass by our window in the still of the night', no matter to whom they may belong. Should anyone attempt to get in via our barricaded doors then, we were told, "You don't ask questions, you just lob grenades out through the bloody fanlights!"

Fortunately the footsteps kept going which was not only a great relief to us but possibly saved the lives of anybody who might have had an inquisitive nature.

During the daytime, from the observation post, we watched the German tank crews playing football around their vehicles – before signalling their positions back to our battery HQ and stopping their game!

On another occasion I was detailed to provide transport for a Dutch liaison officer and we were sent into a newly liberated Dutch town. The officer was to install the new Town Major who was required to re-establish Dutch administration in the wake of the departed German forces.

As the allied liberating forces had already moved on in pursuit of the Wermacht, the Dutch officer and I were the only signs of the liberation army within the town - the reception was rapturous. The euphoria of the inhabitants rose to the greatest of heights when I distributed amongst them my stored packets of cigarettes!

Although for the majority, their joy was 'unbounded', I was somewhat depressed by the sight of some of the inhabitants taking reprisals against their fellow countrymen and women who had collaborated with the Germans. The situation could not have been easy for anyone at that time and it was sad to see the elements of anger and revenge continuing into the new era of freedom from Nazi oppression.

After the crossing of the Rhine the advance across Germany was more or less 'at-the-gallop.' The whole of Germany suddenly became a scene of retreating Germans trying to leave the front and return to their homes supplemented on the congested roads by the thousands upon thousands of displaced persons. No matter whether German or any other nationality it was a very heartrending sight to see those thousands of underfed bodies of all ages clad in tattered clothing and with rags tied on their feet acting as shoes.

I was detached from the regiment and sent to provide assistance at a newly set up UNRRA (United Nations Refugee Relief) centre in Bocholt.

Bocholt had been almost totally destroyed by the combined attacks of the RAF and the American Air Force. Rumour had it that the town was wiped out in some fifteen minutes by the combined high and low level bombing. However long it might have taken, it was terrifyingly thorough. Gaps had been bulldozed through the rubble to act as 'roads', and the rubble was said to be covering the bodies of thousands of the inhabitants killed in the raids.

The UNRRA centre was in what little remained of a Siemens factory on the outskirts of the town. In a word it was 'pitiful'. Most of the refugees had, over the years of slave labour, lost all sense of hope and dignity and had become accustomed to totally uncivilised behaviour - and those three words summarise the situation with which the UNRRA personnel attempted to deal.

The Royal Engineers endeavoured to set up water supplies and had set up rows and rows of communal, side-by-side latrines. Sadly, during my week or two at Bocholt, I witnessed repeated misuse and vandalism of the former and the necessary demolishment and burning of the latter by the Royal Engineers due to the health hazards arising from the state of the latrines.

As the allied armies rapidly advanced through Germany, they discovered the Nazi concentration camps. We were close enough to be able to smell the death and degradation but fortunate enough to have very narrowly avoided the task of going in and helping to clear Belsen. This awful job fell to a sister regiment. One of our officers was sent to report on the findings and returned a few days later, totally haggard and looking twenty years older than he had when he had left us.

When these atrocities were uncovered by our advancing troops, photographs were taken and copies distributed to all units stationed in Germany. These horror pictures were then displayed in every town and village and the local German population made to parade and witness what Hitler and his Nazi regime had perpetrated. Reactions varied from utter disbelief and the accusation that the pictures had been forged as propaganda, to (rarely) sniggers, and to the much more common and human emotions of shame and sorrow. Many tears were shed.

By VE Day, the regiment had moved on through Germany and occupied Uelzen on the river Elbe – and where the Russian Army occupied the opposing bank of the river. The regiment held a thanksgiving service in the field and our role as an active regiment in Europe was over.

The Café de Peel

Leslie Sprigg served in the Coastal Forces

Coastal Forces Recollections

During the war I served in the Royal Navy, Coastal Forces, which consisted of various small craft including Motor Torpedo Boats, Motor Gunboats, etc. My first boat was ML 108, an 'A' Class boat some 110ft long and initially only armed with 0.5 Lewis Guns and an old 3 pounder. Only about twelve of these were built. They had three Hall-Scott petrol engines, which gave a speed near 30 knots. All were adapted for minelaying of which we carried any of three main types. There were ground mines (magnetic), moored mines, which we sank to a pre-determined depth and were activated by a ship striking any one of the numerous prongs, and magnetic mines which were activated by the rise and fall of a ship's engine. As the ship approached, a clapper would start to rise and continue until maximum. As soon as the ship's engine started to fall, the clapper would fall and detonate the mine.

Our task was to lay mines in the coastal shipping supply lanes close to the shores of France, Belgium and Holland. Leaving Dover at dusk, we would zig-zag through our own known minefields and other hazards and head for the coast of France. The engine would be slowed and silenced (by baffles) as we crept along the coast to our laying areas. The flotilla would consist of about six boats, each carrying between five and nine mines, according to the type. When in position, the mines would be laid in twenty second intervals. My job was to call up to the bridge "Out pins No 1, Lay No 1" and so on, until we moved out of line and the next boat continued the lay. Regarding the mines, 'Out Pins' was the process of activating the mines and disengaging the straps. Once activated and entering the water, it took about twenty minutes for the soluble plug to dissolve.

On completion of our mission, we would move away from the area and either return to port or look for small enemy craft to attack. On some occasions, we carried out diversionary attacks to draw some of the enemy away from a gun battle that was causing them problems. Our task then was to head in the general direction of the skirmish and make a lot of noise (gunfire) to try to draw some of the enemy away.

Safely back in Dover, we would tie-up alongside, wash the decks and clean ship before turning in.

Each month we were issued with 'comforts,' which I had to collect from a store in the centre of town. These consisted of a free cigarette and chocolate ration and various knitted items donated by well wishers. On one occasion, I borrowed a bike from a lady dockyard worker, to save the walk into town, and duly collected our allotment. On the return trip, I was cycling along quite happily, when as I headed across the main square towards the dockyard, a rather large policeman on traffic duty, held his hand high. I put the brakes on but nothing happened. I dropped my feet to the ground and skidded along, but too late. I hit him amidships. He sat down rather abruptly! I decided not to hang about so pulled the bike away and pedalled furiously for the dockyard. Unfortunately, in my hurry, I got caught in the railway track alongside the jetty. Off I came and the bike and 'comforts' disappeared over the side, into the drink. The dockyard worker proved to be not such a lady after all although we rescued her bike, and my shipmates were less than pleased at the loss of their month's comforts. I was in fear and trepidation of a large policeman seeking me out.

ML 108 and indeed the rest of the flotilla, were versatile boats. On several occasions we took passengers, (special agents) to row ashore at a designated spot and some days later, returned to collect them. This did not always prove successful. Either they did not get to the pick-up area on time, although we always waited as long as we dare, for the signal, or they had been captured. We would also take special forces over to one of the harbours, row them in, where they would select a suitable-sized ship. Having decided on their target, they would plant limpet mines beneath the hull, swim back to the dinghy, be rowed back to 108 and off home again.

The minelaying continued until 5th September 1943. We were laying magnetic mines and had just completed our lay, when there was a huge explosion aft, which lifted the back end out of the water. We started to fill quite quickly but at a high level it seemed to stabilize. We were taken in tow by one of our sister boats, and headed slowly back towards Dover. Unhappily a large sea swell developed and the boat gave up the struggle and sank by the stern. I well remember our First Lieutenant, Hugh Fordham, swimming round, asking each in turn "Are you all right?" before shepherding us to the rescue boat. All the crew were saved and most of us ended up aboard ML 101.

We lost all our personal possessions of course, and at Dover we were given new clothes and sent to await a new posting. Not a long wait.

George Bainbridge lived in Hartlepool

The 1521

In 1940 I had to report to Salisbury Plain. There I would undergo eight weeks of extensive training, which if successful would transform us from civilians to soldiers. Mind you being a rookie had its humorous side and I was one of the first to partake of it.

It was April and snow covered the plain, we had been kitted out and I had these woollen Long Johns. Looking at the snow, I put discretion before valour. I quickly put a pair on and attended the parade in full marching order. The drill instructor screamed out 'about turn,' 'by the left, quick march'; this left me in the rear rank and I was beginning to slow down. The said Long Johns were slipping down, my pace was getting shorter as by now they had dropped behind my knees and the squad had gone ahead of me. I was in a sweat when I heard the command 'halt.' The NCO came up to me and asked if I was trying to desert.

"No sir, it's these Long Johns, I forgot to put my braces through the tapes provided to keep them up."

They all had a good laugh at my expense.

I left Bullford after six weeks training as a driver in the RASC. I ended up in Kent, via Pontefract. The Battle of Britain was in progress and planes were falling out of the sky like hailstones.

My next posting was to 12th Corp school. It so happened that I went to early breakfast and at the head of the queue a NCO, Corporal Goode was in charge of a gargle issue and to my amazement he allowed each person to immerse their own mugs into the purple liquid. This annoyed me and I walked on into the dining room, the corporal ordered me to "Take that gargle."

I replied "You can have mine."

Next, the orderly Officer confronted me and I refused him also, and I was placed under arrest and marched off to Company Office and charged with the offence of Disobeying an Order given by an NCO. Next thing, I was ordered to collect my kit and board a lorry and was driven to a stable near Harietsen in Kent. It was January 1941 and very cold. They gave me a bucket of water, which froze over and I had to use it to wash and shave and parade at 6am with the guard. After breakfast I was driven back to Tonbridge and faced the Colonel who read the charge sheet and asked me if I would accept his punishment, which I refused to do. I was then bundled off to The Royal West Kent's headquarters in Maidstone where I elected to be tried by court martial. I was under close arrest for forty days; I couldn't get a medical officer to defend me and that convinced me my goose was cooked. One cannot win, even with a stone wall defence. They sentenced me to thirty-five days in a naval prison in Chatham Kent. On release I returned to the 12th Corps school and was posted to a holding unit awaiting orders.

My next move was to West Byfleet. It was a private house with a grim history. Once the home of a doctor who butchered his wife and the servant in the bathroom, which was stripped bare. I lay in bed, couldn't sleep thinking about it. From Surrey to Lancashire and an old cottonmill soaked in oil. If ever it caught fire we would be cremated alive.

In 1943 we sailed from Liverpool on the Dunarta Castle. We had no idea where we were going, I chanced to ask a crewman how long it would take the ship to get there?

"This ship?" he quipped, "You might need another three ships – it's up to our Navy plus the U Boats."

I had very little liking for the sea and even less now I'd asked that question.

Action stations! That means every man below decks which gives the gunners freedom apparently. Searchlights off the coast of Africa had picked us up and we could hear the fireworks and depth charges exploding nearby. Very soon it was quiet and I began to breathe normally, how pleased I was to see daylight breaking. I was looking out for deserts and palm trees but in every direction all we saw was water. After God knows how many days the weather was much warmer but still no Arabs on camels though we could see the coastline in the distance. We were told it was Algeria - how pleased I was to see dry land.

So this is Algeria and we are in the town of Bone and our job is to clear the cargoes as the crews offload the vehicles. I had a very pleasant surprise while working here. I saw a huge salvage vessel in the distance and I thought that I would go to see it at close quarters when it docked. The next day she had berthed and looking up to the bridge was the name Empire Lorrenzo built in Hartlepool, for Ropner. I thought, "this is great, they've come to take me home." I shouted up the gangway, "Is there anyone from Hartlepool?"

"Yes, we all come from Hartlepool, come aboard."

The first man to greet me was the ship's cook Mick Hillier. We had a good old natter and he asked if I wanted anything.

"Yes", I said, "some bread."

We had been living on compo rations and Mick gave me a newly baked loaf and a huge dinner saying, "as long as we are here, come aboard."

I was soon outdone. They moved out to Bizerta to clear the port, we had to go to Tunis which meant a very long journey along the Atlas mountains by rail in trucks. Twenty-two men in each, eleven slept in the daytime, the others at night. It took seven days. The engine was stoked up by burning wood and cork bark. It was so slow we could drop off, wash and shave and still catch up with the train. Our stay in Tunisia didn't last long before we moved to Algiers. The war out here was over and our Platoon embarked on the SS Ormonde. Inside a week we sailed to Blighty.

How nice it was to see the cliffs of Dover homeward bound. Our ship docked at Liverpool and we were given disembarkation leave, which should have been a gift from heaven, but it took me to the gates of the isolation hospital in Bradford.

A few days after I got home I began to feel groggy and I put on a brave face so as not to worry the family. I was glad to report back to Pudsey Leeds, but I was covered with red weeping spots, that and a high temperature, I felt like a bone in a pan of broth.

My pal Hunter Bell tried to find a doctor, which wasn't easy and the Army Doctor took me into a room and told me to strip completely.

He said, "Don't come near me, get dressed and don't leave this room."

He also told my pal not to let anyone into the building.

It was near midnight when an ambulance arrived and two nurses came in with a stretcher and red blankets. They asked for the Smallpox patient then they drove me off to Bradford to an empty emergency hospital and there I remained for five weeks.

My parents were told of the dangers involved and all the bedding and towels were taken away for fumigation. No money to be handled, no visitors or trades people to enter our home, all food rations, milk etc would be placed over the front garden wall until notified. They warned people to be vaccinated. Anyone I might have come in to contact with on buses, in the cinema and the trains - the locals must have cursed me. Mother was paying bills for weeks.

The Matron at the hospital called me to inform me of my release date but I could have an extension if I wished. I hoped to rejoin my unit, which I served with in North Africa. She told me that there would be a posting when I left the hospital. I was given a warrant to report to the RTO in Slade Camp, Oxford. About 3am, a convoy of Bedford carriers pulled in and we all piled into them. From there we were driven to a concentration area in Purfleet, Essex, to work on "Pluto" (though I didn't know that at the time), the pipeline which fed the invasion of Normandy.

The greatest display of military hardware ever assembled was to be put to its intended purpose of totally defeating the might of the German defences that they had built over the period since Dunkirk. Known as the Atlantic Wall, this was soon to be attacked by a mighty force like hell let loose. The sea was black with thousands of ships, the air was throbbing with gun fire, smokescreens and cordite fumes. Whoever planned this assault did a great job. Conditions weren't perfect for an invasion. The attacking forces are very vulnerable and casualties are always likely to be high. It was an experience hard to forget. Hundreds lay dead on the beaches, being swept in and out on the ebbtides. Those people of the Royal Medical Corps were working like demons to cope with the casualties.

I was now in 246 Petrol Company, a small unit of eight men, my OC Captain Pethwick who I was driving, was easy to get along. He was interested in me and the fact that having been posted as a result of being in hospital, I was hoping to see my old platoon again.

We were just over the border of Belgium and the Captain had been called to a meeting at 12 Corp Rear. As luck would have it he said he would be about two hours and I could run around making myself familiar with the area. It so happened that a truck passed by with my old company sign on the tailboard - 1521. I soon got ahead of him and stopped the driver, whom, I didn't know.

"Has your unit been in North Africa?" "Yes", he replied.

"And is your OC Captain Hockley?" I mentioned a few others by name and he said those men were still there. I felt lucky, also very pleased even though I already had a good number with 246 Petrol Depot.

I picked up my OC and told him all about my discovery and their location in Helmond. He told me to sleep on it and we would discuss it tomorrow. This was September 1944. The Captain asked me if I had made up my mind.

"Yes Sir."

"Very well, I'll arrange something."

True to his word, I had to take him to Helmond, find the unit and leave it to him. Soon I took my OC back, loaded my kit onto my staff car and went back to Helmond. The changeover was made with a man named Driver Cole and I remained with 1521 until my demob in August 1946.

Leslie Oppitz recalls incidents in Germany

World War Two – Before And After

Leslie Oppitz (Cpl Oppitz, 4th Royal Tank Regiment) served with his regiment from 1944 to 1948. The regiment arrived at Ibbenbüren in NW Germany just days after the end of the war with Germany. The Party House became Regimental HQ and troops were billeted in various public buildings. A non-fraternisation ban was issued although it became impossible to control with several hundred young soldiers meeting the many German girls who had lost husbands and loved-ones.

This was, however, Leslie's second visit to Germany. In July 1937 he had visited the Rhineland on a school journey. During that tour the party found itself in a Nazi party rally. German tempers were aroused when the party refused to join in the Hitler Salute. Despite this, one young man traded his Hitler Youth badge for an English memento.

Back in 1945 many valuable war medals, iron crosses etc were willingly passed over in return for cigarettes or coffee – for them, rare commodities indeed. The local people had expected brutal treatment from the British but this of course never happened. Even so, the disclaiming of Nazi association was everywhere.

Leslie returned to Ibbenbüren in 2002 and was not really surprised to see how much the town had changed. He found where parades had been held next to the town's church. The church had memories too. It recalled a late evening in 1945, when he entered it to find the organ unlocked. It gave him the opportunity to give his finest rendering yet of 'Lili Marlene' - much to the German folk's displeasure.

During this recent visit he asked an elderly German, 'Do you remember when we were stationed here in 1945?'

'Ach ja', he replied 'And your Naafi was over there'. He pondered thoughtfully for a moment and added. 'But I am surprised you come back in case a lady greets you with "Hullo Papa!"'

Christmas cards from the war

Reg Bowyer spent some time in Italy

Don't Stand on the Doorstep

I joined the Shropshire Yeomanry in 1939. In August 1942, we sailed from Greenock on the Clyde to South Africa in a convoy of eighteen vessels. Included in the convoy was HMS Shropshire. I came on deck one morning only to find we were alone: our ship had broken down - fire in the engine room. It was a great relief when we rejoined the convoy, without having been sighted by enemy U boats. Members of the regiment acted as gun crews for the six week long journey. We stayed in Durban for six weeks, having received a wonderful welcome on arrival. During that time we had many route marches and some training. In November we embarked for Egypt. While sailing there, news of the El Alemein victory came through and so we went to Baghdad. Seventeen hundred miles over land and crossing the river Jordan. This was part of a plan to guard oil supplies in Iran. Later, we sailed from Alexandria for Italy, landing at Taranto, which is on the heel of Italy.

We moved up to the front at Castel de Sangro, the aim being to divert the Germans from the Western side of Italy so the 5th Army could break through to Rome. Very deep snow cut off some units and they were supplied by parachute. As the weather improved, we moved to new positions. Our first casualty was Jock Davidson, caught in a strafing and dive-bomb attack by the Americans. We moved on to Monte Cassino front along a former railroad track. Monte Cassino dominated all the approaches and we had an observation post on Monte Trocchio. New Zealand and Indian troops attacked for eight days and failed. 1000 tons of bombs were dropped and 680 guns shelled the Monte Cassino area and failed. On the 17th May 1944, the biggest artillery barrage the world has ever seen took place. 1100 guns on a 20 mile front, persistent bombing for a week and Polish troops attacking, caused the Germans to surrender. The most frightening experience up to now was a German gun firing seven shells at once. These were known as moaning minnies - they howled as they flew overhead.

Outside of Florence, Sgt Thomas Oswestry was killed by a shell exploding under his bivouac. Also, about this time, Winston Churchill visited one of the gun sites and wrote a rude message on one of the shells. A friend that I went to school with - Sgt John Maslen - was wounded while repairing telephone lines and died shortly afterwards. I wrote to his parents with the sad news. I had my head down in a cellar at that time. Another friend Jack Davies from Ellesmere told me never to stand on doorsteps, as these were often mined. Soon after warning me he stood on a doorstep and was badly injured.

As the end of the war approached we were near Trieste on the Yugoslavian border. Tito's army was trying to take over that part of Italy, including the port of Trieste, essential to us for supplies. Many men in later days had acquired abandoned vehicles, which doubled the petrol used. The C.O. ordered them to be abandoned. As this coincided with the end of the war, our Captain exchanged an Opel car for fifty-six gallons of wine and a good time was had by all. We came home in February 1946 and I found it extremely difficult to settle into civilian life.

Tudor Williams served in North Africa

Berka

As we sailed away from Liverpool Docks in September 1944, I watched the lone policeman stood under a lampost in a sea of fog.

When we landed in Port Said a fortnight later, the sun on the Suez Canal was dazzling. We thought we were off to serve in the RAF in Burma but to my delight we stayed in Egypt. A large group of us had been together for nearly a year and moved on to the Signals Depot not far out of Cairo. With trips into the city, I was in my element. Then the postings came through and as one by one we were on our way, there were partings that were not far from tearful. I too was posted, to a camp near Benghazi and reluctantly made the solo journey by train and gharrie through the Western Desert.

The small camp was called Berka and I signed in and looked for my billet. It was a fair sized room, which I was to share with another who was away on a course. I asked a few questions, received some answers and went off to the cookhouse for a meal. I tried a few conversations and then went back to unpack. More questions, more answers but not much else. The others had a lot to say to one another and particularly about the pantomime they had staged amongst themselves over the Christmas. The photographs were passed around and I made my comments. I also mentioned the latest plays I had seen in London, but no one was interested.

The next day was much the same and so was the next. Whatever I said did not seem to interest anyone whilst they all went on with their own lives.

The missing airman returned and fortunately, he seemed to be as much an outsider as myself. I warmed to him immediately. And so a few weeks went by with myself still wearing my cellophane outfit. I just could not understand it. I had always been reasonably popular, ready to join in on events, with enough to say for myself as an assured nineteen-year-old.

And then the blow struck. A shocked airman returned from having seen that the camp was to be closed - in a week's time! I always feel that this was the day I began to grow up. Instead of shouting the 'whoopee' I longed to or dancing on the mess hall table, I tried to look as gloomy as the rest. I tried to sympathise; I tried to say the right word - or even keep my mouth shut.

The days sped by in a flurry of activity and then the most joyous news of all. I was to return to the Signals Depot from which I had come four long weeks ago.

We loaded up, many with tears in their eyes and myself as dry eyed as I had ever been. On our trip back, they began talking to me and I slowly realised that I was viewed as the one who had come to break up their close knit community of men who had been through a joined experience and who resented the intruder. They were also afraid of what I represented - the outside world to which they would have to return.

It was like coming home for me to see the barricaded gates of the Signals Depot and suddenly I was the 'gen man', as the leaves they had taken were in Alexandria and they knew Cairo not at all, whereas yours truly considered himself an expert.

The next day we went into town. I showed them the Tedder Club, the YMCA, Groppi's, the cinemas, nightclubs. The next day we went again and then the next.

Unfortunately the next time, I realised that my pay was fast running out with still another week to go to pay day. When they asked me why I did not want to go, it was a case of them saying, "you come, we'll pay." Of course they had all their non-spent back pay and I was their guide and guest.

A pleasant month went by and we became like blood brothers - I was accepted into the group. And then another blow- my posting to the sunny Sudan, but this time I had a big send off from the Berka boys, some more tears in eyes.

I felt I had learned a lot and maybe I had even grown up more than the few months I had been with them.

Brian Moran recalls a dramatic incident in Italy

Vesuvius

In 1943, a letter came telling my father that he was to enlist in the army and report to a barracks in Suffolk, where he was drafted into the infantry. A few weeks later he was reassigned to the Royal Army Medical Corp.

By the end of that year, he had been drafted overseas to somewhere in North Africa attached to the 8th Army, then sent on to a place called Noceta Inferior near Sorrento, in southern Italy and not all that far from Amalfi and Naples just across the bay.

On the 23rd to the 25th of March 1944, Mount Vesuvius erupted with such great force that many people living on the side of it were evacuated. Dad was one of the many who were sent to help in the evacuation. He managed to send home a glass file containing all the different types of ash that had fallen each day. Every day was a different colour and a different size of ash. The first day started with large particles of deep black ash just like coal dust. The next day the ash had changed to a reddish brown then orange and the last day of the eruption the ash had turned to a fine grey. How that tube got through the post without breaking I shall never know.

At times, mum would receive cards from dad with just 'Love from your husband Alf' written on it, because the censor had obliterated all the other writing out.

Lots of wives and sweethearts never did get a full letter explaining or telling them where their loved ones were or how they were getting on. Many times there would be no letters for weeks on end and then all at once, a whole batch would come through the letterbox. Many who had not had a letter for quite some time would wait at the gate for the postman to arrive and say, "Anything for me today?"

Many a time the answer would be "None today dear."

It must have been a very worrying time not getting a letter so that you knew whether your loved one was still alive. The worst thing to be delivered to you was the telegram, telling of a death or missing in action; a little better news was that he had been captured and was now a prisoner of war.

Here is a letter from dad to mum about Vesuvius:

My Dearest Edie,

I hope this will find you OK. The top where the crater is was one huge column of smoke and at frequent intervals, as if being forced by a pump, a vast quantity of red hot liquid was sent thousands of feet into the air.

The stream of red-hot lava ran down the side, a very nice picturesque sight at night. With these eruptions came showers of black ash, which being sent up a tremendous height were carried by the wind, which fell like rain. Instead of being wet, it was black ash which came down covering everything and if it caught you anywhere on the face and hands you got stung.

Well here's how I saw it. The volcano itself during the eruption was a very spectacular sight. The whole thing was like a red-hot heap of coke only instead of coke it was lava. It was an act of nature which thousands of people would have given pounds to see. That great rolling mass of liquid rock could be seen clearly rolling down the volcano's side at night. This grand spectre although an experience, bore with it disaster to many homes and arable land, that was already set with plants they hoped would serve them in the way of food.

You remember that picture called the White Sisters at the Tivoli? Well that gives one a crude idea as to how we saw it.

This vast mountain of destruction has once more changed its shape; instead of two peaks there is only one gigantic slope. An everlasting monument in my memory although I may be able to give you a far better idea when I come home. I will bring home some pictures.

The weight of the ash causes many roofs to collapse, but there it is, one can never foretell what is in store for us.

Well my dear I have done my best to describe to you how I saw it and take it from me it was no picnic for any of us.

It has now left a layer of ash all over many parts of the places it happened to fall, it will take years to remove this, I can tell you.

Well I hope you are OK. This is the first time I have been able to tell you about this adventure, which I must say has given me something to write about.

Well honey this is all for now as it is bedtime.

Bounno Notte (good night)

Yours forever, love and kisses, Alf.

Edith Ward served in India

Christmas Eve 1945

The place is a British General Hospital near Rangoon, a gaunt stone building, built in a square round a courtyard with balconies on every floor. This evening the balconies are alight, and in the jungle the frogs and cicadas croak endlessly. The air is hot. Every ward has its little Christmas tree decorated with shining things and small parcels. The balconies are crowded with men - standing, sitting, in wheel-chairs, even beds pushed to the open doors. All in white pyjamas. Bandages, splints, crutches in evidence and deep invisible wounds that only a few know of. The pushing sergeant, the shy artistic mechanic with secret ambitions, the Brigadier General who surreptitiously asks the welfare girl to teach him to knit for his coming baby, ("but never tell anyone!") all crowded on the balconies, their faces lost in wonder and amazement at the beauty that is happening in the middle of the courtyard. Reflecting maybe the awe that once poor shepherds, inn folk and kings felt when they were confronted by the new-born Christ. A choir and small orchestra have visited the hospital and are singing 'The Messiah,' as it has never been sung before!

Pat Stephens recalls the days after D-Day

D-Day and Beyond

Pat Stephens, having finished four years training as a nurse at Scarborough Hospital, Yorks, in January 1944, volunteered to join Queen Alexandra's Imperial Military Nursing Service Reserve and a few days after D-Day was sent to France with the 74th British General Hospital. She was the youngest QA in the Army at the time.

We settled in Watford and began to pack a 600 bedded hospital into huge wooden crates, which we had to mark - thermometers, bed pans, microscopes, theatre equipment, bedding, tents etc.

6th June was D-Day and about a week later, it was our turn. We were taken to a huge enclosed camp at Eastleigh, allowed no contact with the outside world and told to make our wills! We set off for Normandy from Southampton in a hospital ship, which after leaving us at the British Mulberry harbour returned with wounded from the front line.

Our destination was a large apple orchard near Bayeux where we were confronted by an enormous mountain of our packed crates. The boys dug 3ft trenches to hold our bedding, which would allow us to sleep below ground level, safe from shrapnel. That first night we slept in our clothing and tried to get some sleep, before attacking the packing cases next morning and assembling our hospital, tents, beds etc. There was much amusement when we found hessian draped over poles and inside wooden boxes with holes in for our 'Loos.' As there was no roof, the RAF had great fun swooping low overhead, when we were all seated there in the mornings!

After this, the real work began. Convoys of ambulances came over the hill from Caen and each sister in charge of a tented ward had to admit twenty-five British and twenty-five German casualties to her ward. 'Hectic' is really not the word. Blood soaked, filthy, exhausted men had to be sorted into categories of injuries. Some were sent straight to theatre, some for blood or saline drips, wounds had to be treated and less severe injuries sent back home by 'plane to England from an airstrip at the end of the orchard. During theatre duties, the Pioneer Corps lent valuable assistance by wheeling patients in and lifting them on to the tables. Some of the boys were so ill that they were calling for their mothers but my most vivid memory is the smell in resuscitation where the most severely wounded went after surgery.

Life in the camp was spartan. We had no bread, just 'hard tack' for a week and each sister was only allowed two pints of water per day for washing herself and her clothing and each night brought the hope of only a few hours sleep in our clothing. "Come back on duty as soon as you wake, Sister." Some of the surgeons would go three days and nights without a break. When shrapnel started falling we placed pillows on the boys' heads before diving under the beds ourselves.

Normandy was hectic, but had its lighter moments. One day during a busy dressing round an orderly came into my ward to announce the imminent arrival of General Dempsey accompanied by the Matron and one of the surgeons. I knew that I would be expected to meet them and show them round a spick and span ward. "Leave it to us" said the boys. Having met the General, the surgeon stopped by a bed, explained the case history and asked for the bed cradle to be removed to see how the patient's injuries were being treated. Removal of the cradle revealed a pile of beer bottles, cigarette ash, loaves of bread etc. A hush descended. All the men were lying to attention and the Matron's face was red. Fortunately, the General started to guffaw, the whole ward broke into laughter and I never heard any more about it.

One night we were told to be ready to retreat and we had to pack our personal belongings. This was just before Caen fell.

In the autumn of 1944 we moved to Belgium where we set up hospital in Bruges, in the old St John's Hospital which we took over from the nuns who returned to their quarters. I was in charge of a whole floor and it was here that we treated the airborne troops from Arnhem. We were billeted in little hotels, which was luxury after the mud of Normandy. There was nothing in the shops except perfume and cheese.

One evening, an orderly came in and said that someone was looking for me. It was Alan Brown, an old school friend of mine who was the same age. He was now the captain of a motor torpedo boat. I said, "I don't believe it, you can't be in charge of an MTB" and he replied, "And you can't be in charge of a ward!"

From there we moved to Luneburg, setting up our hospital in a German cavalry barracks. It was here that William Joyce, better known as Lord Haw Haw, was admitted after his capture, and it was here that our pathology staff did a post-mortem on Himmler. We also witnessed the huts of Belsen being burned to the ground.

Bert Thompson travelled to Yalta

The Big Three

On the 29th January 1945, a cavalcade of VIPs aboard the array of RAF Transport Command's AVRO Yorks, Liberators, and Sir Winston's personal Skymaster, took off from Northolt Airfield.

I had been with Transport Command since its creation in March1943 and had seen Sir Winston and many VIPs in their comings and goings; but this was the first occasion I had been seconded to a York crew and it was obvious that something big was in the offing. My only information was that the journey would be in two legs - first to 'MAGNETO' and then to 'CRICKET' and that the ultimate destination would be somewhat primitive!

The VIPs allocated to our York proved to be Admiral Sir Andrew Cunningham, General Sir Alan Brooke, Air Marshal Sir Charles Portal and their three ADCs. Sir Anthony Eden and his party occupied another York and so on in order of position and standing. All took their places on the assembled aircraft and at intervals of fifteen minutes we were airborne.

Seven hours later we touched down at 'MAGNETO' which in reality was LUQA airfield in Malta. Here, among the crowd of service personnel was Earl Alexander of Tunis waiting to greet our passengers.

The following day President Roosevelt and the American delegation flew in. We also learned that one of our Yorks had crashed into the sea somewhere off the Italian coast and many precious lives had been lost.

At the end of the fourth day we took off for 'CRICKET' under cover of darkness. In the early light of the following morning we landed amidst a vastness of snow and ice at SAKI airfield, in the Crimea, USSR. With the arrival of Joseph Stalin in a lease-lend Dakota - such a contrast to all our pomp and circumstance - the whole world soon learned that the 'Big Three' were meeting at Yalta, for a conference that shaped the post-war world.

Two weeks later the conference over, the homeward journey began. For some of us this proved to be a change of plan. This probably had some bearing on the loss of the York on the outward journey.

After a six-hour journey by Russian lorry, we reached Sevastopol, on the Black Sea. Awaiting us there was the 'Fratikonia.' The journey via the Black Sea, Bosphorus, Dardanelles and Mediterranean to Liverpool took three weeks. I came home in the knowledge that a tremendous piece of history had been made.

Dorice Lindsay lived near Paris

War from an Occupied Perspective

I lived in the town of Chatou about seven miles from Paris. During one of our frequent air raids our eyes were, as usual riveted toward the sky and our excitement reached a crescendo as we saw B-17 Flying Fortresses in the distance, heading our way. They bombed Villacoublay airfield, bridges, factories and rail centres not far from us. One day, they bombed a bridge two miles from us and the next day, pieces of human bodies floated down the Seine river across from our garden. Arms, legs and other body parts would get caught in the weeds along the river.

We had been under the German occupation for four long years and looked forward to being liberated.

Across the street from us was a Rest and Recreation (R&R) home for SS troops who had been wounded on the Russian front. The Gestapo had arrested my father, a Frenchman, and after spending eight months in Fresnes prison near Paris, we were told he was in the concentration camp of Buchenwald, where he was allowed to write us a censored letter, in German only, once in a while. We knew he was alive but had no idea Buchenwald was an extermination camp. The Germans across the street told us that he was in a 'work' camp, and was being well treated. (Little did we know … !)

My father came home after the war weighing less than six stone, a living skeleton and spent months in bed after his return. He had been arrested for the following reasons:

1. A dead German general was found floating down the river Seine in Paris.
2. Theft of documents from German offices in Paris, where my father worked as an Interior Decorator.
3. Treason against the 'Great Reich.'

After his liberation from Buchenwald, he was made Commander of the Legion of Honour for services to the French Resistance and the Allies.

My father had unlimited access to the German occupied airfields since the Germans asked him to make 'black-out' curtains for the windows of the Luftwaffe barracks. As a result, he was able to gain information about the number and type of 'planes possessed by the Luftwaffe, details of which he relayed to the Allies. He always said that he did it because it was his duty, and never wanted credit for it. However, he was credited with saving the lives of thousands of Allied pilots.

During an air raid, instead of seeking cover in our basement, we would quickly go outside in our garden and look for the first 'planes to arrive. It would not take long to spot the B-17s in their large formations, leaving vapour trails behind them. The Germans would immediately begin trying to shoot them down. We would watch in horror as a 'plane was hit, and one day we saw three 'planes shot down overhead, the date was September 13th, 1943. A wing broke off on one of the 'planes and circled down to the ground while the 'plane crashed and some of the men bailed out. Some airmen had their 'chutes deployed, others didn't. Our hearts broke as we witnessed these sights. I am still haunted today by these scenes.

I remember seeing two bodies plunge to the ground without the 'chutes opening. I saw one airman come down with his 'chute deployed and watched with horror as our German neighbours machine gunned him. His head tipped down all of a sudden, and we knew he was gone.

Another parachuted to safety on an island across the Seine, very near to where we lived. He was so close, we could watch him wrap up his 'chute and hide it, about a hundred yards from us, then disappear in the woods.

Suddenly our German SS neighbours rang our doorbell and demanded to borrow our small sailboat to get across the river to find the airman. We told them this was impossible for it was a sailboat and it would take a long time to get it ready and there were no oars.

They were upset and left, but realized that the boat would not be of much use to them. Then they noticed our small motorboat on blocks, in our garden. We mentioned to them that the motor was not working and we had no gas anyway. The nearest bridge to access the island was about five miles away and we found out later that the Germans had blocked the access to the island to prevent French people from trying to locate and rescue the airman. The Germans went on the island but never found him.

Late that night our doorbell rang. Cautiously, my mother opened the window. It was our town's assistant mayor, who knew my mother was a US citizen and wanted to know if she could come and speak with the airman.

Knowing that the Germans lived across the street and were watching our every move, that my father was in Buchenwald and that she would have to leave us all alone in the night, she offered money and food instead. She did not want to leave us, tempted as she was to go and see this airman, her first American soldier. We heard later that some members of the French Underground crossed the river with a rowboat, after dark, found the airman and brought him back to the town hall. His name was Rudolph Richer and he was a radio operator on the B-17. He was the only survivor of his crew and was sent back to England via Spain. The whole process took two months.

The day before the liberation of Paris, August 25th 1944, we heard rattling noises in our street. I ran to our gate to see what the commotion was all about. German tanks were retreating. I opened our gate to take a closer look, when the Germans immediately pointed their machine guns at me. You never saw a fourteen-year-old close a gate so fast!

The next day, we found out that these same troops had murdered eighteen Frenchmen, making them dig their own mass grave, shooting them and pouring water into their grave to drown those who were not quite dead. There is a memorial at that spot, in Chatou.

Mr Adamek is Polish

A Young Man's War in Poland

A few weeks after I had killed my pigeons (when we thought that we were going to flee from the Germans and then didn't) more Germans soldiers arrived and this time things were very different. War had really started. There were shootings and the Germans began to treat the Polish people very badly. There was no public transport. The railway was taken over by the German army. Day and night, a never-ending stream of trains roared by, some carrying troops and others equipment and guns, going further into Poland. This went on for about six months. We tried to carry on life as usual. I still went to school. Gradually the Polish teachers began to disappear until eventually the school closed for a year. The local people then decided to open the schools again, but they could now only teach the German language and eventually banned Polish speaking in schools.

The Germans then decided to register the population, to find all the useful males to train for the German army. There was no choice - to object meant you were sent to the concentration camp. The persecution of professional and learned people began.

By the time I was fourteen years old my parents received a letter to say that I would be recruited to a Workers Corps. I was given a spade instead of a gun and trained as a soldier using the spade in place of a gun. Myself and the other lads were given all sorts of dirty jobs to do.

In 1943 I was moved to Germany, near Hanover. For six months I was properly trained as a soldier, but treated and worked as a peasant. I was able to witness the British bombing of Hanover. It was a spectacular sight from the distance with everything lit up by phosphorous flares. I was glad to be away from the city. I was then sent home as a civilian and told that when I was sixteen years old I would be called up to join the German army.

When this happened I was taken by train to Clermont-Ferrand in France and began training to be a soldier in earnest with guns. After the training I was sent to Sete in Southern France and back to doing the dirty work (latrine cleaning, etc) for the Germans. The Germans were short of food and ammunition. Soon, fighting started in real earnest when the Americans began their offensive. I spent the next three months in retreat-walking all the way to Luxelle on the German/Belgian border. These three months were part of my teenage years. I was crawling with lice - there was no water to waste on washing or drinking. I drank water from dykes and puddles. There was no food. The soldiers killed their horses for meat. I stole food. I still have signs of that long walk. My feet are misshapen and my big toes are black. Eventually order broke down. The Polish boys fared better. The French people were kind to us and gave us food. Some tried to escape and were shot. At Luxelle we stopped for a few days. I told a French farmer who I was and that I wanted to escape from the Germans. They suggested I hide in the hay in a barn and they fed me. When the Americans closed in a few days later the farmer handed me over to them. Because I was a Pole they kept me (and other Poles) separate from the German POWs. They fed me and were kind to me. After two weeks, other Poles and myself were taken to Marseilles where we were taken by ship to Brindisi in Southern Italy to join the Polish army under British command. I was in very poor shape. I was de-loused, washed, shaved and fed properly and given two weeks rest. I was then retrained for the Polish army. I was in the Signals Corps. Later I was sent to the Adriatic Coast to Ancona to fight the Germans, who were in retreat. By the time the Poles reached and liberated Bologna the war was finished.

The British Government gave the Poles the choice of returning to Poland, or going to England, Canada, Australia or New Zealand. I was afraid to go to Poland as the Russians were there and it was no longer a free country.

When I arrived in England at a camp in Amersham, I thought what a wonderful clean and beautiful country it was. I decided then that England was to be my new country where I could start a new life as a human being. I was transferred to a rehabilitation camp in Lilford, Northamptonshire, where I met my wife. We had five lovely children, who between them have so far produced thirteen super grand children.

My family in Poland were delighted to hear from me in 1946, they thought I was dead, as they had received a letter from a German Officer to say I was missing. I now have that letter- it ends 'Heil Hitler' but my mother scribbled over and over that part, in a fit of desperation. I was not allowed to visit them until 1961 by which time my parents had died. I visit regularly now. After all that, I am now a very happy man.

Mr Adamek's 'walk'

Romuald Lipinski also left Poland when he was deported by the Russians

Leaving Poland

The soldiers came on June 19, 1941 at about 2.30am. They just knocked and came in. I remember my mother woke me up and immediately I realized what was going on. They told us to take what we needed and be ready in one hour. We packed our belongings, some potatoes, clothing, etc. and my mother asked if she could take some medicines for the heart. The officer refused. My mother asked if we can take the mattresses which were just made before the war. To our surprise the officer allowed us to take them. We were the last in their round-up for the night and they had some room on the truck, so he didn't object.

We were taken to a railway station, where on the side tracks were awaiting freight cars. There was a long freight train ready, the box cars with iron bars in the windows, and people were being brought from all over the area.

Most of the families were without men, they were either arrested earlier or separated at the time of deportation. In our case, we were lucky - my father was apparently too old to represent any danger to the Soviet Union. When I think about the reasons for selection of the deportees I get lost. There seem to be none. There were people from all walks of life: young, old, poor, rich, educated, uneducated, in other words everybody. There was a family of Russians, two sisters with their children, their husbands had been arrested before. They spoke among themselves in Russian. There was also a Russian Orthodox priest with his son.

In our boxcar there were about fifty people. We were held at the station the whole of the next day. They let us out a couple of times to go to the station latrines. When I went with my father (men were taken separately from women) we looked at each other - it was easy to run away and hide ourselves in one of the railroad employee's houses. But mother was on the train and we could not leave her to be all by herself. We went back. People were coming to the train bringing things to eat, clothing, and expressing their compassion. But at that time our spirits were good. There was no despair.

There is something I never understood. The Russians came 'to free the peasants from the yoke of the Polish landlords' and yet, many of the poor peasants were deported with us to Siberia. Sometimes you could see whole families, old people and small children, arrested and deported. In our box car there was a grandfather, age 72, and two of his grandchildren 5 and 7. What crimes against the Soviet Union did they commit in their lives? But this was an example of 'Soviet justice'.

During the night of 21st June we heard the train moving. All of a sudden it became very quiet in the car and then somebody started to sing. Some women started to cry. I don't think that at that time I realized the seriousness of the situation and the dramatic consequences of this moment for the rest of my life. It was somehow inconceivable to me that I would leave Poland forever. I visioned myself returning to my native land as a grown-up perhaps, after many years, to find everything the way it was when I was a boy. Somehow, it was our destiny that practically every generation had to go to Siberia. My father went there twice: once as a Russian soldier and then as an exile; my great grandfather died in Siberia; and now it was my fate to be exiled.

I spent many hours at the window trying to get a glimpse of the countryside. One could see that it was not a happy land. We were passing villages with small houses with thatched roofs. People going about their daily chores seemed to be subdued, without a smile. At railroad stations there was the everpresent NKVD.

At nights, I listened to the monotonous sound of the wheels, thinking that every sound takes me further and further away from my country. Couple of times, I don't remember where, we noticed the stations bombed and the rumours about the war between Germany and Russia were confirmed.

After twelve days of travel we arrived to the city of Barnaul - which is in Altai Country. It is a beautiful country, resembling Vermont or New Hampshire. I will never forget the scene when we were being detrained and a group of Russian women came to us and asked if we wanted anything to eat or drink. They told us that they were exiled there from somewhere some ten years ago in similar conditions. I learned later that to be exiled from one place to another was part of normal life in Russia. This was due to Stalin's paranoia and communist system.

We were put in a large hall. These were sort of local community clubs that served as all-purpose assembly rooms, movie houses, meetings and every other purpose imaginable. Of course, every meeting or other communal activity had to be sanctioned and approved by the local party boss. In Soviet Russia nothing, absolutely nothing could be done without approval of the Party. We were sleeping on the floor, next to our things without any privacy whatsoever. There were about four hundred people in that room.

After a few days, the NKVD told us that those who work would have a priority in getting accommodation in the permanent barracks. My father was not eligible to work (too old) but my mother and I volunteered. My job was to carry mortar to the plasterer. Every once in a while the plasterer, usually a woman, would yell at the top of her lungs "Rastvoru" (mortar) then we would get a couple of shovels of the mortar and bring it to her. They were working on the permanent barracks. We were paid for work, but it was not much and there was practically nothing that one could buy with this money; it was more profitable to go to the river and fish. At least you could get something that you could eat. The Ob, the second largest river in Russia after the Volga, at that time, was full of fish. It was not unusual for me to bring home 15-20lb of fish. We had fish in every possible shape and form.

As soon as it became known that my father was a physician, many Russians, having more confidence in a Polish doctor than their own, started to ask my father to see their sick. My father, in return for the medical visits, since he was actually not licensed to practice, didn't take any money but did not refuse if they offered something to eat. So, more fish, because the Russians hardly had anything else. But soon after us, there arrived a lot of Lithuanians (usually rich farmers) and they brought with them large amounts of food. When they started to call my father he would bring home a piece of pork lard or something like that. My mother would save it for winter, which everybody was afraid of.

We were getting 500g of bread per day. Under normal conditions there would be enough of other things to eat and one would not be hungry. If one gets only the bread and nothing else, 500g is definitely not enough. I remember once we were fishing and a Russian boy, who was fishing next to me asked me to take care of his 'zakid.' A Zakid is a long string that has several hooks attached to it. One end of the string is anchored to the bank of the river and the other has a stone that is thrown into river. After some fifteen minutes you pulled the zakid out of the water and usually there were several fishes on the hooks. So, this boy disappeared for a while. After half an hour he came back and said: "Well, I've just had my 500 grams of bread, and that's until tomorrow."

To me, this simple incident symbolized the quiet resignation with which Russian people accepted their fate in times of war.

Heinz Barthel left his home in Germany and fled in the opposite direction

Retreating From the Russians

While fleeing from the advancing Russians my mother, my sister and I, an eight-year-old boy from Potsdam, still had our pillowcase full of raw coffee. For this I had had to climb into a huge food wagon in a military train for my mother while we were still on the other side of the Elbe struggling through the chaos of shortage and surplus of military supplies. Sacks of coffee, sugar and beans were stored there. The coffee appealed to my mother.

"Everyone can help himself to his heart's desire" called a German soldier from under the wagon. "Pretty soon there won't be much more of it to be found anyway." He had been ordered to prepare the truck for the explosion that ensued a short time later. Whilst I was shovelling the coffee into the pillowcase, I was greeted by the noise of shell and rifle fire from all directions, interrupted by several large explosions. It was impossible to make out whether the noise announced the approaching Russians, or whether drunken soldiers were firing into the air for fun or shooting at the land mines which had been laid. Perhaps the SS, who were hidden in a villa on a little hill not far from the bank of the Elbe, were trying once again to shoot at those German soldiers who were trying to reach the American-occupied west bank of the Elbe.

A short time later this whole freight train with all its good things was blown up in the middle of the milling mass of people. The German military had carried out the order not to let anything fall into the hands of the Russians. But now we had got our pillowcase safely over the River Elbe and it gave us, gram by gram, good service in reserve currency.

We hid it (the coffee) as if it were a pillow right at the bottom of our pram. And my mother counted out the coffee beans whenever she could get something edible in exchange for them, a jug or milk from a farmer or just a place to sleep for the next night.

As quickly as we could, we left this place where the horrors of war seemed to have caught up with us all over again. It was difficult then for people to behave in a rational way that we now take for granted. The instinct alone, the absolute priority, which everyone feels inside for survival, dictated one's behaviour.

So my mother set off towards the South, to Weida in Thuringen, her hometown, where she sought safety. Over 300km lay ahead of us, on foot, on country roads in the scorching sun. Our remaining treasures of clothing, blankets and food were all stowed in a large-wheeled pram, which we found abandoned along the way and which accompanied us to the end of our wandering through the Germany of 1945. It was like a dream to us; a landscape seemingly unaffected by war. Every day brought a new adventure …

"Quickly quickly" shouts a man in an American uniform (how come he speaks German?) "The hall is needed for wounded people! Pack your things and get going!" And so began the first morning of peacetime for us.

The ballroom floor of a small village guesthouse near the west side of the River Elbe had been completely covered with straw. People were lying in tightly packed rows, old and young, many children. They were refugees from the eastern part of Germany, some of whom had been on the move for the four months since January 1945. They were fleeing from the ever approaching War Front - fleeing from the Russians, the Red Army. The fear that drove them on was written all over their faces, faces that bore the evidence of indescribable strains and stresses.

Their fear was a terrible mixture, from the horror stories of the Nazis: "Now these sub-human creatures are coming to take dreadful revenge!" Everyone knew those ugly Bolshevik faces - they had been portrayed almost daily in the 'Volkische Beobachter' and these were now buried deep in our souls, especially for us children. And there were the horrors of the nights of perpetual bombing from which we had escaped. And worst, there were the reports from eyewitnesses among the refugees, some of whom had escaped from the Russians several times and in the process had lost members of their families. There were those who had had to watch as others, mostly women and children, paid with their lives for the horror that the Nazis had started among Eastern Europe's peoples. And there were the German soldiers fleeing, often for good reasons, from imprisonment by the Russians. Whole SS Panzer Divisions were pushing towards the West in the hope that the Americans would unite with them to drive the Russians out of Germany again.

And now today, no reason for fear anymore. We had finally and happily arrived in the land of peace on the west side of the Elbe with the Americans.

It was the 2nd or 3rd of May 1945 - still very early in the morning and still no end to the war, but we were, or so it seemed to us after the peaceful night, safe.

When the people who had been lying on the floor realised that the man who spoke German had been serious with his order to empty the hall, they quickly piled together their remaining possessions. A woollen blanket for sleeping on at night. Some food, mostly from the German army's 'iron rations': choca-cola (fliers chocolate), the fruit bars that the very young German soldiers had slipped to us the previous day, still on the Russian side of the river. They were sitting in their trenches, obviously waiting to go into action. Also tins of preserved pork and daily rations of crisp-bread whose cardboard packs the soldiers could use as postcards.

And even before the last refugees had left the room the medical orderlies pushed in, carrying stretchers and tipped their sad loads onto the straw. We knew at once that we had already seen these bloodstained groaning bodies. These were those same very young German soldiers from the trenches on the other side of the river. No doubt they were members of the Hitler Youth, who had quickly been pushed into military uniforms and sent off to fight the Russians, just to gain one or two days in which the fleeing German soldiers at the front might succeed in being captured by the Americans. That's why they risked their lives and now the 'leftovers' were being brought into our nightly shelter ...

Kees Vanderheyden recalls an incident in Holland

Khaki Helmets

My memories of the war are of a young Dutch boy living under the German occupation and finally being liberated by the Canadians and the British. The war was literally in my backyard, with a German General's staff, his radio listening post, the allied airmen hidden far away in the garden and later, the Canadian military field hospital in our living room, with blood and wounded soldiers around us. It was a strange, terrible and sometimes even exciting period for an eleven-year-old boy.

One beautiful September day in 1944, the overhead rumble of planes was so deafening that the daily flights of the Allied bombers seemed a simple buzzing noise in comparison. That afternoon, plane after plane flew over, very low to the ground.

These weren't the usual bombers, but big planes towing motorless square gliders, brushing the tops of the trees as they flew past. We could even see the pilots and wave to the crew. It was absolutely incredible and terribly exciting.

The German anti-aircraft defence guns rattled endlessly, but the procession stayed on its course towards an unknown destination. We became convinced that they were coming to liberate us that very day. After several hours of racket and cheering as hundreds of planes flew by, all was quiet again. But we were worried. Mostly, we were disappointed. Not a single American or Canadian was in sight.

The Germans were nervous, but they were still lords and masters. Neighbours reported that one of the gliders had been shot down and crashed near the village, killing American soldiers in the accident. We were aghast.

Early the next day, I went to Saint-Peters-Banden church, where I sang in the choir. There was blood on the church steps, and the wrought-iron gates to the cemetery were open. German soldiers were busy with wheelbarrows on which they had placed long, bloodstained, brown paper bags. I understood that bodies had been placed in these bags for burial.

The soldiers were tossing the bags into a row of graves they had dug near the cemetery gates. What had happened? Who were the dead? Were they Germans, or were they the Allies who had died in yesterday's plane crash? I had no answers for the moment. First, I had to serve mass. But as soon as mass was over, I dashed to the cemetery.

The Germans were gone, but the gates were still open and a crowd of curious onlookers was examining the freshly dug graves. I drew closer. Much to my surprise, there were five wooden crosses with khaki-coloured military helmets perched atop them. Most of these helmets were damaged or crushed. And they weren't German helmets either. What a distressing sight!

Maybe the dead were the people we waved to yesterday. Now they were buried in our cemetery, next to a row of German graves marked with similar crosses without helmets. I grew heavyhearted as I took it all in. I hadn't yet really seen death, but I'd found its sad monument.

Olga Gerbers also lives in Holland

Liberated by the Canadians

Leiden is in the western part of the Netherlands. In 1943 we were evacuated out of The Hague. The area where we lived was transformed into a fortification, because the ReichsKommissar Seyss Inquart lived in a property not far from our home. Because of the strike on the railways, which started in September 1944 at the same time as the attack on Arnhem, we were effectively cut off from the rest of the country. There was no electricity or gas. There was no fuel, so no public transport. The same applied within a short time, to the availability of food or clothing. The occupation by Nazi-Germany was felt totally.

In Leiden we lived in a sort of loft level apartment together with an elderly couple. In 1945 there were six of us. We were a family of four and two grandparents, who had fled by bicycle during the attack on Arnhem. The living room measured about 2.5 x 2.5 metres. Once a day the stove was lit to warm the food. This was heated with 'brickets' (compacted coal dust). The food was placed in a 'zakpan' made from an old basin; this allows you to put the pan right into the stove - the only way we could warm the food. My parents had placed all our furniture in storage in The Hague, apart from those which were absolutely necessary. We shared access to lavatories with the principal tenants. These were downstairs. We had a water tap from which we could get water for cooking and washing.

I went each day to the cook-shop for the six of us. In addition, being a pupil in Oegstgeest, I received an extra little pan of food. I was also expected to find out whether there was any food to buy in any shop. We were able to get some sugarbeets, potatoes, wheat, brown beans and tulip bulbs. I also remember making an expedition to Rijnsburg, with a sledge, to fetch winter parsnips. We also went, once per week to Oegstgeest to get a loaf of wheat-and-tulip bulb meal baked, until the day came that the baker ran out of fuel. Possibly some bread was also being distributed. Naturally I well remember the half loaf of Swedish white bread together with half a packet of margarine, to which I had a right. Also, the airdropped food parcels, the souplike grey ditch water, which during the last two weeks of the war was made available from the cook-shop, and finally bread, sausage and similar, which were provided by the German military to us children, when they were sitting behind our house while they were waiting to capitulate.

The schools were closed because there was no heating fuel. Moreover, the Wehrmacht had requisitioned them. Twice per week we had school in a freezing church hall. On a food expedition my father had bought ice-skates for me, so I spent a lot of time learning to skate in a flooded meadow. I roamed a lot through the meadows and small woodland with a friend, or I played at the home of a girlfriend who had also lived in The Hague. It was a large house inhabited by various people. The piano playing, brown haired Miss van der Linden, was found after the war to have been a Jewish girl in hiding. I heard afterwards that several people had been in hiding in a cellar, which I never dared to enter. There was nothing at all to read.

It was only too obvious that the Wehrmacht were around. We had an alarming experience once when two Wehrmacht soldiers rang the bell and knocked on the door. No one opened the door. My mother was afraid that my father's bicycle might be requisitioned. Later we heard that they had just mistaken the address.

The liberation came just in time. There was no longer anything to eat. I can still see us looking out of the loft window for Netherlands flags. We witnessed the entry of the Canadians. There were festivities for children. In the end both my sister and I ended up in hospital because someone from the B.S. (Inland Army) ran us down. We were carried to the hospital on the bonnet of a Jeep. Actually, I knew nothing about this because I was unconscious for hours. In August 1945 we returned to The Hague to find that our district was still a fortification. I needed a 'permit', which certified that I was allowed to be in the district.

The 1940s - Month by Month

1947
January
- Britain's coal industry was nationalised
- Al Capone died

February
- Lord Louis Mountbatten was appointed the last Viceroy of India
- Heavy snow swept across Britain in one of the worst winters on record

March
- Heavy floods affected many parts of Britain as the snow melted
- The Dead Sea Scrolls were discovered

April
- Charlton Athletic beat Burnley 1-0 in the FA Cup final
- The school leaving age was increased to 15

May
- The government approved the proposal for the Partition of India

June
- The 'Marshall Plan' was unveiled, with the USA pledging to help fund the rebuilding of Europe after the war

July
- The engagement of Princess Elizabeth to Lieutenant Philip Mountbatten was announced

August
- British rule in India came to an end
- Austerity measures were announced by the government due to the growing financial crisis

September
- Striking miners caused the closure of Yorkshire steelworks due to a shortage of coal

October
- Pilot Chuck Yeager became the first man to fly through the sound barrier, reaching a speed of 670 mph

November
- Princess Elizabeth married Philip Mountbatten at Westminster Abbey

December
- Stanley Baldwin, former Prime Minister died aged 80

After The War

Charlie Miller grew up with his mother in Rochdale

The Homecoming

I was born in September 1939, two days before World War II broke out. The following year my father was called up and he spent the next few years fighting for His Majesty in 'countries various'. I spent the war learning to walk, talk, read and write in Rochdale with my mother and assorted aunties but not many uncles.

In late 1945, mother told me that my father was due to come home soon. I couldn't remember him at all so there was not quite the same level of excitement within me as there obviously was within mother. She was beside herself with anticipation and didn't know whether to sit down, stand up, walk around the room or go to the toilet so she did all of them – repeatedly.

Suddenly, aunt Margery burst through the door. 'He's coming Joan, he's coming!' (or something like that).

Mother rushed out of the door pulling me behind her. Walking quickly down the street towards us were two soldiers in khaki uniform, kit bags thrown over their shoulders. I remember wondering which one was my Dad. This query was soon answered as the taller of the two men dropped his bag on the pavement and ran towards us. Mother let go of my hand and fell into his arms when he reached us. Tears ran down both their faces. After a moment or two, dad looked down at me. 'Hello young Charlie, have you been looking after your mum?'

Before I could think of an answer he bent down and picked me up with one of his strong arms and held me close to him, with mum still crying on his other shoulder. I can still remember the smell, a mix of dad's uniform and mum's perfume.

Playing in the Road

Roy Cox recalls an incident whilst stationed in Cheltenham

POWs

In January 1946 I was stationed in Cheltenham as a driver in the RASC. We were often sent on detachment to a nearby German POW camp. The POWs were waiting for repatriation and we were waiting for demob, the atmosphere was generally relaxed. This particular day I had to pick up my two trustee Germans, Heinz and Walter. They had been assigned to me as loaders many times before and I trusted them implicitly. I had to drive back to Cheltenham, then take a two-ton trailer to Tetbury to fill up with potatoes.

Heinz and Walter did a good job and they sat on the potatoes in the lorry to make sure that no sacks fell off. It was starting to get dark as we returned to the POW camp and I heard a thumping on the lorry cab. I stopped and got out. Heinz and Walter pointed to the front trailer wheel on which the tyre had burst. We had no spare and we were about ten miles from camp. I didn't know what to do. Heinz suggested that I unhitch the trailer, take Walter back to camp and he would guard the trailer until I returned. This we did and I went to report to the catering officer.

He asked me who was looking after the trailer of potatoes.

"It'll be OK, sir", I said, "One of the POWs is looking after it."

The look of amazement on the officer's face was something to see.

"You've done WHAT?"

It dawned on me then how stupid I had been.

"If it's not still there when you go back, you'll be taking his place inside!" he informed me.

I had to wait for two hours before the workshop sent out a spare wheel. I drove back to the trailer, all the time praying that Heinz would still be there. As I rounded a bend in the road I saw him in the headlights. He was very cold and I thanked him for not running away.

"Where would I go?" he said.

To show my relief, I gave him a packet of Woodbines.

He and Walter and all the rest in the camp were repatriated soon afterwards.

Allan Taylor left The Orkneys

An Invitation from the King

I was born on a December morning in 1929 on one of the storm-lashed Orkney Islands. Eighteen years later, I received an invitation from the King, our present Queen's father, not so much an invitation as an order, to become a member of one of his forces and here's me not ever knowing or spoken to the gentleman in my life!

The letter said I had to report to what was a Salvation Army canteen in our capital town, Kirkwall. So off I went and on arrival, there were one or two other boys there who had received the same invitation. As soon as I entered the door things started to change. Sitting, eyeing me up and down were three men each wearing a uniform; the navy, the army and the air force. Having working for a shipping company since I left school, I thought it would be the navy for me. It must have been a Thursday because I was handed the local weekly paper, 'The Orcadian' and I was asked to read a small piece from it. With this, all three gentlemen seemed fairly pleased. I was then pointed to another room where there was a man dressed in a white jacket. He asked me to strip to the waist, then he hung something from his ears and touched me with the other end both back and front. Then he asked me to drop my trousers. I must have looked surprised and he said, "Your pants as well."

There was this man with a soupspoon in his hand looking at my private parts. Anyone who has been in a wooden hut in the northern latitudes in the dead of winter will know how cold and draughty it can be. There he took a grip and said, "Cough."

This was the last thing in my mind at that time. Then it was "Put your clothes on" and I was handed a small bottle and asked for a sample. With this I was pointed to another small room in the corner. Not feeling too comfortable after what I had just been through I struggled, then once I got started I could not stop and could have filled a dozen bottles or more!

I then went and sat on a form and after about half an hour, I was told I had been accepted in the Royal Air Force and to go home. I awaited further instruction.

On a February night during a blizzard, I received a brown envelope from the King, well that's what it said - On His Majesty's Service - and the address read 'Aircraftsman 2nd Class Taylor TA.' I was asked to report to RAF Padgate in Lancashire and enclosed was a railway ticket from the wilds of the Orkney Islands to Liverpool. At that time I had never seen a train. On the morning I left the islands I caught a steamer to mainland Scotland with my little suitcase in my hand and climbed up to sit beside the funnel for warmth as the ship heaved and rolled on its three hour journey across the Pentland Firth. We arrived in Lime Street about four o'clock the next afternoon, by this time there was about twenty boys with suitcases. No more Mr Taylor, it was "Airman," shouted by a man with stripes on his uniform. We were all herded into the back of a truck with a canvas top with wooden forms to sit on. At the guardroom at Padgate, another man with stripes on his uniform informed us that he was the corporal and as he clicked his heel once more also informed most of us that we did not have a father, or words to that effect. Then we were made to march to our hut and each given an iron bedstead with a straw mattress and four blankets. By the look of the blankets we were not the first users. We also had our set of irons - fork, knife, spoon and enamel mug. These, like your number, you kept until you were demobbed. That was my first day in the RAF, number 2384727.

After a few days we all met these kind men called drill instructors and one thing I am sure of, none of them had a known father! But to end on a happier note I would not have liked to have missed my time in the Royal Air Force. There I met my wife Jean and we have now been together happily for fifty-six years.

Gladys Davey set up her first home

Squatters

1946, my most memorable year. My husband was demobbed, no house to call our own, so we squatted in a disused WAAF hut. Sixty feet long, twenty foot wide, an NCO's room in one corner and combustion heater in the middle. No electricity, no water though we were lucky enough to boast a toilet just inside the door. Cement dust flew each time a brush was put on the floor. Oil lamps, Primus stoves, candles and all water carried from the wash house on the site, which was quite a task when my third child was a home birth, but all our neighbours were in the same position and we all helped each other.

Eventually the electricity was established and water pipes laid. The old combustion heater was replaced with a kitchen range.

Thanks to the efforts of all the menfolk, who scoured building sites where houses were being renovated, we had wooden partitions to make bedrooms, carpets from second-hand shops and lino paint kept the cement dust from rising.

How hard we all worked, to make our 'homes' and how great was the friendship between everyone. But as each family was allocated a council house and moved away, sadly, something was lost. I now keep in touch with only one fellow squatter who is in Canada.

I have no regrets over that five years in the hut. It took courage, but we were happy and together, a great thing after the separation of war.

Stanley H Jones remembers the celebrations in Trowbridge

Celebrations

When it was obvious that the war in Europe was nearly over, the victory celebrations in Trowbridge had already been planned. Posters were going up in shop windows amid red, white and blue rosettes. Only the date of VE Day had been left out. As we left school on Monday 7th May the teachers told us that if there was an announcement during the evening that Germany had surrendered, there would be a holiday for the next two days. The announcement came - and no way were we going to school, but some children and one or two teachers obviously did not listen to the wireless. As we went into the town where bunting was already being put up we passed the school and there on the steps, with the doors locked, was a small queue of children and my teacher.

My next memory is in the afternoon - a large crowd had gathered outside the Town Hall - loudspeakers had been erected and at three o'clock Winston Churchill made a broadcast to the nation, and in his wonderful and dramatic way told us that war was over - Hitler had been defeated. Churchill also reminded us that there was still much to do - Japan was still at war with us - but this was the great day.

On down to the People's Park, and sure enough Albert Taylor, the organisor of the pre-war carnivals and manager of Fosters menswear, was there, almost as if he had been waiting in the wings. Soon the children were enjoying sports. Before tea there was still time for an icecream. Apart from a shop in town, the only place we could buy icecream was from the backyard of a house almost adjoining the gas works. It was about half a mile from home and we bought either penny or threepenny cones. There was then a dash home before the icecream melted, across rough land where buildings had been demolished under pre-war slum clearance. I don't expect these days the icecreams would have met health and hygene regulatons but these icecreams were homemade and delicious.

Duncan Hamman took up a new hobby in Cheshire

One Big Step

Sometimes you may do something, which you feel is quite insignificant at the time yet it can have a massive effect on the rest of your life. This is what I did one Sunday in the summer of 1947.

On this day, as a fifteen year old, I went out on a day's ride with a cycling club, little did I realise this would involve me in over fifty years of pleasure and excitement and bring me a huge number of friends.

I cannot remember the reason but I had received a new bike, which had been bought from Jack Sibbit's shop on Stockport Road, Longsight, and as it had dropped handlebars, I called it a Racer. I remember it had cost £15 and everyone was amazed at how expensive it was.

In 1947 my brother Jim was doing his National Service in the Royal Navy. I could never understand why Jim chose to travel all the way from Plymouth to Manchester, when he had a weekend leave, just to go out with his cycling club on Sunday, yet he did.

I was quite surprised when one Sunday Jim, who was home on weekend leave, ordered me out of bed and told me that I would be coming out with the cycling club. I wasn't very keen on the idea but as big brother had spoken, I had no choice. A couple of hours later I was riding along the road to the meeting place at Cheadle.

The war had only ended two years earlier and petrol was still rationed. This meant that only the police, Fire Service and other emergency services were allowed to use petrol. There were a few civilians permitted to buy petrol but they were under strict control as to when and how they could use it in their cars. To get a permit to buy petrol the motorist had to prove that he/she could not possibly do their job without a car. He was expected to walk, cycle or go by bus or train so it was unusual for a permit to be issued. The permit might authorise him to use the car only between Manchester and Bolton and on Monday to Friday after 8am and before 6pm. If he were caught driving outside these times and places he would be arrested. This meant that the roads were almost completely empty of motor traffic. Many thousands of people used a bicycle to get to and from work and other journeys. Trafford Park had massive bicycle traffic jams every morning and evening as thousands of cyclists headed into and out of the Park to their daily work.

We did see occasional cars on the roads during the week but at weekends the roads were almost completely empty and it was possible to cycle on Sunday and see, perhaps, only two or three cars all day! I remember we used to ride six abreast on the climb of the Cat and Fiddle road. One Sunday the whole club of about 60 or 70 riders sat in the middle of the Buxton to Leek road, at the top of Axe Edge, and enjoyed a picnic. We didn't have to move once. This same road is now full of heavy traffic and every time I drive along it I think back to that picnic in the middle of the road.

With cars not being used, many people took up cycling and hiking as spare time activities and they became very popular pastimes. In fact it was the cyclists and hikers who kept the country pubs open with their custom during the years of petrol rationing. Sadly when petrol came off ration (in about 1953, I think) many pubs put up 'No Cyclists or Hikers' signs as they welcomed the motorist back to the roads.

Cheadle was the traditional meeting place for many Manchester cycling clubs and on Sunday mornings there would be many hundreds of cyclists each with their own particular club meeting point.

Jim and I were going out with the South Manchester Racing club. Cycling was so popular that club run attendances of 60 or 70 riders were quite common and, with dozens of clubs meeting, Cheadle became a cycling town each Sunday. It was a fantastic atmosphere as there were a lot of friendly insults flying between various clubs.

I was a little nervous at meeting all these strangers but was amazed at how quickly I settled in. I was introduced to everyone as Jim's kid brother and was soon chatting to everyone. With the roads being empty of traffic such huge groups of cyclists didn't cause any problems. We were, without doubt, the Kings of the Road. In my innocence I thought things would always be like this and had no idea of the traffic problems that loomed in the future. I suppose it was a good thing we didn't know what the future held for us. We were able to enjoy those wonderful years of fun, laughter, friendship, healthy exercise and adventure without a care in the world.

I cannot remember much about my first day with the cycling club. We rode out into Derbyshire and there were plenty of tough climbs but I cannot remember finding them hard at the time. I also fell off my bike on the descent of Mam Tor into Castleton, which made me feel very stupid. Suddenly Sunday had changed from being the most boring day of the week into the most exciting.

I was not very happy employed at the Watch and Clock Repairer so when I saw an advert in the Manchester Evening News stating, 'Youth wanted to learn cycle trade' I decided to apply. I was most surprised to discover that the job would be at Jack Sibbit's shop, the same shop where my own bike had been made. I got the job and so cycling became not only my hobby but also a means of earning my living.

Jack Sibbit had been one of Britain's top Track Racing Cyclists in the 1920s. He had competed in several World Championships and Olympic Games (including the 1936 Games in front of Adolph Hitler) and was very famous in the cycling world. His business was building cycle racing frames and they were renowned throughout Britain and I was employed to help Jack, as there were only the two of us working at the shop.

On my first day at work I had a nasty surprise as I found my new boss was very short tempered, swore all the time and he frightened me to death. I began to wish I had not left the watch and clock shop. My first job was to learn how to build spoked cycle wheels, quite a complicated process, and every time I made a mistake, which was frequently, Jack would shout and swear at me. It took me a long time to realise that underneath his rough exterior he had a heart of gold and we later became very good friends and he treated me more like a son.

Jack's son was doing his National Service in Egypt with the RAF and Jack was so sad that he showed little interest in cycling. I remember him saying to me once "God knows what will happen to my business when I am gone." His fears were well founded as a few years after his death in 1950, his son closed the shop and the famous Sibbit Racing Cycles were never made again.

I worked at Sibbit's shop for about three years, until I had to leave to do my National Service in the RAF. Between us we built hundreds of cycle frames – Jack doing the brazing and me doing the other jobs. I also served in the shop and gradually built up my knowledge of bikes and all things to do with bikes. I also managed to bring Jack into the modern era and, I like to think, I helped to improve his business. This is how it happened.

As far as cycling and cycling equipment was concerned Jack was one of the old school. He thought British was always best and anything that wasn't British, was a load of rubbish. At that time a lot of new modern cycling equipment was coming in from the Continent but Jack wouldn't entertain it. "I'm not putting that rubbish on my bikes" he would say. Many cyclists thought of Sibbit's bikes as being very good quality but a bit old fashioned.

One day Jack took me by surprise when he suddenly asked, "What do they say about my bikes in the cycling clubs?" I decided I would tell him the truth about them being old fashioned and he seemed upset and I was sorry I had spoken out. A few days later one of the reps from the wholesalers came in and Jack called me into the shop. "What do you think of these?" he asked. On the shop counter were sets of lugs, fork crowns, front and rear ends and fork blades, all very modern and not a bit like the usual fittings used by Sibbit. "These are fantastic," I said. "They are really modern." To my surprise Jack started ordering the new stuff and, when the rep had gone he said, "We'll give it a try but if these frames don't sell you are in trouble."

We made about half a dozen frames with the new fittings and I thought they were great although Jack looked a bit doubtful. "Foreign muck." he would say. The first frame to come back from the chrome platers and enamellers was placed in the shop window and we waited to see what our customers thought and as the days passed it was clear that everyone thought the new frames were fantastic. Orders started coming in for the new modern Sibbit frames and Jack grinned at me "I won't be sacking you after all."

There was a funny experience when Jack nearly blew himself up. He couldn't resist a bargain and one day he came into the shop with several large ex-army Jerry Cans. "These will come in handy," said Jack but they had been used to store oil and would need cleaning out. At first he tried to clean them by using paraffin but this didn't work then he had one of his ideas. He would use the brazing torch to heat them up until they were red hot, this would remove the oil – or so he thought.

I was working on the other side of the workshop when there was a great explosion. The room was filled with fire and smoke and Jack appeared from out of the smoke. His face was black and he had lost his eyebrows and a lot of hair and he was very dazed. I took one look at him and burst out laughing. I couldn't help it. For a minute he just stared at me then he started laughing too and we stood there screaming with laughter. When we had regained control Jack looked at me and said, "What do you think you are laughing at? Brew me a cup of tea before I sack you."

Suddenly, Jack had a stroke and was very ill. He had always been so active and full of life so it was strange when I called at his house in Stretford, to see him lying in bed and looking very weak. This meant that Jack's son took over at the shop and the business started to go downhill. Young Jack didn't like getting up in the morning and never arrived at the shop before 10am, so I had to wait on the doorstep about an hour each morning. Instead of working he would chat with his friends in the shop leaving most of the work to me. I decided it was a waste of time arriving at 9am so started getting to work at the same time as Young Jack.

One morning I arrived at 10am and was surprised to see the shop already open. Inside was (old) Jack with a face like thunder. He yelled, swore and cursed me and I thought it was the end of my job but he knew what had been happening while he had been ill. He resumed command and (young) Jack had to start working again. Only a short time later he had another stroke, much worse this time, and he found it very difficult to speak and was confined to bed.

I was due to take my annual holiday and I was going with the club cycling down to Cornwall for two weeks. I went to see Jack before I left. His last words to me, which were said with great difficulty were, "Have a great time and tell me all about it when you get back." When I returned from holiday Jack had died and Young Jack was back in charge. It was only about six months before I was due to go in the RAF so I knew that when my National Service was over I wouldn't be returning to Sibbit's bike shop.

Anne Trent lived in Hayes

TV and Weightlifters

I recall VE Day, the 8th May 1945. I was eleven years old. My dad had cycled off to work before 7am to his job as a coppersmith at Fairey Aviation, Hayes. He hadn't got far before a lady ran out and said to him "Go back home, the war is over, nobody will be going to work today." It was a day of great joy for my mum, sister and myself. Us children couldn't really recall real peacetime as even in 1938 my father was digging a trench in the garden in preparation for war. I felt such a sense of relief, although I was only eleven. Everything seemed wonderful - my father took us for a walk in the fields and it was so peaceful, the air smelled fresher, the birds seemed to be singing louder. I felt so good inside myself.

The man next door was one of the pioneer workers in TV before the war. When the war ended he went to work on TV at EMI. They had a TV many, many years before anyone else. I remember seeing it for the first time, on a screen the size of a postcard, in this neighbour's house. I thought it was absolutely fantastic.

The neighbour would call our family in on a Saturday night to see a cabaret hosted by a funny little old Frenchman called Pierre Auguste. I believe that sometimes a French lady called Helene Cordet would appear on this cabaret too. At about 10pm the only TV station would close down.

During the 1948 Olympic Games in London, the weightlifters and 'strong' men were housed in the school I went to - Greenford Grammar School. Since we had no TV we didn't follow the events like we do today. However, I recall standing outside the school which was just opposite our house, with my autograph book (autograph books were very popular in those days) with many of my school chums and neighbouring children. Sadly I no longer have the autograph book in which I got the signatures of many of the weightlifters from the Middle East.

Another event I recall in January 1949 was the disappearance of a British South American Airways' airplane called 'Star Ariel.' My aunt's neighbour, Mrs Rettie who had a toddler daughter, had her husband George on board. He was the radio operator and I recall being at my aunt's when the news came in. Mrs Rettie came to my aunt's house and for the first day was joking that maybe the plane had landed on a desert island. However, as the days went by she became more and more anxious. As far as I know the Star Ariel was never found and remains to this day a big mystery. I believe the area the plane went missing was in the Bermuda Triangle.

INSTRUCTIONS TO PENSIONERS.

Read this Form or have it explained to you.

WHO MAY APPLY

1. An applicant must be a habitual user of tobacco (whether pipe tobacco, cigarettes or any other form of manufactured tobacco) or snuff, and must be in possession of a pension order book for one of the following pensions :—

(a) If aged 70 or over, a contributory or non-contributory old age pension of any weekly rate ; or

(b) If aged 65 to 70 (man), or 60 to 70 (woman), a contributory old age pension of more than 10s. a week exclusive of any supplementary pension ; or a widow's pension under the Contributory Pensions Acts of more than 10s. a week, exclusive of any child's allowance or supplementary pension ; or

(c) a blind person's pension under the Old Age Pensions Act, 1936, of any weekly rate.

WHEN TO APPLY

2. Persons in receipt of pension by 15th November, 1947.
Persons who are in possession of a pension order book for one of the pensions described in paragraph 1 are advised to apply as long before 15th November, 1947, as possible.

3. Persons not in receipt of pension by 15th November, 1947.
If by 15th November, 1947, you are **not** in possession of a pension order book for one of the pensions described in paragraph 1 you **cannot be granted duty relief**—

until you receive your first pension order book on being awarded a **non-contributory** pension or blind person's pension.

Eligible Old Age Pensioners could apply for Tobacco Duty Relief Tokens

Barry Ledgard recalls a holiday in Blackpool and life in Bradford

Blackpool and Plot Night

In August 1945, my family was on holiday in Blackpool, staying, as a special treat, at a seafront hotel, 'The South Crest' in the centre of the resort. The final victory of the war was due at any time, and I went to bed one evening leaving my parents in good spirits downstairs in the bar, celebrating the expected event. I was awakened in the early hours by noises outside on the promenade, and on looking out of the window, saw hundreds of people dancing and cheering in the streets. The air raid shelters, which had been built every hundred yards or so along the front were being invaded, the wooden benches dragged out, and pushed up onto the shelter roof where they were added to the massive bonfires burning on each shelter. It was a magic sight, particularly after the darkness of the previous six years, and made an impression upon me, and after nearly sixty years I can recall the picture with absolute clarity. My wife was born at the end of April 1946, nine months after the victory over Japan was announced, and I like to think that she was conceived at the moment I was gazing out onto the Blackpool Promenade watching the victory celebrations!

By the end of the war we had left our small back to back house and moved up in the world (up the street that is) and we lived above and behind a shoe shop. It was a big improvement to our previous house in that we had a bathroom in the attic although we still had an outside toilet. The bath was ancient and had been repainted many times which gave it a strange lumpy interior and the tap strained to produce hot water from the boiler at the back of the kitchen fire. It was a luke warm flow of such miniscule proportions that it took thirty minutes to achieve a water level of four inches, after which it seemed to sigh and just give up. My brother and I slept in the other attic room, and on the first floor was my parent's bedroom. Our front room, which was above the shoe shop, was the place where we lit the fire at Christmas, but I don't recall spending much time in there on other occasions.

The focal point of our life was the living kitchen where my mother did her best to prepare meals for the family of four on a single gas ring at the side of the sink. There was an oven at the side of the fire, as an additional cooking facility (providing the fire was lit.) In summer it was a great strain for my mother to prepare Sunday lunch, with a roast and Yorkshire pudding, when the fire had to be lit to provide the oven heat, irrespective of the weather conditions outside. I can see her face now, flushed and perspiring as she struggled to prepare the meal. At the time it meant little to me, but as I look back I can see the love and devotion that went into that Sunday morning torture she endured weekly in summertime.

Fish and chips were a good alternative to preparing a meal, and there seemed to be fish and chip shops on almost every street corner, providing succulent haddock and crisp chips in yesterday's newspaper. Fish was about two old pence, a fishcake one and a half pence and chips one penny. A good meal at an affordable price, and available for lunch or an evening meal.

Lister's Mill, world famous velvet weavers, was just up the street, and provided work for the majority of the community. Woe betide you if you were sent for fish and chips for lunch, and you got behind one of the apprentices from the mill who had been sent out from the shed in which they worked with the lunch order for their workmates. "Fish and chips thirty six times, cake and chips fifteen times, and twenty bags of chips with two dozen buttered teacakes!" The wait for your turn to be served took forever!

November 5th, 'Plot Night' was always a big feature of our calendar, in memory of the actions of Guy Fawkes. We started to go 'chumping,' that is gathering wood for the fire in September and it was retained in the back gardens of several of the gang and watched carefully to avoid it being stolen by other gangs. As the day drew near, excitement grew, and after the war, fireworks became available again. We raced home from school on the day of the fire, and the whole community began to build the bonfire on the cobbles in the middle of the street. There seemed to be a bonfire on almost every street throughout the city and not, as these days in public parks and areas. The fire was lit at about six thirty in the evening and burned with such ferocity initially that it seemed that the adjacent houses, no more than twenty feet from the fire, would be consumed by the flames. Fireworks followed - Catherine Wheels, Little Demons, Ripraps, Roman Candles, fountains of all sizes, Golden Rain, and for the less well off the 'sparklers' which were pieces of wire coated with a mixture of iron filings and saltpetre and were a devil to light!

The food came next. One neighbour would provide the 'plot toffee', thick sugary pieces that stuck to your teeth, and then 'parkin' - huge slabs of dark ginger cake made with treacle, and then it was pork pies and mushy peas that had been warming in someone's oven. As the night drew to a close, potatoes were thrown into the edge of the embers and extricated by a tree branch sometime later as charred black cannonballs of charred potato skin which cracked open to reveal the cooked white potato innards. We slapped butter on them and ate the lot, charred casing as well! If the fire started to go out before we were ready to leave, more wood had to be found. Many people got up the following morning and found their wooden garden gate missing! The following day we came home from school to find that the fire ashes had been collected together by the gardeners of the community and carted off for fertiliser - nothing wasted.

In the immediate post war period, Bradford received a number of immigrants from war torn Europe to provide necessary employees in the mills and factories, which were short of workers. Men and women from Lithuania, Estonia, Latvia, Poland, for example arrived and settled into our community with little fuss. The only difference between them and us was the language - there was no difference in appearance and I think this made integration much easier. I can recall as a small boy accosting men in the street who were known to be DPs (Displaced Persons) and asking if they had any foreign coins. We quickly built up a collection of base metal coinage and improved our knowledge of geography to boot!

There were nearly as many cinemas as fish and chip shops and we used to visit regularly, including the Saturday morning Kid's Club, where we saw Flash Gordon and Emperor Ming in a weekly battle of wits. We had the wonderful benefit of seeing films in 'Glorious Technicolour' at the peak of the film industry successes in the USA and travelled with John Wayne to Monument Valley, with Enrol Flynn through Sherwood Forest, with Tyrone Power on the Spanish Main and into the bull rings of Spain! That experience, with the reading of books from the public library, gave us knowledge, imagination, and writing ability that has served us well in adult life

I enjoyed Grammar School, within the limits of my ability. It paid not to be too prominent for whatever reason. One of my new schoolmates made an enemy of the French master on the first day and as his punishment was led around the classroom by this master with a dog collar around his neck at the end of a dog lead! I got the message.

We were not a well off family, by any means, and my father had a penchant for horse and dog racing which consumed such money that he had. I didn't begrudge him that - he worked very hard and was entitled to some pleasure. We all knew if he had done well at the dog track on the Saturday night because early on Sunday morning we were roused from our beds and told "we are off to the seaside!" It happened at least once a year! Dad raced down to the Alhambra Theatre in Bradford centre where the coaches left each Sunday for seaside destinations, fixed tickets through one of his contacts, and after packing sandwiches we hurtled down to the Manningham Park gates where the coaches stopped to pick up passengers. We had great days at the seaside. One thing about my dad - when he had money he spent it. Sadly, usually he hadn't any!

We always had new clothes for Whitsuntide, even if they were from a catalogue and we were paraded up the street or to relatives, to show that we were able to dress well for one week in the year at least.

Then the fifties dawned - and what a surprise - sweets were still on the ration! So nothing changed there then!

Yvonne Fischer grew up in India

The National Anthem

I was a twelve-year-old boarder in a school called St John's Vestry High School in Trichinopoly, South India. In August 1947, Idependence was granted to India. Months ahead of this celebration we had to learn the new national anthem – Jana Kana Mana.

On the big day, the pavilion was decorated, the governor, the headmaster and other very important people were seated. The school was assembled in the front. The juniors stood right in the front and the seniors behind us, all of us in our very best uniforms. The Union Jack was lowered and the Indian flag raised. The singing started, the seniors at the back singing God Save Our Gracious King and the juniors in the front singing Jana Kana Mana. It was quite embarassing for our headmaster!

The next day we had to assemble in our beautiful chapel and were given quite a dressing down and told that we had to accept this as our new national anthem.

Most of the Anglo-Indians could not accept this and left for other countries – the UK, Canada and Australia, etc. I wonder how many other Anglo-Indians at my old school, if still around could remember this?

Ruth Warburton lived in Germany

A Canadian Teenager in Germany

In September 1946, when I was fifteen, my mother, two sisters, younger brother and I set sail from Nova Scotia, in Canada, to join my father in Dusseldorf. He had been posted there as part of the Military Government established after the war to help with the re-settlement and re-organisation of Germany.

We were excited and somewhat apprehensive of this new world we were about to discover so soon after the end of the war. Our father had certainly not embellished the facts, but we were not prepared for the appalling destruction that we saw, or the hatred that we encountered.

At times the loneliness and boredom would bring on waves of homesickness. I had no books to read, no friends at first, just two hours of German lessons every morning and a piano lesson once a week. Occasionally an evening at a club in Dusseldorf, a Church Army service on Sunday, once in a while a movie in one of the two remaining theatres in town or a symphony concert in the bombed-out opera house. We also had the British Forces Network on the radio. We walked around town a lot, I remember.

I recall our first Christmas in 1946. We found and cut down a tree, not as big as those we had had for Christmas in Canada, but it was an evergreen. Of course we had no decorations, but thanks to an ample cigarette ration, we were able to make balls of the silver paper from cigarette packs and cut very thin strips of silver paper for icicles. We made paper chains from coloured pages cut from the Eaton's catalogue that we had brought with us.

Wolfgang, the German boy who lived across the road, made clamps and holders for tiny candles which, as I recall, were never lit. Looking back it really wasn't much of a tree, but it was our first Christmas together as a family since 1939 and we were happy. For Wolfgang and our German neighbours we were a source of cigarettes and liquor and the occasional good meal; we were tolerated only. I think they were glad when we finally returned to Canada, because by that time their life was slowly beginning to improve and return to normal.

Then in July 1947 I was sent to Prince Rupert School in Wilhelmshaven, a school set up for the children of the British Forces of Occupation. I look back now on that time as a most unique experience. The Colonel's daughter and the Sergeant's son were thrown together with no social or racial barriers and I have happy memories of those months at the school and how the whole 'German Experience' changed my life forever.

Barbara Fuller recalls a happy time!

A Memorable Week

During the summer of 1946 I went to Stafford to spend a holiday with my friend Barbara. She was living there while her husband was in the Army in Palestine, while mine was serving with the Welsh Guards in Germany.

One hot day we went on a long walk through the country lanes, we had to stop for a drink of water to quench our thirst. Eventually we came to a lovely old church where we were able to rest and to pray for the safe return of our husbands. We also had pleasure in finding a jug of water in the vestry.

As the sky began to look rather stormy we decided to start on the way back again. Our feet were so hot and sore that we took our shoes off and walked bare foot. Much to our surprise a black Rolls Royce passed by, then stopped. A chauffeur in uniform put out his arm and opened the back door, so we got into this plush car, hastily putting on our shoes once inside. We were driven to Stafford railway station, where obviously he had to meet someone. We left the car expressing our grateful thanks to the chauffeur, who never once spoke a word to us.

A week later, on returning to my flat in Fulham, I found a parcel and a card showing a picture of the Queen Mary, on which my friend Rene had recently sailed to join her American husband. She had sent me a gorgeous pair of white leather sandels decorated with gold studs, also a box of Hershey chocolate bars. What luxury! Further to this delightful surprise was a dozen letters from my husband Reg.

I sat there late at night wearing the shoes, enjoying a bar of chocolate while reading my husband's letters. The final one told me that he would be coming back to England in a few days time. I felt that my prayers had been answered.

This was certainly one of the happiest days of my life!

John Wood-Cowling remembers the arrival of the NHS in Glasgow

The NHS

The NHS arrived in 1948 - our area thought it was Christmas every day, you've never seen so many plastic teeth in your life! The minister, Nye Bevin realized it had to stop - all of a sudden guys could see a whole new world. Free glasses, that had to stop! One old guy in our street had lost his left leg in the Great War, he was a peg leg. Another guy said to him "You can get a free metal leg from the NHS and you can wear two shoes." Charlie made inquiries. As luck would have it his pal had lost his right leg and he took a size eight shoe. After they got fitted with their new NHS legs, they bought a pair of size eight shoes and shared them!

Charlie got his pension on a Thursday, he had no money for a pint by Tuesday, but he had kept his peg leg so he put it back on and pawned his NHS leg till Thursday. We kids would chase him down the road "Pawned yer leg! Pawned yer leg." You couldn't make it up! Women would pull up their blouse in the street, "Have you seen my operation?"

"For God's sake lassie give us a break!"

Those were the days.

Derek Allen recalls an embarrassing incident in London

Mistaken Identity

Once a week in the summer of 1948, I went to the People's Palace, Mile End Road in London's East End, where the BBC broadcast a radio show starring my friend Ralph Reader – 'It's Fine To Be Young.'

The cast comprised of almost unknown artistes including Mary Naylor, Jack Beet and Norman Fellows known as 'The Twizzle Sisters' from Ralph's RAF 'Gang Show', the 'Four Yeomen' and a young comedian, Bob Monkhouse. Bob had no car at the time, so I would sometimes give him a lift home to his flat at Beckenham.

Each week there would be a guest artiste; these included Petula Clark, Denis Compton and Squadron Leader Douglas Bader. At the pub opposite the theatre, where we went for a drink after the show, I would get autographs for my kid sister.

One week a newcomer joined the show, a young comedian who did very good impressions. Ralph introduced him as Peter. The two impressionists called Peter that I had heard of were Peter Brough and Peter Cavanagh and I knew that it was not Peter Brough.

At a convenient time I asked politely "May I have your autograph Mr Cavanagh." With a straight face he asked my sister's name, wrote something in the autograph book and handed it back to me. He then joined in conversation with the rest of the party.

Arriving home my sister read the latest addition to her collection; it read "Love to Molly, Peter Sellers."

"Who is Peter Sellers?" she asked.

Annoyed that I had asked an unknown person to write in her book. I replied "I don't know, but keep it, he might be famous one day!"

A few weeks later, Ralph Reader compered a show for the RAF at the Royal Albert Hall, with Vera Lynn and Richard Attenborough. Although he was not on the programme, Ralph also introduced Peter Sellers, who was a great success.

By this time I knew who he was and realised that he was much younger than Peter Cavanagh. We chatted for a long while backstage, but neither of us mentioned my stupid mistake.

Valerie Simpson recalls a cold winter

Nutty Slack and the New Look

The very severe winter of 1947 was an ordeal, so soon after the worries of the war. A travelling salesman in a caravan asked to park in our backyard for the ten days that he would be in our area. The snow came and he was stuck there for ten weeks! We were very used to Romany gypsies with their horse drawn traditional caravans but this one was pulled by car and was modern and cosy, with an anthracite stove. Fuel was very short that winter, nutty slack and briquettes appeared. The last was coal dust shaped like bricks. It filled the back of the fire.

Young ladies were delighted when nylon and the 'new look' in clothes arrived, so feminine after the wartime austerity. We all wore matching hats, shoes and gloves to go shopping. After clothes rationing, to be able to go clothes shopping was a special pleasure. Also not many books were about in the war. I had lots of second hand books for Christmas for years and the books coming back to the shops were so nice. Going without lots of things made all of us very appreciative of the simple things of life.

The winter of 1947

W Garner also remembers the winter in Shropshire

Frozen Rabbits

In 1947, I was in the army stationed at Craven Arms, Shropshire. We were moving munitions, which were stored in shelters at the side of the roads. Snowdrifts twenty feet deep and seeing rabbits jumping over telephone wires was weird. We wore our denims and the water travelled up to our waist. We hung our trousers over the bottom of our beds. In the morning our trousers were frozen solid and we had to get into them and let the heat of our bodies melt the ice. It took about five minutes to get my trousers on! If you dropped your soap it froze and you couldn't pick it up.

Also after the snow had melted you could see half way up the trees where the rabbits had chewed the bark to keep alive.

Shirley Cowan worked in Somerset

Wellington Boots

In 1947, when I was fourteen years old, I got a job on a farm in Somerset, 'training to be a farm labourer.' The farm was about twelve miles from Taunton. It was very primitive, no gas, no electricity, no water. Water came from a spring in the yard.

My job was to look after two hundred and fifty chickens, that was after I had brought up the eight cows from the fields for milking every morning by 6.45, put them in the barn for the farmer and two boys to milk. Breakfast was at 7.30 but I never got to have it because by that time, I was busy mixing hot mash for the chickens and going down the fields to feed them, clean out the henhouses and collect the eggs. All day long I worked like a slave, if I complained, I was told it was all part of the training. Lunch was at 12.30. I did get that but for me that was the only proper meal of the day. Then I had to clean out the pigsties and stable. Help with all the other animals too. And if I had any free time, I had to work in the house cleaning windows, scrubbing floors, or helping to deflea the dogs and cats!

That winter was very bad. The snows started to fall in early November and for one whole week we were cut off from the outside world. I still had to tend my chickens, only now they were shut in their houses all day long but I still had to clean them out every day. My feet were frozen in my Wellington boots. I'd only been there four months, but I was hating the job. I had to sit in a chair all night and it was so cold in my bedroom that icicles hung inside the windows. I wanted to run away but I couldn't because the farmer had my money. When I first went there he said he would put when wages of £2.50 a week into a Post Office book but I didn't know until I left that I hadn't had any wages at all. He had paid nothing. Luckily my dad sent me a ticket for the train to come home for Christmas that year. I couldn't wait so forgot to get my wages. The farmer said I could go the day before Christmas Eve but had to be back the day after Boxing Day. As it turned out, I never returned to the farm as it was found I had gangrene. My feet were so bad that they were black but my father's doctor managed to save them. The dye from the socks I wore had poisoned my open chilblains and then the snow down the wellingtons had frozen my feet. The doctor had to saw off my boots with a surgical saw and my feet were put into neat disinfectant. How I screamed!

I couldn't walk properly for nearly three months.

Kay Vallance lived near Watford

Ice Skating

In the winter of 1947 the River Colne had flooded in to the surrounding fields near Watford. I lived in one of the bungalows nearby and my friend Marian lived at the bottom of Bushey Mill Lane. We were ten-years-old at the time and thought it great fun to go skating on the now frozen, flooded fields. We were having a wonderful time when suddenly there was a cracking noise and Marian fell through the ice into the water. Luckily, her father had been watching us from their house and quickly came to the rescue. Fortunately, the water was only a few inches deep but even so, one now realises how dreadful the outcome could have been.

Joan Hunter lived in North London

The Spring Bride

In 1947, I was living in North London. Bill and I planned to marry on Easter Saturday, the 5th April. In February, we managed to find a flat at the time that the bad weather started. The flat needed a lot of decorating and every time that we went there, we had to dig ourselves up the front path.

Coupled with the bad weather, we also had power cuts. I can remember going to have my hair permed for the big day. We would get halfway through when off went the power for goodness knows how long. Off I went home with a towel wrapped around the curlers, to go back after the power was restored to finish off.

We had heavy snowfalls, the roads were very icy and travelling was difficult. Not much petrol about for normal use, although my father had a van for his business with 'C' Coupons and he could go to Finsbury Park Station to collect the bridesmaids when they came for their dress fittings. I begged, borrowed and acquired clothes coupons from whoever and wherever I could to get my Going Away outfit.

Food was in very short supply, due to the aftermath of the War and the extremely bad weather. Most of the food for the Reception was bought on the 'Black Market'. The wedding cake was made with dubious ingredients for the princely sum of £5.5.0d.

My father and husband were both measured for new suits at the '50 Shilling Tailors.' These were made in Leeds but because of the conditions they didn't get them until Whitsun, so they had to make do with what they already had.

Flowers were also in short supply. I ordered roses and carnations but two days before the wedding I was called to the florist to be told there were no flowers in the market at all. I had visions of walking down the aisle with a pot plant but I left it to the lady to do what she could for us and we ended up with Blue Iris for myself, Pink Tulips for the bridesmaids and Snowdrops for the buttonholes.

We eventually got our flat decorated in spite of the weather and my hair was finally permed. Unfortunately, many guests could not make it South from Durham where my husband came from. It snowed on Good Friday but the sun shone on the Easter Saturday and at 1pm we were married and off to Margate for a long weekend honeymoon, as that was all the time we could take off work.

June Muller emigrated to Australia

Extracts from June Muller's Mother's Diary of their journey to Australia

We reached Tilbury where we had a preview of the 'Orcades'. Unfortunately our luggage happened to be in the back of the train so by the time we walked back, we thought all hopes of a porter had gone. George was struggling best he could when up came a St. John's Ambulance nurse who promptly took charge of Barbara and the pram, gave Peter to me to carry. George was told to get all necessary papers ready, leave the luggage where it was and follow her. A fishing fleet in full sail was nothing to what we were then. One word from the nurse and she pushed a pathway through the crowd with the pram, helped by a voice of authority, and there we were presenting papers, giving up ration books, identity cards, etc., and were again hustled along to the customs shed.

"Have you any exports?"

"What do your cases contain?" and we were through and up the gangway aboard the 'Orcades'. Goodness, it was barely five minutes since we had left the train. I did feel a small pang for the people who were still waiting because of us - but here we were at last aboard, ready to start this long talked-of journey. For better or worse we had taken our feet off English soil.

Taken to our cabins. George has managed to change his cabin over to ours so we are all together after all.

We have a very nice steward, nice speaking voice. I've found out he's Irish and his name is Noel.

By the time we had recovered our breaths and dumped things in an unholy mess in the middle of the cabin, the bugle went for lunch. Up two stairways - called companionways - brought us to the dining hall. We found our seats on Table 25. It consists of roughly 20 seats. Our waiter proved to be Irish again, quite young. After getting over the shock of reading the menu:- Soup, boiled beef, vegetables, peaches and custard, we thought we'd do justice to it.

Back to our cabins to do a spot of sorting out and to try and convince Peter we were really on a ship and intended staying on it for about three weeks. Eventually Peter and

Barbara were persuaded to sleep and so George, June and myself went on a tour of inspection. After getting lost quite a few times we found the lounge. It was now the middle of the afternoon. We had been on board roughly four hours and learned we weren't likely to sail for another four hours and could send letters if we wished. Paper and envelopes were provided so just a note home and one to Australia to say we had really started and a gong was going for 4 o'clock tea. We took this in shifts so we could look after the kiddies. The children should have tea at 5.15 but today things were a bit haywire so they had late dinner at 6.30. The engines started and we moved off at 7pm. I had a queer sensation in the pit of my stomach as we moved but just now it's part of the excitement of watching everything that's happening.

June 22nd

We're up on our feet after a surprisingly restful night. I expected to come out of my top bunk unceremoniously in the middle of the night but I apparently stayed put. We all went to breakfast at 7.45. Cereal, kidneys, bacon, toast and marmalade. Yum! Yum!

We arrived back to our cabin to find our steward putting the finishing touches to our cabin, bunks made, everything tidied up, so we just walked in and out again, and once more went to discover the whys and wheres of the ship. Things are beginning to get a bit organised now. Dancing tonight, also Housey-Housey, a games committee is in the offing, also volunteers for the church choir. They certainly get things going.

Roast pork, etc. for dinner tonight. I don't know if it was intentional but soon after dinner we started to pass through the Bay of Biscay. By now we are really rolling.

George says he's definitely going to bed. I think I'll go dancing - mainly while I'm still on my feet. On the way I called into the Housey-Housey game. That was a good idea on my part. I won 10/-.

A few people have gone under with sea-sickness. Some have gone under because they were making too much of the bar being open most of the time, which is rather silly at this stage. I've only had one iced ginger ale which is a pleasant drink and not likely to do things to you.

June 23rd

Breakfast has to be seen to be believed, even more so to see me eating it. This morning's consisted of porridge, Yarmouth bloaters, fried eggs, bacon and potatoes, toast and marmalade and as many cups of tea as capacity allows. George got very hungry yesterday, waiting from 7.45 until 12.30 without anything to eat, so he woke this morning with the firm resolve to wade through everything that was on the menu - he did - so did I, which was an even bigger wonder.

June 24th

We awoke this morning feeling very tired; didn't realise why until much later, we'd forgotten to alter watch and clock - we're losing 20 minutes every day now.

Passed Cape St. Vincent early this morning through to Cadiz now onto the Rock of Gibraltar at about 10.45. This morning we had the Rock of Gibraltar on one side, and Tangier and Morocco on the other.

June 26th

Our first Sunday on board. There are no social events on the entertainment board for today so it's a case of just waiting to see what happens. We sighted our last bit of land this morning - Tunis - until we sight Port Said about 6am Tuesday. We're allowed ashore then for a few hours before we go down the Suez Canal.

June 28th Tuesday

As we dock at Port Said today, there's been a bit of excitement through the ship. Most people have been finding quiet corners to write airmails, cards etc, ready to post. Wondering if we'll receive any mail. We got up early this morning, about 5.30, so we wouldn't miss anything. As we arrived on deck, the pilot had just been picked up - he'd climbed aboard from a launch up a rope ladder - apparently a special man has to pilot the ship through the mouth of the Canal.

By now most passengers were on deck and everything was buzzing with excitement. There in front of us was an opening our huge ship had to go through. We docked intact and dropped anchor at roughly 6.30am, engines stopped for the first time in seven days.

Within minutes it seemed small boats were coming from all directions. Officials and Police complete with fez and rifles. We soon had other things to attract our attention for alongside in small boats came dark swarthy skinned natives selling merchandise. Their selection of goods was vast, ranging from leather cases, handbags, hats, necklaces, rugs, down to watermelons, coconuts, and peanuts. Some things were really lovely, especially the rugs. Soon the fun started. A number of passengers had done this journey before and knew how to barter with the men. It wasn't long before we were all at it, offering about a quarter of the price asked. Some had real bargains. I indulged in a huge straw hat, fez hat for June, hat for Peter, also a small handbag, rather nice one with a camel on the outside - for 5/-. Considering the prices in England it was a fair bargain. I wanted a suitcase, could have one for 1/- but as we're told we'll have a repetition of it at Aden in two days time, we may as well wait. Passengers were allowed ashore 9am until 12am. We didn't go, mostly we didn't feel safe taking the children. They are supposed to be hostile to British people, also we had warnings from the Purser not to go off the main streets. Unfortunately photos are not allowed to be taken in the vicinity of Port Said or the Suez Canal. We could have had some really good ones too because as you leave Port Said to go into the actual Canal it's a sight really worth remembering. All buildings and houses have pink mostly or pastel shaded roofs. I've seen Technicolor films of the Middle East and always had an idea the colours were a bit artificial but they're not. That colouring is real, very real. Everything has a pink glow about it. Most official buildings are flanked by trees bearing a brilliant red flower. This adds considerably to the picture.

We left Port Said with regrets because from the ship it was all so beautiful. It seemed impossible that behind all that beauty were sordid back streets trading in and with the lowest, a city of blackguards ready for all evil, but still to the passing world showing such a movingly beautiful outer covering. Away from Port Said into the Suez Canal, very slowly now - strange to have land on both sides. One side just desert, sand as far as the eye could see with not a thing to relieve it. On the other - British - running parallel with the Canal there's a perfectly straight road where occasionally a car, but mostly Army lorries would go along, the troops tooting madly or waving and shouting at us as we sailed by.

At about 3.30 after going about 20 miles down the Canal, we had to pull in anchor to allow a smaller ship to pass. The Canal itself starts off quite narrow, perfectly straight, then blossoms out into two bulges, one called the Great Bitter Lake, one small bulge obviously called the Little Bitter Lake, after which it reverts back into a narrow strip again.

By the time we had finished dinner at 7pm, we were getting a bit browned off with missing the sights of the Canal. Even a Gala Dance couldn't make up for it. So up on deck again we went to see what could be seen in the lights of the ship. It wasn't the same of course as it would have been in daylight but nevertheless worth seeing. The lights making a great arc around the Great Bitter Lake was quite a sight.

30th June

Went to our first cinema show on board tonight. It's rather a queer experience at first. It's held on the top deck of all, that's one reason that it attracted people because being right at the stern of the ship, you just must get a breeze of some sort. A screen is hoisted, deck chairs placed facing it so we are facing wherever we've just come from. The film was quite good 'This Time for Keeps' and a few shorts. Tomorrow should see us in Aden.

July 1st

I'm just reflecting this morning that for two whole days we've just sat and sat, got hotter and hotter. I'm beginning to realise why white people through the ages have been pictured as little tin gods letting the black people wait on them. The humid atmosphere just saps all energy one might have had and one is very grateful to anyone who feels like working just to let them get on with it. It's not a good way of acting but it's just how the heat affects you.

Our luck seems to have left us after Port Said. We were sailing along so nicely to see Aden when we ran into a sandstorm. What a mess! Everything down to our cabins was nothing but sand. We eat it, we wipe it out of our ears, eyes, our hair was smothered. We were all turning ginger by degrees. We are informed sandstorms last anywhere up to two hours so it didn't look hopeful. We were so near and yet so far to Aden. We had sighted land once, now it was blocked from view by sand. We'd promised June in a rash moment we'd take her ashore but still the sandstorm was raging. Dinner at 6.30pm. By 7.30 still no sign of a break. In desperation we put June to bed about 9 o'clock and we hung around hopefully but even we in the end went to bed. We collected ourselves and June and eventually went ashore about 1.30am. Talk about being mad. There we were on land again after seventeen days walking along a filthy street in Aden, peopled with even dirtier people selling odds and ends. By dodging persistent black taxi drivers, we managed to find some shops open for the occasion. We started to regret we hadn't taken more advantage of Port Said goods because either it was an unearthly hour and goods weren't displayed or goods were not there. We returned to the ship after about an hour with a feeling of disappointment but at least we had been ashore. Now we were due away again at 3.30am. So we wouldn't see much of Aden.

July 2nd

I'm feeling a bit rough. Haven't been feeling too good all morning. I've only just realised why; the smell of Aden seems to have got right inside me. Everytime I eat or drink I seem to taste it. I'm told it's the smell of the East - well, they can keep it. It seems to contaminate everything.

We didn't sail at 3.30 this morning after all. When we awoke we were still in port. On making enquiries we learned that when the rope was being released from the buoy, it had got wound around our propeller so we had a view of a diver doing his stuff. Eventually we sailed at 9am, through the Gulf of Aden into the Arabian Sea.

It's still hot and the Aden smell seems everywhere, even now. I've heard and seen old souls with their fans in the past and always given a silent snigger and thought it a spot of swank but believe me, I've dropped into one of those dear old souls and a fan became a must buy at Aden. To see me sitting on deck fanning myself surely was a sight worth seeing.

July 6th

Colombo. Five days since Aden, two of which were taken up battling the storms of the Arabian Sea. We've booked to go on a motor-coach trip when we land at Colombo. It seems better with children to do it that way than just land and wander anywhere.

By 2pm we'd had lunch, had our papers stamped by the Colombo Police, also changed English money into rupees, 13 to the £1. For purchasing purposes, a rupee was generally counted as 1/6d. As our motor tour was booked, all we had to do was get into a launch, be driven to the quay, pass through the barrier straight on to the coach. For dirt, filth and squalor, Colombo must be the worst place on earth - in parts at least - I thought Aden bad enough but Colombo - phew! We drove along through dirty streets, passed houses if they could be called such, some even may have been mud huts - naked children were everywhere mixed up with rickshaw runners, fruit shops, all the trades imaginable. Laundry was being done by the side of the road, men sitting sewing away at shirts, dresses etc. I understand they are very clever at it. Dresses could be made up perfectly finished off from your own selection of material, in two to three hours. We took in these sights on their face value as we drove along because obviously this was the native quarter of Colombo because we were gradually passing residences of quite a different kind. Possibly English residents or at least the better class Ceylonese. One particular part was very impressive, just an avenue flanked on either side with flamboyant trees, tress as big as normal English trees but bearing a mass of flame-coloured blossom. Now out into open country to come to a huge building with beautifully kept lawns in front, an official building obviously but as we couldn't find out what, we turned our attention to a snake-charmer by the side of the road. Some got out of the coach to have a closer view, but as my love of snakes isn't great, I decided I could see as much as I wanted to in my seat. It was the real thing and very interesting. There was the native playing some kind of weird music and out of the basket uncurled the snake and emerged rearing its head and looking very vicious.

We stopped at a hotel for tea, very clean - although served by natives, quite an English air about it. The waiters were very correct, very polite. The only thing strange was hot milk instead of cold for the tea. It all came to 2 rupees, 20 cents; that's near enough to 3/6d, which was very reasonable. One of the waiters told us he had a daughter the same age as Barbara. I suppose he thought that gave him an excuse to pick her up and nurse her. He should have known better, being a father himself, but Barbara enjoyed herself. She doesn't mind what colour they are as long as they make a fuss of her.

We returned to the ship just in time for children's tea at 5.15.

July 7th

We're now definitely the other side of the world. At approximately 2am this morning we crossed over the Equator. I'm told the 'crossing of the line ceremony' has died out so the event passed with only a few realising it. The children have been given certificates to mark the occasion, which I thought was rather nice. I think we'll get them framed when we get on dry land again.

Although we have nearly a week to go before we reach Fremantle, a rustle seems to have gone through the passengers, a suspicion of a feeling that we have been living in a dream with the strange sights of the East, and now when we next see land it will be so much like the life and land and people we have left behind in England. Our first hint of all this was the issuing of forms to be filled in for each passenger before we reach Australian waters. A duplicate has to be made for each so someone has to fill out ten forms in our family, plus a customs baggage form.

July 8th

We're now in the Indian Ocean and have lost sight of land for the last two days until we reach Australia - seven days with just nothing but water. The deck competitions are being played off to the semi-finals and finals. We have a wrestler on board, a few boxers, so tonight there are exhibition bouts to be seen.

July 10th

Our last Sunday on board. It's colder now, silk dresses have disappeared, costumes and coats are coming out. I've seen a man with overcoat and thick scarf on. I understand while we're getting colder, in England a heatwave is going on. It will be winter when we reach Perth in three day's time.

July 12th

Winter with a vengeance now. Topcoats are definitely the things of the day. There's a tidy gale blowing; what with that and the boat rolling, it's a job to stay on deck. But we must because we have a medical examination to pass before we can land tomorrow. First we have to queue for quarantine cards, then join another queue to pass the doctor who looks at foreheads and arms for signs of smallpox. We apparently passed OK.

July 13th

Today is the day! I suppose a day to remember all our lives. We were called at 6.30am although I was already up and dressed and had been watching distant lights that meant land was in sight again after seven days.

Before breakfast could be served everyone on board, crew as well as passengers, had to pass the doctor again, an Australian doctor this time. This was no five-minute job. Long before it was finished we were tied up alongside at Fremantle, where crowds lined the quay waiting for friends, relations or sponsored emigrants. Breakfast was a fiasco because first sitting people were still waiting to be served while the second sitting had turned up for theirs. We spotted uncle from the ship but although we waved and yelled, he didn't see us. He was eventually allowed on board where we officially met. Last minute packing, farewells, leave-taking of stewards, waiters, all who had helped to make our journey as comfortable as possible. Our baggage to be seen off then off the 'Orcades' into Australia.

The customs was a lengthy affair, but eventually we were in the car en route for Perth. What now?

The 1940s - Month by Month

1948
January
- Mahatma Gandhi was assassinated in New Delhi
- The railways were nationalised

February
- Communists seized power in Czechoslovakia
- The Winter Olympics were held in St Moritz

March
- Jan Masaryk, Czech Foreign Minister, died after 'falling' from his flat in Prague

April
- The GCE exam replaced the School Certificate

May
- The state of Israel was founded and British troops withdrew from Palestine
- The Empire Windrush brought the first organised party of West Indian immigrants from Jamaica to the UK

June
- The Russians began a blockade of West Berlin, hoping to force the Allies to withdraw. The Allies airlifted supplies in to the city

July
- The National Health Service came into operation
- The first Oxfam shop opened
- The Olympic Games opened in London

August
- The Olympic Games were hailed as a great success, despite being staged on a very low budget

September
- Mao Tse Tung declared 'The People's Republic of China'

October
- The Morris Minor was launched at the Motor Show

November
- The Polaroid camera went on sale in the USA
- Prince Charles was born

December
- Seven senior Japanese war leaders were hanged following their conviction for war crimes
- Dennis Compton scored a record breaking 300 runs in 181 minutes playing for the MCC against a Transvaal cricketing eleven

=================

The 1940s - Month by Month

1949

January
- Ben-Gurion's Labour Party won the first election in Israel

February
- A truce was declared between Egypt and Israel, ending the first Arab-Israeli war
- The first rocket was launched in to outer space from New Mexico

March
- NATO was formed
- Clothes rationing ended
- The first non-stop flight around the world was completed by a B-50 bomber called Lucky Lady II. The journey lasted 94 hours

April
- Wolverhampton Wanderers beat Leicester City 3-1 in the FA Cup Final

May
- The Soviet blockade of Berlin ended
- Europe's first Launderette opened in London

June
- US Tennis player Gussie Moran caused a sensation at Wimbledon by wearing lacy knickers

July
- The first commercial jet airliner, the De Havilland Comet made its maiden flight

August
- Dr Konrad Adenauer won the first elections to be held in the Federal Republic of Germany

September
- The Pound was devalued from $4.03 to $2.80
- Mao Tse Tung was elected Chairman of The People's Republic of China
- The Berlin Airlift ended after almost 277,000 flights

October
- China was declared a Communist Republic
- The East of Germany occupied by the Soviets was established as a communist Democratic Republic

November
- Two 'planes collided near Washington killing 55 people, the worst air disaster in US history

December
- The Israeli capital was moved from Tel Aviv to Jerusalem

I Remember When I Was Young

Rob has also published a previous collection of peoples' memories. Entitled 'I Remember When I Was Young,' this is an absorbing collection of half a century of personal memories, covering the decades of the 1920s through to the 1960s; 400 pages of pure nostalgia.

Each chapter contains a wide range of peoples' personal memories from childhood, early adulthood and later life. Some recall humorous or emotional incidents unconnected with the world around them; others describe episodes that have a direct connection to the major events of the day. Written in a variety of styles, all recall a time very different to the present day and all who lived at that time will feel a sense of belonging and possibly a tinge of regret that this time has now passed.

Each decade begins with an overview of the main historical events of the time. Important discoveries and 'firsts' are highlighted, together with notable anniversaries. The main focus, however, is not on well-documented historical events but on ordinary people's own personal reminiscences. Everyday stories, which will make the reader laugh, cry, ponder and remember.

This is available for Kindle or iPad/Laptop (via the free Kindle Reader App):

20th century memories

I Remember When I Was Young can also be ordered at all good bookstores, internet book retailers or from your local library. Alternatively, you can order a signed copy direct from Rob (see below). When ordering, please quote ISBN number 1-58832-083-9

E mail: rob@intheforest.co.uk
Website: www.20thcenturymemories.com

Acknowledgements and Thanks

The following individuals and organisations have generously contributed to this book. Copyright of individual's specific memories remain with that individual. I would like to express my sincere thanks to all of those people who took the time and trouble to help me with this project. Many of the memories submitted by contributors have been edited, to a greater or lesser extent. I have tried not to detract from the original emphasis of any of the pieces and I hope that this has been achieved throughout. If I have missed anyone, or 'misspetl' any names, please accept my apologies for the oversight.

Personal Contributions

A Slice of Life: Barry Chatfield, Laura Turner, Gordon Brown, Bill Luke, Alan Birmingham, Katie Smith, Margaret Chatters, Muriel Stirling, Jack Shepperd, Stanley H Jones, Alan Everson, Eric Cornfield, 'Mary Lou' Potter, Beryl Worthington, Norma Service, Joyce Mellor, Roy Cox, Doris Parr, Leslie Oppittz, Mrs H Phillips, Edna Turner, Judith Keel, Alan R Irons, Norman Heath, Olive Soutar, Beryl Pearmain, Colin Bartlett, Mary Oldfield, Patricia O'Driscoll, John Dymock, Doreen Garner, Connie Coates, Geoff Bartlett, Mike Minson, Joy Riley, Brian Moran, Jillian Kearns, Marjorie Williams, Ernest Wallace, Diana Moyse, Eunice Jones, Sheali Stafford, Mrs M Leith, Irvin Stewart, Barbara Algar, Iris Campbell, Lucy Baruch

The War at Home: Miss P Strickland, John Rogers, Rachel Noble, Ruth King, Mr R Francklin, Nora Wilson, Alphra Marshall, Mabel Johnson, Alastair Barclay, Mrs A Howarth, Ted Humphreys, Rosemary Mary Somerville, Geoff Darby, Bryan Jones, Pat Jones, Janice Aves, Maurice Darling, Mike Golding, Sheila Chugg, Dorothy Bass, Joyce Williams, Fred Lacy, Jean Macpherson, Joan Lloyd-Davies, Mrs J Turner, Barry Thorpe, Doreen Gale, Mary Singleton, Eileen Yeldham, Joe Rider, Eileen Kelly, John Bennett, Dennis Devier, Eve Fielder, Doris Parr, Alan Everson, Bob Turrell, Mrs W Ferris, Joyce O'Shea, Vera Walton, Edith Higgins, Maurice Rudge, Peter Rook, Pat Collins

Childhood: Pat Barham, Sheila Darzi, Eileen Smith, Christine Goodhugh, Valerie Simpson, Mavis Grant, Sheila Brown, Brian Sewall, Barry Ledgard, James Gunn, Mr P Evered, Mrs Dennett, Mrs B Halton, Archie Beggs, John Wood-Cowling, Ann Davis, Fred Harket, Duncan Hamman, Mrs M Dance, Derek Hyamson, Patricia Saxon, Judith Keel, Elizabeth Diggens, Yvonne Wright, Pete Hepper, Don Goodwin, Betty McCrea, Shelagh Crompton, Babs Henderson, Michael Yarrow, Margaret Weeks, Ann Bush

The Blitz: Frank Stonard, Jillian Elms, Jean Williams, Dennis Darney, Alan Ottoway, Roy Bartlett, Denis Sheehan, Mr J Shepherd, Brian Moran, Derek Allen, Leslie Oppitz, Mr A Gilleland, Elsie Warren, Mrs M Rudge, Mary O'Boyle, Ted Watson, Colin Holloway, Doris Parr, Mary Beech, Michael Barrett

Evacuees: Joyce Ambrose, Olive Hoyles, Betty Goble, Miss P Strickland, Mrs B Norfolk, Anne King, Mr Duquemin, Maurice Rudge, Dianne Scapens

Doing My Bit: Alistair Duncan, John Barfoot, Richard Wright, Dr Tony Husain, Alexander Duncan, Barbara Algar, Eric Wilson, Marguerite Lloyd, Shirley Lingwood, Charles Butland Horlock, Esme Hurn, Winnie Ponting, Fred Bishop, Sheelagh Aranha, Jeremy Woods, John Scrivens, Joyce Watson, Kathleen Dicker, Mrs Marjorie Harvey, Rona Reardon Smith, Audrey Mason, Jeannette Howell, Bert Triggs, Roy Cox, Lionel Barnett, John Chambers

The View From Over the Water: Joan Thompson, Pat Barham, Tom Dunn, Joe North, Jack Shepperd, Leslie Sprigg, George Bainbridge, Leslie Oppitz, Reg Bowyer, Tudow Williams, Brian Moran, Edith Ward, Pat Stephens, Bert Thompson, Dorice Lindsay, Mt Adamek, Romuald Lipinski, Heinz Barthel, Kees Vanderheyden, Olga Gerbers

After The War: Charlie Miller, Roy Cox, Allan Taylor, Gladys Davey, Stanley H Jones, Duncan Hamman, Anne Trent, Barry Ledgard, Yvonne Fischer, Ruth Warburton, Barbara Fuller, John Wood-Cowling, Derek Allen, Valerie Simpson, W Garner, Shirley Cowan, Kay Vallance, Joan Hunter, June Muller

Other content
The historical events which form the backdrop to the time covered in this book are obviously in the public domain. However, a number of organisations and individuals have helped me to gather together the personal contributions. I am particularly grateful to these:
Gladys Shaw, Saga, The Office for National Statistics, The Open University, Brighton Evening Argus, Tenby Observer, Westmorland Gazette, Nottingham Evening Post, Guernsey Weekly Press, Malvern Gazette, The Swan, Dickie Riding, Yours, The Royal British Legion, Revival, Irish World, Western Daily Press, Southampton Library Service, Hampshire Record Office, The Western Mail, Lincolnshire Life, South Wales Argus, The Royal Air Forces Association, Liverpool Echo, North Cornwall Advertiser, Sunderland Echo, The Courier, Kettering Evening Telegraph, Bournemouth Evening Echo, Southampton Evening Echo, Bristol Evening Post, Oxford Mail, Newcastle Evening Chronicle, Shropshire Star, Sunday Sun, Yorkshire Evening Press, Manchester Evening News, Coventry Evening Telegraph, Northants Evening Telegraph, Liverpool Daily Post, Western Morning News, Gloucestershire Echo, East Anglian Times, Emma Broadbent, Vicki Green-Steel.

Photographic images

The following organisations and individuals kindly gave me permission to use their photographic images. All copyright and trademarks remain with the original owners. I am very grateful to them all.

1940s montage, 1940s movie stars - photos copyright Tracy Dolphin (www.wickedlady.com);
The Concert Party – copyright Roy Cox;
The Animals, Contemporary Cartoon, A Long Day, Visit to Edinburgh, Winter 1947, Tobacco Relief – photos copyright Judith Keel;
The Fat Ration, Fire Precations – photos copyright Sheila Brown;
Identity Card, Evacuees, Anderson Shelter, Castle St Bristol, Playing in the Street – photos copyright Maurice Rudge;
Stewarton Home Guard – copyright Alastair Barclay;
The Crossing to France – copyright Mike Golding;
POW – copyright Dorothy Bass
Christmas Cards – Dorothy Bass and Sheila Brown;
Radar – from a drawing by Eileen Yeldham;
Ann and Leonnie Bush – copyright Ann Bush;
Coventry Auxiliary Fire Brigade – copyright John Bevan;
Jeremy Wood's letter – copyright Jeremy Wood;

Morse Code, Café de Peel – photos copyright Colin Paine;
Mr Adamek's walk – copyright Mr Adamek;

Last but not Least

A special thankyou goes to the following people:

My wife Karen, who encouraged me and didn't complain too much as I worked on the book for hours on end.
My sister-in-law Sally Denny-Morley and niece Beth Denny-Morley, who both helped with the typing.
Charlotte Brookes, my proofreader, who noticed all of the missing punctuation marks and grammatical inconsistencies.

=== THE END ===

Printed in Dunstable, United Kingdom